INTRODUCTION TO OBJECT-ORIENTED PROGRAMMING WITH C++

Anita Millspaugh
Mt. San Antonio College

THE DRYDEN PRESS
Harcourt Brace College Publishers

Fort Worth Philadelphia San Diego New York Orlando Austin San Antonio
Toronto Montreal London Sydney Tokyo

Publisher   George Provol
Acquisitions Editor   Christina Martin
Product Manager   Debbie K. Anderson
Developmental Editor   Larry Crowder
Project Editor   Colby Alexander
Art Director   Carol Kincaid
Production Manager   Eddie Dawson
Electronic Publishing Coordinator   Deborah Lindberg

ISBN: 0-03-023621-5
Library of Congress Catalog Card Number: 98-86371

Copyright © 1999 by Harcourt Brace & Company

All rights reserved. No part of this publication may be reproduced or transmitted in any form or by any means, electronic or mechanical, including photocopy, recording, or any information storage and retrieval system, without permission in writing from the publisher.

Requests for permission to make copies of any part of the work should be mailed to: Permissions Department, Harcourt Brace & Company, 6277 Sea Harbor Drive, Orlando, FL 32887-6777.

Address for Orders
The Dryden Press, 6277 Sea Harbor Drive, Orlando, FL 32887-6777
1-800-782-4479

Address for Editorial Correspondence
The Dryden Press, 301 Commerce Street, Suite 3700, Fort Worth, TX 76102

Web Site Address
http://www.hbcollege.com

THE DRYDEN PRESS, DRYDEN, and the DP LOGO are registered trademarks of Harcourt Brace & Company.

Printed in the United States of America

8 9 0 1 2 3 4 5 6 7   0 4 8   9 8 7 6 5 4 3 2 1

The Dryden Press
Harcourt Brace College Publishers

I would like to thank my family and my students for their support and input.

The Dryden Press Series in Information Systems

Adams
First Steps Series
  Word 97
  Excel 97
  Access 97
  PowerPoint 97

Coorough
Getting Started with Multimedia

Fenrich
Practical Guidelines for Creating Instructional Multimedia Applications

Fuller/Manning
Getting Started with the Internet

Gordon and Gordon
Information Systems: A Management Approach
Second Edition

Gray, King, McLean, and Watson
Management of Information Systems
Second Edition

Harris
Systems Analysis and Design: A Project Approach
Second Edition

Larsen/Marold
Using Microsoft Works 4.0 for Windows 95: An Introduction to Computing

Laudon and Laudon
Information Systems: A Problem-Solving Approach
(A CD-ROM interactive version)

Licker
Management Information Systems: A Strategic Leadership Approach

Lorents and Morgan
Database Systems: Concepts, Management, and Applications

Martin
Discovering Microsoft Office 97

Martin/Parker
PC Concepts

Mason
Using Microsoft Access 97 in Business

Mason
Using Microsoft Excel 97 in Business

Millspaugh
Introduction to Object-Oriented Programming with C++

Morley
Getting Started with Computers
Second Edition

Morley
Getting Started: Web Page Design with Microsoft Front Page 97

Parker
Understanding Computers: Today and Tomorrow
98 Edition

Parker
Understanding Networking and the Internet

Spear
Introduction to Computer Programming in Visual Basic 4.0

Spear
Visual Basic 3.0: A Brief Introduction
Visual Basic 4.0: A Brief Introduction

Sullivan
The New Computer User
Second Edition

Martin and Parker
Mastering Today's Software Series

Texts available in any combination of the following:

  Windows 98
  Windows NT Workstation 4
  Windows 95
  Windows 3.1
  Disk Operating System 6.0 (DOS 6.0)
  Disk Operating System 5.0 (DOS 5.0)
  Microsoft Office 97 Professional Edition
  Microsoft Office for Windows 95 Professional Edition
  Word 97
  Word 7.0 for Windows 95
  Word 6.0 for Windows
  Corel WordPerfect 7.0 for Windows 95
  WordPerfect 6.1 for Windows
  WordPerfect 6.0 for Windows
  WordPerfect 5.1
  Excel 97
  Excel 7.0 for Windows 95
  Excel 5.0 for Windows
  Lotus 1-2-3 97
  Lotus 1-2-3 for Windows (5.0)
  Lotus 1-2-3 for Windows (4.01)
  Lotus 1-2-3 (2.4)
  Lotus 1-2-3 (2.2/2.3)
  Quattro Pro 4.0
  Quattro Pro 6.0 for Windows
  Access 97
  Access 7.0 for Windows 95
  Access 2.0 for Windows
  Paradox 5.0 for Windows
  Paradox 4.0
  dBASE 5 for Windows
  dBASE IV (1.5/2.0)
  dBASE III PLUS
  PowerPoint 97
  PowerPoint 7.0 for Windows 95
  A Beginner's Guide to QBASIC
  A Beginner's Guide to BASIC
  Netscape Navigator 4.0
  Internet Explorer 4.0

PREFACE

The trend in programming design is moving towards an object-oriented approach. This is due to many influences in the evolution of software and hardware. As many systems become graphically interfaced and the demand for "easier-to-use" software increases, the program complexity expands dramatically.

A solution to the complexity of programs is to develop them using an approach closer resembling the real-life relationship of objects. The traditional structured approach to programming is limited through its treatment of data and actions as distinct entities. By dealing with data and instructions as interwoven items, the ability to develop reusable code is enhanced. Object-oriented programming in C++ requires an understanding of encapsulation of data and functions (classes), polymorphism (overloading), and inheritance of classes.

This text is oriented towards teaching C++ with an emphasis on object-oriented design and programming. The introductory chapter introduces the terms related to OOP including encapsulation, polymorphism, and inheritance, which are then covered in more detail throughout the course. The first chapter also includes the iostream.h functions, cout, and a printer object. Projects containing multiple functions are demonstrated and encouraged in the solution of the chapter exercises.

The second chapter covers data including constants and variables. Structures are introduced towards the end of the chapter. This leads into chapter three, classes, which combines the data with the functions. Public, protected, and private data and functions are examined. The following chapters introduce loops, calculations, and decision.

Pointers and arrays are treated as a unit because of their close relationship. The coverage of pointers includes an understanding of the levels of indirection to minimize errors resulting from illegal assignments of pointers.

The reading level of the text should be easier than most on the market. The technical nature of the C++ language does not mean that the text should be hard to understand. Students should have some programming background before attempting the course in C++. The text can be used in a quarter or semester course in C++ for a two-year or four-year institution.

Each chapter of the book contains the chapter objectives, a chapter overview, a chapter summary, and a list of key terms. In addition, self-tests with answers are located between the subtopics of each chapter. Additional review questions are at the end of the chapter along with computer exercises. The Hayley Office Supplies is a series of projects that relate to the same company. Some of the projects build upon assignments from previous chapters.

I would like to thank reviewers Mark Terwilliger, Lake Superior State University, and Steve Peralta, for their contribution to the accuracy and timeliness of this book. At The Dryden Press, I would also like to thank Christina Martin, acquisitions editor; Debbie K. Anderson, product manager; Larry Crowder, developmental editor; Carol Kincaid, art director; and Eddie Dawson, production manager. Special thanks to Colby Alexander, project editor, for all of the work that he has done on this project.

ABOUT THE AUTHOR

Anita Millspaugh holds a BS in Computer Information Systems and an MBA. She has taught at the community college level since 1975. Since 1980 she has been a member of the Computer Information Systems Department at Mt. San Antonio College and spent eight of those years as department chair.

In addition to classroom teaching, she has been involved in facilitating and training leaders for teaching seminars that examine methods of improving classroom teaching across the curriculum. She has also participated in research programs in collaborative learning and classroom assessment techniques.

INTRODUCTION TO OBJECT-ORIENTED PROGRAMMING WITH C++

by Anita Millspaugh

CHAPTER 1	*An Introduction to C++*		1
CHAPTER 2	*Basic Data Types and Structures*		19
CHAPTER 3	*Creating Objects*		45
CHAPTER 4	*Processing Data: Calculations*		63
CHAPTER 5	*Decisions*		83
CHAPTER 6	*Loops and Arrays*		109
CHAPTER 7	*Creating Menu Programs Using the switch Statement*		137
CHAPTER 8	*Pointers*		165
CHAPTER 9	*Pointers and Arrays*		189
CHAPTER 10	*File Input/Output Using Structures*		223

INTRODUCTION TO OBJECT-ORIENTED PROGRAMMING WITH C++

by Anita Millspaugh

CHAPTER 1 An Introduction to C++ / 1

Chapter Objectives   1
Chapter Overview   1
The History of C++   1
Object-Oriented Programming   2
    Characteristics of an OOP Language   2
    Advantages of C++   3
        Portability   3
        A Large Selection of Operators   3
        Flexibility   3
    Disadvantages of C++   3
        Cryptic Appearance   3
        Operator Confusion   3
        Misused Pointer Access   4
Running a C++ Program   4
    Editors, Compilers, and Linkers   4
A First Program   4
    The main() Function   5
    The Include Directive   6
Output   6
    Screen Output   6
    Advancing to a New Line   7
    Ending a Line with endl   8
    Sending Output to the Printer   9
    Skipping Blank Lines   10
Documentation   11
Dividing a Program Into Parts   12
    Creating Functions   12
    Declaring a Function   12
    Defining a Function   12
    Calling the Function You Create   13
        Having Trouble Getting Printer Output?   14
    Programming Style   14
Programming/Debugging Hint   15
Key Terms   16
Summary   16
Review Questions   16
Exercises   17
Hayley Office Supplies   17

CHAPTER 2 Basic Data Types and Structures / 19

Chapter Objectives   19
Chapter Overview   19
Data Items and Data Types   19
    Constants and Literals   20
    Identifiers   21
    Named Constants   22
    Variables   23
        Declaring a Variable   23
        String Variables   23
        Declaring Multiple Variables of the Same Type   24
        Location of Declarations   24
        Initializing Variables   25
        Initializing String Variables   25
        Multiple Variables and Initialization   25
        Assigning Values to a Variable   26
        Assigning a Value to Multiple Variables   26
        Assigning Values to a String Variable   27
        Moving a Portion of a String   28
        Printing Variables   28
Formatting Data   29
    Column Width   29
    Justification   29
    Avoiding Exponential Format of Numbers   29
    Combining Multiple Flags and Manipulators   29
    Precision of Decimal Numbers   30
    Resetting Manipulators   31
    Setting the Manipulators Before the Print Line   31
Entering Data   32
    Solving the Skipped String Entry Problem   32
    Prompts   33
Structures   35
    Structure Variables   36
    Size of a Structure   37
    Referring to a Field within a Structure   37
    Structures within Structures   38
Programming Style   40
Key Terms   40
Chapter Summary   41
Review Questions   41
Exercises   41
Hayley Office Supplies   43

CHAPTER 3 Creating Objects / 45

Chapter Objectives   45
Chapter Overview   45
Creating Data Types Containing Functions   45
    A Structure with a Member Function   46
    Functions Defined Outside of the Structure Declaration   46

  Use of Properties by Methods 47
  Classes 47
  Objects 47
Constructors 48
  Inline Functions 49
Data Types for Functions 50
  Returning a Value from a Function 51
  Using the Return Value from a Function 51
Constructors with Arguments 54
Overloading Constructors 55
  Default Values 57
Overloading Operators 57
Destructors 58
  Naming a Destructor Function 58
  Contents of a Destructor 58
Programming Hint 58
  Creating Header Files 59
  Implied Object 60
Key Terms 61
Chapter Summary 61
Review Questions 61
Exercises 61
Hayley Office Supplies 62

CHAPTER 4 Processing Data: Calculations / 63

Chapter Overview 63
Arithmetic Operators 63
  Binary Operators 63
  Precedence of Operators 64
  Modulus 65
Unary Operators 66
  Increment Operator 66
  Decrement Operator 66
  Prefix versus Postfix 66
  Another Look at Precedence 67
Assignment Operators 68
  Precedence 70
  Mixing Data Types in Calculations 70
The sizeof Operator 72
Exponentiation 72
Using Calculations in a Method 73
Manipulating String Data 73
  Combining String Fields—Concatenation 73
  Concatenating the Beginning of a String 74
Key Terms 78
Chapter Summary 78
Review Questions 78
Exercises 78
Hayley Office Supplies 81

CHAPTER 5 Decisions / 83

Chapter Objectives 83
Chapter Overview 83
Making Comparisons Using Relational Operators 83
    Comparing Numeric Data 84
    Comparing Character Data 84
    Implied Conditions—True or False 86
The Logical Operators 86
    Precedence of And and Or in Compound Conditions 87
String Comparisons 88
    Comparaing a Specified Number of Characters 88
    Comparing Strings and Ignoring the Case 89
    Finding the Length of a String 89
Decisions—The if Statement 90
    Using if in a Member Function 93
    Nested if Statements 93
    Compound Conditions 94
    Conditional Operator 96
Precedence of Assignment, Logical, and Relational Operators 100
    Combining Assignment and Increment Operators 101
    Combining Increment and Logical Operators 102
Programming Style 104
Key Terms 105
Chapter Summary 105
Review Questions 105
Exercises 106
Hayley Office Supplies 108

CHAPTER 6 Loops and Arrays / 109

Chapter Objectives 109
Chapter Overview 109
Loops 109
    The while Loop 110
        Infinite Loops 110
    Priming Input 111
    The do loop 113
    The for Loop 114
        Multiple Initialization, Condition, or Action 116
Nested Loops 118
Highest/Lowest Logic Using the if 120
Single Dimension Arrays 121
    Declaring an Array 122
    Initializing an Array 122
    Initializing an Array of Unspecified Size 122
    Partially Filled Array 123
Subscripts 123
for Loops and Arrays 124
    Using a for Loop on Partially Filled Arrays 125

A Report Program   128
Key Terms   131
Chapter Summary   132
Review Questions   132
Exercises   133
Hayley Office Supplies   136

CHAPTER 7 Creating Menu Programs Using the switch Statement / 137

Chapter Objectives   137
Chapter Overview   137
The switch Statement   137
    Break   138
    More than One Alternative for a Case   138
    Using the switch for a Range of Values   143
Menu Programs   145
    Structure of a Menu Program   146
    Using Letters or Numbers for Menu Options   149
Menu Hints   151
Creating a More Generic Menu Class   153
Running Executable Files or DOS Commands from the Menu   156
    Clearing the Screen   157
Using Menu Bars   158
Programming/Debugging Hint   161
    Reverse Video   161
    Printers   162
Key Terms   162
Chapter Summary   162
Review Questions   162
Exercises   163
Hayley Office Supply   164

CHAPTER 8 Pointers / 165

Chapter Objectives   165
Chapter Overview   165
Pointer Variables   165
    Pointer Operators   166
    Declaring a Pointer   166
    Assigning a Pointer to the Address of a Variable   166
        Combining Declaration and Assignment of Pointers   167
    Dereferencing a Pointer Variable   168
    A Pointer Contains an Integer   168
Summary of Pointer Characteristics   170
Pointers to Pointers and Levels of Indirection   170
    ***Decreases, &Increases**   171
Pointers as Function Arguments   172
Function Call by Reference to a Local Variable Address   173

Reference Operator   174
Passing Addresses of Functions   175
Menu Revisited   176
    The Header File   176
    The MENU Program   178
Multiple Level Menus   179
Inheritance   180
Key Terms   186
Chapter Summary   186
Review Questions   186
Exercises   186
Hayley Office Supplies   187

CHAPTER 9   Pointers and Arrays / 189

Chapter Objectives   189
Chapter Overview   189
Pointer Calculations   190
Pointers and Arrays   191
    Accessing a Single-Dimensional Array with Pointers   192
    Accessing a String Using Pointers   192
Multidimensional Arrays   193
    Initializing Multidimensional Arrays   194
    Accessing a Two-Level Array with Nested Loops   194
Multidimensional Arrays and Pointers   196
    Pointers to Pointers and Multidimensional Arrays   196
    Incrementing the Pointers   197
    Accessing a Multidimensional Array with Pointers   198
    Accessing a Multidimensional Array as a Single Array   198
    Accessing Data in an Array   199
Searching an Array   200
    Serial Search   200
    Binary Search   203
Sorting Data in an Array   208
    An Exchange Sort   208
    Using the qsort() Function   209
The Compare Function in qsort() and bsearch()   211
Pointers and Structures   212
The new and delete Operators   215
Programming/Debugging Tip   217
Key Terms   217
Chapter Summary   217
Review Questions   218
Exercises   218
Hayley Office Supplies   222

CHAPTER 10   File Input/Output Using Structures / 223

Chapter Objectives   223
Chapter Overview   223

Sequential vs. Random File Access   223
    Using Structures in Data Files   224
Random File Access   224
    Data Files   224
    File Modes   224
    Attaching a File to a stream   225
        The open() function   225
    Closing a File   226
    Testing If the File Exists   227
    Writing to the File   227
    Reading Data from a Disk File   228
    The seekp() function   229
    The seekg() function   229
    The tellg() Function   229
Updating a Random File   230
    The Class for the File   231
    The Write Routine   232
    The Read Routine   233
    Using the Same Screen   233
    Adding Records to the File   234
    Deleting or Editing a Record   234
        Flagging a Record for Delete   235
        Using a Delete Code   235
    Editing Records   237
    Listing Records from the File   239
        Printing to the Screen   240
        Printing to the Printer   240
        The List Routine   240
    Replacing Deleted Record Positions during Add   242
Complete Update Class   242
Programming/Debugging Tip   255
    Hash Addressing   255
    Hashing Algorithm   255
Key Terms   257
Chapter Summary   258
Review Questions   258
Exercises   258
Hayley Office Supplies   261

AN INTRODUCTION TO C++

CHAPTER 1

CHAPTER OBJECTIVES

By the end of this chapter you should be able to:
- Understand the relationship between the ANSI C language and the C++ language.
- Be familiar with the terms *encapsulation, inheritance,* and *polymorphism* as they relate to object-oriented programming.
- Know the history, advantages, and disadvantages of the C++ language.
- Grasp the purpose of the main() function.
- Write a program that will output constant/literal data to the screen or to the printer.
- Know the importance of documentation, indentations, and blank lines for readability of code.

CHAPTER OVERVIEW

This first chapter introduces programming in C++ with a short program. Demonstrating the use of punctuation is an important aspect of this program. Functions for producing output to the screen or to the printer are used. In addition, this chapter begins a discussion of style and the importance of documentation and spacing to produce code that is easy to read and to debug.

```
#include <iostream.h>


void main()
{
     cout <<"Welcome to Programming in C++";
}
```

THE HISTORY OF C++

C++ originally began as an object-oriented extension of the C language by Bjarne Stroustroup called "C with Classes." The word *class* refers to the object-oriented approach of the C++ language. The name evolved to C++, using the C operator for increment (++) to mean beyond C.

Dennis Ritchie of Bell Labs originally developed the C language. It is based on two languages that did not contain data types: B, created by Ken Thompson, and BCPL, written by Martin Richards. C++ is an extension of the C language.

The trend in programming is toward object-oriented design, and C++ contains features from Simula-67, a forerunner in the field. However, the C++ language is considered a hybrid because some features are not totally consistent with pure object orientation. C++ compilers are currently available on a number of operating systems, including DOS, Windows, and Unix. As the use of the language has grown, the American National Standards Institute (ANSI) has been meeting to develop and adopt a standard for the language.

Because C++ was written as an extension to standard C code, it is backward compatible to existing C code. A goal of C and C++ is hardware independence: therefore, the standard should run on any compiler without requiring changes to any of the code.

OBJECT-ORIENTED PROGRAMMING

C++ is an extension to the C language that provides the capability for **object-oriented programming (OOP).** Object-oriented refers to the analysis of data and related functions into abstract classifications or classes.

Programming using classes is an attempt to model the way in which items in general are broken down into classifications within the "real world." For example, a general class of objects is automobiles. Automobiles have many different features or attributes that resemble each other. The term automobile may then be used without referring to any details about a specific type of car.

An extension to the analogy of an automobile is that the car is really a class within the class of vehicles. Vehicles is a class within modes of transportation. Each one of these classes has specific traits that become more general as the class becomes more general.

Any example within an office environment can also be related back to an object. Consider customer information that may be used in many different applications or an invoice which may take on specific characteristics within a specific use.

Characteristics of an OOP Language

Three characteristics of an OOP language are encapsulation, inheritance, and polymorphism. Although the terms are introduced at this point they will be covered in more detail later in the text.

Encapsulation combines data structures with the actions that are used to manipulate the type of data. In C++ encapsulation is denoted with a structure that contains both data and functions, called a **class.** Classes will be introduced in Chapter 3.

Inheritance is a feature of object-oriented models that allows one class to be derived from another class. The **derived class** has similar features and actions but requires greater specificity than the **base class** with which it is associated. The automobile would be a derived class from vehicle base class. The concept of inheritance leads to a relationship of classes known as a **hierarchy** of classes and promotes reusability of code. It also allows features to be added without altering code that is already in use. This topic will be covered in more detail in Chapter 7.

The ability to have many versions of the same function and to select the appropriate version at run time is called **polymorphism**. This allows functions to be written for various data types; the compiler selects the proper function to be used in a particular execution of the program. In C++ polymorphism is referred to as **overloading**. Both functions and operators can be overloaded.

Advantages of C++

The advantages of C++ include its portability, its power due to a large selection of operators, the way it lends itself to object design, and the flexibility of the language. The popularity of C++ is due to its power and flexibility despite the small size of the language.

PORTABILITY

There are very few reserved words in the C++ language. Most of the programming done in the language uses a variety of functions that are stored in header files and libraries. The function names remain the same from one machine to another. The machine dependent code is written inside the standard library functions. The contents of these library functions may change from system to system, but the calls to the functions used by the programmer remain the same.

A LARGE SELECTION OF OPERATORS

Despite the small number of reserved words, C++ has a large number of operators that often make the code look cryptic. The ability to overload (redefine) operators means that operators can be used differently, but this may also result in increased confusion if not properly documented.

FLEXIBILITY

C++'s ability to manipulate data addresses allows programs to be written at almost an assembly level. With the large number of operators and library functions, it can also function as a powerful high-level language. These two levels of programming in C++ make it a very versatile language.

Disadvantages of C++

Some difficulties also arise from the language's compact style. The code may become difficult to read. It may contain difficult-to-find logic errors due to misuse of operators that do not generate syntax errors. Incorrect memory locations may be inadvertently accessed through the misuse of pointers.

CRYPTIC APPEARANCE

Because of the ability to write very compact code with embedded logic, C++ can be very difficult to read. It is critical in C++ to write well-documented programs and to use white space effectively to improve readability.

OPERATOR CONFUSION

Another common error for beginning C++ programs results from the large number of operators. It is very important to be familiar with and to refer to the precedence tables of the operators. Operators may be used anywhere, regardless of context. The assignment operator (=) could inadvertently be used when the conditional equality (==) is intended. In addition, the same symbol is sometimes used for different operations depending upon the context.

MISUSED POINTER ACCESS

Because this language allows the programmer to manipulate data at the bit level and to access data and functions by their memory address, some difficult-to-find bugs may be introduced. With the use of pointers, one of the powerful features of C++ that allows the programmer to access the address of an item, it is possible to inadvertently access anywhere in memory. With a poorly specified pointer, the program might accidentally access the storage area of the program or even the operating system. Such errors in logic may be very difficult to locate.

Fortunately, C++ has an advantage over C in that it includes the use of references and greater error checking, which can reduce the potential for damage by misuse of pointers.

RUNNING A C++ PROGRAM

C++ programs are created with an editor and then processed by a compiler. The programs in this text have been compiled with Borland C++ and Microsoft Visual C++. There may be some differences depending on the compiler. Be sure that your program has the extension .CPP to use the C++ options.

Editors, Compilers, and Linkers

In order to code and run a program in C++ it is necessary to have a text editor, a compiler, and a linker. The text editor may be a part of your C++ environment or it may be an independent editor. The **text editor** is used to enter the program into the machine and should provide the ability to easily edit your programming code (**source code**). These edit features usually include cut and paste, and searching operations. Such capabilities will help speed up the development time of your program.

A **compiler** translates your source code into **object code** (machine instructions). As the compiler attempts to perform this translation, it will be able to locate any syntax errors. Syntax errors consist of punctuation or spelling that cannot be translated by the compiler. The level of this error checking can usually be set as part of the environment.

After the program is compiled, the **linker** will be accessed to combine all necessary object files and data files. This step is done automatically for the programmer.

The text editor, the compiling process, and the linking process are all a part of the total environment provided by the Borland programming packages.

A FIRST PROGRAM

Let's take a look at a short C++ program.

```
#include <iostream.h>


void main()
{
      //Output to the screen
      cout << "This is a C++ program";
}
```

> **NOTICE THAT:**
>
> 1. The first line starts with #. This is not really a line of C++ code but rather a **preprocessor directive,** which specifies some action to be taken prior to the compilation of the program. In this case, the preprocessor calls for the inclusion of a file called iostream.h. Files from the library with an .h extension are called **header files** and contain definitions that will be used in the program.
>
> 2. The word main() is preceded by the word void and followed by () parentheses. The word void indicates that this function will not be returning any values to the location that called the function, upon the completion of the function. The parentheses contain any values or arguments received by the function. In this example the empty parentheses indicate that no values are being received.
>
> 3. The braces{} enclose the statements or instructions within the function.
>
> 4. C++ provides the ability to use single-line comments within a program. A **comment** is information contained in the source code that is not translated by the compiler. The symbol for these comments is two slashes //. The compiler will not translate this line. Comments should be used liberally to explain the program code for future reference by the programmer or others.
>
> 5. The cout statement within the main function ends with a semicolon. Most C++ statements will end with a semicolon. The cout is an object used for output that has been defined in the iostream.h file.

The main() Function

All C++ programs contain a **main() function** that controls execution of the entire program. The program will always begin and end execution in the main() function.

```
void main()
{
     program statement(s)
}
```

The instructions in this main() function are enclosed in braces{ }. Other programmer-created functions will also be enclosed in braces. The **braces** are used to mark the beginning and the end of a series of statements called a block. The main() function is an example of a block.

The set of parentheses following the word main() is used to enclose any informational items that need to be sent to the function. In our first example, you will not be sending any information to main() so the parentheses are empty. Any items that are enclosed inside of these parentheses are called **arguments**. All function names will be followed by the parentheses whether they accept arguments or not.

SELF-TEST

1. What function is required in all C++ programs?
2. What is the purpose of the braces { } in C++?
3. Is cout a reserved word in C++?

ANSWERS

1. All C++ programs must have a main() function.
2. The braces { } in C++ are used to enclose a group of statements called a block. In the earlier example the braces were used to enclose all of the statements that compromised the contents of the main() function.
3. No. The cout object in C++ is stored in the library files. It is not really a reserved word but rather an object that could be examined by listing the source code in iostream.h.

The Include Directive

Preprocessor directives begin with a # sign and do not have a semicolon at the end. The lack of a semicolon is due to the fact that these are not really C++ statements but rather instructions that insert other code into your program prior to compilation of your program. These directives cause some action to be taken prior to your program: hence, the name "preprocessor."

With an include directive, the appropriate file containing the library function definitions will be included in your object code. You will not see the actual lines of code unless you list the source code of the header file. However, as the program compiles, the line count of the header files is included as the contents of the header files are included into your object code.

Notice that the punctuation is the symbols < >. These symbols around the header file name indicate that the file may be found in the default disk directory for header files. You may use any path name for header files if you enclose the path and filename inside of quotes:

```
#include "a:iostream.h"

#include "c:\\cprog\\my.h"
```

It may be necessary to insert the double backslashes when giving paths to avoid confusion by the compiler with escape sequences. The escape sequences that are mentioned later are inside of quotes and are preceded by a backslash. Therefore "a:\test" would be interpreted as containing a \t escape sequence which is a tab.

OUTPUT

You will start the programming in C++ by creating output. The most common destinations for output are the screen and the printer. Data files are covered in Chapter 10.

C++ uses objects to produce output rather than reserved words, demonstrating the ability to remain hardware and operating system independent. The two output objects are cout and one you declare for the printer.

Screen Output

The object used to place information on the screen is the cout. Following the word cout is an operator << which is called the insertion operator. The format of the cout is:

```
cout<<items to be printed;
```

The items to be printed may be variables or constants. Variables are covered in the next chapter. For now, consider the cout in an example that prints a constant. The words to be printed are enclosed inside of double quotation marks.

```
//Ch01Pr01.cpp

#include <iostream.h>

void main()

{

    cout << "This is my first C++ program";

}
```

NOTE: To make this book easy for you to read, all code examples are double-spaced. This does not affect the output, but as you type your code, most editors will generate single-spaced code. The example at the left would look like this:

```
//Ch01Pr01.cpp
#include <iostream.h>
void main()
{
    cout << "This is my first C++ program";
}
```

OUTPUT

| This is my first C++ program |

The program prints exactly what is inside the quotes, printing it all on one line.

The following code produces exactly the same output:

```
#include <iostream.h>

void main()

{

    cout << "This ";

    cout << "is ";

    cout << "my ";

    cout << "first ";

    cout << "C++ ";

    cout << "program";

}
```

Each use of cout will print what is inside the quotes, and it will print on the same line because no instruction is given to advance the line. This could also have been coded on a single line with multiple constants using multiple insertion operators.

```
#include <iostream.h>

void main()

{

    cout << "This " << "is " << "my ";

    cout << "first " << "C++ " << "program";

}
```

Advancing to a New Line

The \n can be used inside of quotes to tell the output device to go to a new line. This will assure that the next item to print will not print on the same line. The \n (newline character) can be used anywhere in the quote. To leave a blank line, use one newline symbol to exit the current line and a second one to skip a line.

```
cout<<"1\n2\n3\n";
```

would print as:

```
1
2
3
```

Remember, when no newline symbol was included, the second print continued on the same output line as the previous print.

Watch what the output will be for the following program.

```
#include <iostream.h>

void main()
{
      cout << "Happy ";
      cout << "Birthday!!\n";
}
```

OUTPUT

```
Happy Birthday!!
```

The newline symbol or character is at the end of the second line, so that if there are additional cout calls, they advance to a new line. In this case, both words printed out on the same line because there was no newline character inside the quotes on the first call to cout or before the word "Birthday" in the second call to cout.

If you wish to print three letters on three separate lines, you do it with a single cout or with multiple couts.

```
cout << "A\nB\nC\n";
```

is the same as

```
cout << "A\n";
cout << "B\n";
cout << "C\n";
```

The newline character is the first example of an escape sequence.

Ending a Line with endl

Another way to indicate a new line at the end of a cout line is to use endl, a constant for the newline that is defined in the <iostream.h> file.

```
cout << "A" endl;
cout << "B" endl;
cout << "C" endl;
```

Notice that a second << operator is used prior to the endline endl. You can use many endl(s) on the same line.

SELF-TEST

1. Write a cout object that will print

    This is fun!!!!

2. Write a single cout that will print your name on the first line and the date on the second line.

3. What is wrong with each of the following:

    a. cout "Programming in C++";

    b. cout << I know what's wrong with this;

    c. cout << "OOPs, another wrong one;

    d. cout << "Maybe this one is correct"

    e. cout << "Print and then go to a newline"\n;

ANSWERS

1. cout << "This is fun!!!!";
2. cout << "your name here \n then the date";

    or

    cout << "your name here" << endl;

    cout << "then the date" << endl;

3. a. The << operator is missing.

    b. The information to be printed should be in quotes.

    c. The closing quotes are missing.

    d. There is no semicolon at the end of the statement.

    e. The \n newline character must be inside of the quotation marks.

Sending Output to the Printer

Sending output to the printer is accomplished by assigning an output device with an ofstream statement, and then using an object that you will create instead of cout. The printer object will require the use of the fstream.h file. The fstream.h includes the functions from the iostream.h eliminating the need to include both files.

The format for assigning a file is:

ofstream objectname("DEVICE");

where device is:

DEVICE SPECIFICATION	DEVICE
"LPT1"	Printer
"CON"	Console

This device assignment statement must be placed prior to the use of the printer object. This code may not work on some printers or networks. See the suggestion later in the chapter.

```
#include <fstream.h>

void main()
{
    ofstream Printer("LPT1");
    Printer << "This will go to the printer" << endl;
    Printer << "\f"; //Used for form feed
}
```

Of course, multiple calls to the printer object can be used to produce several lines of output or to continue the first line depending on the use of the newline escape sequence.

Note, however, that some printers require a carriage return as well as a newline sequence. If your printer goes down one line but keeps the same position across the line where it left off on the previous line, you will need to use \n\r to go to the beginning of a new line. The \r is the escape sequence for a carriage return and the \f is for formfeed.

Skipping Blank Lines

To skip a blank line using either a cout or a printer object requires the use of two newline symbols as in "\n\n". This also occurs if one output constant ends with a new line and the next output constant begin with a new line. The effect is the same as having put both of the newline symbols together.

If you want to print the title and column heading for a report, you would probably print the title on one line, skip a line, and then print the column headings. This is easy to accomplish with a series of printer calls.

```
Printer << "          Alpha Company\n";
Printer << "         Inventory Report\n\n";
Printer << "   Product          Quantity      Unit\n";
Printer << "   Description      on hand       Cost\n";
```

Would print as:

```
         Alpha Company
        Inventory Report

   Product      Quantity   Unit
   Description  on hand    Cost
```

■ SELF-TEST

What output will the following statements produce and to what output stream, assuming that an ofstream Printer("LPT1") has been executed?

1. Printer << "X\n\nY\n\nZ Corporation";

2. Printer << "XYZ Corporation\n\n";

3. cout << "Client name: ";
4. Printer << "\n Name";
5. cout << "\nName";

■ ANSWERS

1.
    X
    Y
    Z Corporation
    (Would be sent to the printer.)

2.
    XYZ Corporation
    (Would be sent to the printer, followed by a blank line.)

3.
    Client Name:
    (to the screen)

4.
     Name
    (Printer, skips a line and then a space because of the space after the \n.)

5.
    Name
    (Screen, no space before the word "Name.")

DOCUMENTATION

Good programs will contain comments as necessary to make the code easier to interpret. It is important not only for other programmers who will need to understand the logic to make modifications to your code but also for yourself. You may have discovered in your past programming experience that if you go back to make changes to a program that you've written awhile back, it may be hard to follow quickly some of the steps in the code.

A comment line can be included in C by bracketing with slashes and asterisks all information that you don't want the compiler to translate.

/* this is a comment line and may go anywhere */

A dangerous fact about the C method of commenting is that it can be opened anywhere and will continue through until the closing symbols. You may turn several lines of code into a comment. This is handy when debugging but can be frustrating if actual instructions are commented out by accident. The comment will continue until a closing */ is found.

A better alternative is to use the C++ convention of commenting out single lines using //. This notation for comments will only comment out a single line but does not need a closing mark.

```
#include <iostream.h>

void main()
{
    //Will print on one line
    cout << "Have ";
    cout << "a ";
    cout << "nice ";
    cout << "day!!!";
}
```

DIVIDING A PROGRAM INTO PARTS

Creating Functions

In addition to the ability to call C++ functions that are stored in a library, it is possible to create functions. The functions you create can also receive arguments and/or return a value. Passing arguments and returning values are covered in Chapter 3.

A **function** is a block of statements that performs some action. A program is divided into functions according to the role or purpose that the statements are intended to serve. At this point, you have sent output to the printer and to the screen. For a program that will perform both of these jobs, you can place each task in a separate function. To create a function to be called, it is necessary to declare the function and to define the function.

Declaring a Function

To create a function, you must declare it by giving it a name followed by parentheses containing the data type of any arguments. For now, you will not pass any arguments but you must still use the (). The function declaration is referred to as a **prototype.**

```
void PrintToScreen();
```

```
void PrintToPrinter();
```

The function must be declared before any function calling it, specifying what the return value will be. The declaration follows the #include directives at the beginning of the program. If there are no return values, use the return type of void just as you have been doing before main().

Defining a Function

The function definition contains the contents of the function. Enclose the function contents in braces. The first line contains the function name. Below the function name are the braces { } enclosing all of the statements that are a part of the function.

```
void PrintToScreen()
{
```

```
        cout << "Name:    ABC Incorporated\n"
        cout << "Date:    September 5\n";
}
```

Notice that there is no semicolon following the function name at the beginning of the function definition. This distinguishes the line from a function call or function declaration.

Calling the Function You Create

When the function is to be executed, it can be called by referencing the function name. A semicolon follows the function name because the call is a statement. The function may be called as many times as necessary. The function call will not contain void.

```
PrintToScreen ();
```

In the example below, main() will call the two functions: PrintToScreen () and PrintToPrinter (). Typically, you will put the main() first followed by the other functions.

```
//Ch01Pr02
/*********************************************
Programmed by:    A. Millspaugh
Date:             1997
Purpose:          Project containing multiple functions
*********************************************/
#include <fstream.h>
#include <conic.h>

//Function Declarations
void PrintToScreen();
void PrintToPrinter();

void main()
{
    PrintToScreen();
    PrintToPrinter();
}

//Function Definitions
void PrintToScreen()
{
    //Display output on the screen
```

```
        cout << "Demonstrating that what displays on the screen\n";
        cout << "will not always be the same as the printer\f";
}


void PrintToPrinter()
{
        //Print output on printer
        ofstream Printer("LPT1");
        Printer << "This will print on the printer \f";
}
```

HAVING TROUBLE GETTING PRINTER OUTPUT?

Some newer printers cannot deal with the LPT1 designation without setting them up to receive DOS commands. Another alternative would be to send the report output to a text file and then print from Notepad or another text editor.

To send output to a text file, use the name and path of the text file for your device name.

```
ofstream Output("a:\\report.txt");
```

After the program has completed execution, you will open the text editor and print the output.

Programming Style

The indentations and blank lines that are placed in a C++ program do not affect execution of the program. The use of both indentations and blank lines is for readability of the program listing.

```
#include <<fstream.h>


void main()
{
        ofstream Printer("LPT1");
        Printer << "This will go to the printer\n";
}
```

In the program discussed earlier, you will notice certain things about the spacing. The preprocessor directive is usually placed first in the program. Following the #include is a blank line. Use a blank line at the end of all preprocessor directives to separate them from the actual C++ code.

The main() is placed on a line by itself; place the function name on a separate line. The braces that indicate the beginning and end of the main() function are aligned. Later, you will use more sets of braces so it will become very important that each opening brace is aligned vertically with its closing brace.

The statement(s) inside of the braces should be indented to make it easier to spot the braces at a quick glance. The indentation may be a few spaces or an entire tab stop.

There will be further discussion of programming style as more statements are introduced.

PROGRAMMING/DEBUGGING HINT

Use the fact that Printer can output to the screen and to the printer to your advantage. When you are testing a program, you may wish all of the output to go to the screen so that you can see it before you actually send it to the printer.

Write your program with Printer using ofstream Printer("CON");. After you are satisfied with the way the output looks, you can change CON to LPT1. The program will then send the output to the printer.

If you need to have both printer and screen output, you can use the copy feature in your editor to duplicate your Printer line, and then have one function call to the screen and one to printer.

```
//Ch01Pr03
//Project using an ofstream for printer and console
#include <fstream.h>


//Function Declarations
void PrintToScreen();
void PrintToPrinter();


void main()
{
    PrintToScreen();
    PrintToPrinter();
}


//Function Definitions
void PrintToScreen()
{
    ofstream Screen("CON");
    Screen << "Demonstrating that what displays on the screen\n";
    Screen << "will not always be the same as the printer\f";
}


void PrintToPrinter()
{
    //Print output on printer

    ofstream Printer("LPT1");
    Printer << "This will print on the printer";
}
```

Key Terms

argument	insertion operator
base class	linker
braces{ }	main() function
class	object code
comment	object-oriented programming
compiler	OOP
derived class	overloading
encapsulation	polymorphism
function	preprocessor directive
header file	prototype
hierarchy	source code
inheritance	text editor

Summary

C++ is a portable language that is used in many environments. The language is very flexible and is often considered the closest to assembly-level language of all higher-level languages. The use of standard functions stored in libraries allows the hardware-dependent information to be removed from the programmers' realm and implemented as a part of the language functions.

All C++ programs contain a main() function that may be located anywhere within the program but must exist. Other functions will be called or created as needed.

Two objects providing formatted output are the cout and the Printer. The cout outputs to the screen only, which is considered the standard output device. The Printer allows the output stream to be specified.

The programmer may divide programs into functions that serve a specific purpose. Each function must be declared in a prototype and be defined.

Review Questions

1. Why is the #include required when using a cout?
2. What will the following code produce?

   ```
   cout << "Have a nice day!!!"
   ```

   Modify so that each word is printed on a separate line.

3. Modify the example in number 2 so that one cout is required to print each word in the phrase "Have a nice day!!!"
4. What is the significance of the main() function?
5. Explain the use of the following punctuation marks:
   a. { }
   b. ( )
   c. ;
   d. //
6. Is it necessary to place each statement or instruction on a separate line? If not, why bother doing it?
7. What is a comment?
8. Why has C++ become such a popular language in such a short time?

9. Some people feel that C++ is a low-level language like assembler, and others consider it a high-level language. Discuss what is meant by each of these views.

10. What is the relationship between a text editor, a compiler, and a linkage editor?

Exercises

1. Create a student survey printout. Print information on the screen and the printer about yourself. The output will contain name, phone number, major, previous programming background, and a reason for taking this class. Each item will be on a separate line. Include the appropriate information about the program as comments at the beginning of the program and before each function definition.

2. Write a program that will produce the following form on the screen:

          Ace Designs   Date:

    Customer Name:

    Customer Address:

    Customer Phone:

3. Write a program that will print out 5 features of the C++ language to the screen and to the printer. Include a title and your name at the top of the list. Leave a blank line before the list and after the title. Print each feature on a separate line.

4. Create a program to print a list of names and phone numbers to the printer. Include title and column headings at the top of the list. Leave a blank line between the title and column headings and another between the headings and the first name and number. Double space the lines that contain the names and the numbers.

5. Write a program that will print a memo on the printer indicating that hours will be extended to 8 a.m. to 6 p.m. effective July 1. The memo should include a heading with the current date and topic, change of hours, and a "from" line containing your name. Leave a blank line between each of the heading lines, and double space before the body of the memo.

6. Write a program that will print out a cover sheet for your assignments. The sheet will be sent to the printer and will contain your name, course title, time, and days that the class meets.

7. Write a program to write out a short-term and long-term plan of your goals: educational, career, and personal.

Hayley Office Supplies

Write a program that will print a letterhead for Hayley Office Supplies. The letterhead should be centered at the top of the page and will include the company name, address, and phone number.

Sample Output:

Hayley Office Supplies
1111 Main Street
Chino, California 91711
(909) 555-1111

CHAPTER 2

BASIC DATA TYPES AND STRUCTURES

CHAPTER OBJECTIVES

By the end of this chapter you should be able to:
- Understand the difference between constant and variable data and the ways they are declared.
- Assign numeric values.
- Assign(copy) string data with string functions.
- Enter data using the cin object.
- Design prompt screens for the entry of data.
- Combine variables with a structure.

CHAPTER OVERVIEW

This chapter builds on the print functions covered in the previous chapter by introducing the use of variables. The data types for individual fields are explained as well as the combination of fields into structures. Data entry functions are also introduced to create interactive programs.

DATA ITEMS AND DATA TYPES

Data items may be variable or constant. As with other languages, data that is **variable** may be changed during the execution of the program while **constant** data remains unchanged during execution.

The way that data is handled is determined by its **data type.** The types of data in C++ are integer, floating point, double precision, and character. These may be modified as long integer, short integer, signed integer, or unsigned integer.

The different types of data require different amounts of memory for storage. This varies from 1 byte for a character to 8 bytes for a double precision number. The amount of storage required may vary from one machine to another.

DATA TYPE	STORAGE USED	CONTENTS	POSSIBLE VALUES
char	1 byte	character data	−128 to 127 (ASCII characters)
int	2 bytes	integer data	−32,768 to 32,767
long	4 bytes	long integer	−2,147,483,648 to 2,147,483,647
signed	2 bytes	signed integer	0 to 65,535
float	4 bytes	floating point numeric	7 digit precision
double	8 bytes	double precision float	15 digit precision

Constants and Literals

Constants will not change values during the execution of the program. Constants are either numeric or alphanumeric. Numeric data is for use in calculations while alphanumeric may contain numbers as well as letters and punctuation marks.

Numeric constants may be an integer such as 5 or a floating point value that contains a decimal such as 5.05. These numbers can be used in a calculation, assigned to a variable, or used in an output function.

A characterconstant contains only one character and is enclosed in single quotes such as 'c'. Character constants may be a single letter, a digit, a symbol, or they may be escape sequences.

Escape sequences are typically used to represent white space, such as a tab or new line, or to represent unprintable characters, such as the bell: They are preceded by a backslash \, such as the newline escape sequence \n from Chapter 1. The backslash can also be used in C to allow certain special characters to be used in a print string that might otherwise be interpreted differently. For example, if you want to print a quote you cannot place the quotation marks inside the print quotes because the compiler would interpret the quote as an opening or closing of what was to be printed. However, you can actually print the quotation marks if they are preceded with a \. This means that the escape sequence \" used inside an output constant will cause quotation marks to be printed.

Common escape sequences include the following:

ESCAPE SEQUENCE	PURPOSE
\a	Bell (the a comes from "alert")
\b	Backspace
\f	Formfeed
\n	New line
\r	Carriage return
\t	Tab
\0	Null character
\'	Single quotes
\"	Double quotes
\\	Backslash
\%	Percent sign

Some printers require a carriage return at the end of each line. The tab can be used for spacing out the print line and aligning columns of text.

A **string literal** is a constant containing multiple characters and is enclosed in double quotes, such as "This is my first C++ program." String literals can be used in other situations besides printing.

Examples of Constants and Literals

Integer	5
Float	.05
Character	'c'
Character	'\n'
String	"literal"

■ SELF-TEST

1. What is the difference between a character constant and a string literal?
2. Are the following constants, numeric, character, or invalid?
    a. 5
    b. .05
    c. 5%
    d. '5'
3. To test the tab stops on your system, type in the following program and execute it.

```
#include <iostream.h>

void main()
{
    cout << "\t\tHelp!!!!\n\n";      //print tabbed info
    cout << "1234567890123456789"; //count positions
}
```

■ ANSWERS

1. A character constant contains only one character or an escape sequence and is enclosed in single quotes, while a string literal may contain multiple characters and is enclosed inside of double quotes.
2. a. numeric, integer
    b. numeric, floating point
    c. invalid—cannot have the % unless the two characters are inside of double quotes, a string literal.
    d. character

Identifiers

The programmer makes up names for the variables, called variable names or identifiers, but the names do not necessarily tell the type of data unless the programmer uses a variable name which denotes the contents.

RULES FOR IDENTIFIERS

1. Up to 32 characters.
2. May contain only letters, numbers, and underscores.
3. No embedded spaces.
4. Must begin with a letter or underscore.
5. C++ is case sensitive so it matters if you use upper or lowercase.
6. No reserved words.

In addition to the rules for naming variables you should also follow naming conventions that allow the code to be more easily read and understood.

NAMING CONVENTIONS

1. Use meaningful names.
2. Precede the variable or constant with a prefix indicating the datatype.
3. Place constants in all capital letters (except the prefix) with underscores to separate words.
4. Use mixed upper and lower case for variable names with a capital to separate words.

Prefixes for identifiers by data type:

DATA TYPE	PREFIX	EXAMPLE
char	c	cLetter
double	d	dWeight
float	f	fBalance
int	i	iCount
long	l	lSum
string	st	stName

Named Constants

Use the reserved word **const** to assign a name to a constant value. The value assigned to the name cannot be changed during execution of the program but it provides an opportunity for improved readability of the source code.

To declare a constant, specify the keyword const, along with the data type, the constant name, and an assignment of the value. The sequence of the data type and const is not critical. If no data type is specified the default is int.

```
const datatype identifier = value;
```

As an example the following statement creates a named constant called fPI, which is assigned the value 3.14.

```
const float   fPI = 3.14;
```

It is a convention for C++ programmers to use uppercase for named constants while variables normally are lower or mixed case.

When working with a word such as a company title, it is necessary to use square brackets after the constant name to indicate that there are multiple characters (an array). A more complete explanation of character arrays is found later in the chapter within the topic on variables.

```
const char stCOMPANY[] = "XYZ Corporation";
```

■ SELF-TEST

1. Define a constant called fTAX_RATE with a value of .065.
2. Create a constant called stMESSAGE1 containing "Please try again."
3. What data type will a constant default to when no data type is specified?

■ ANSWERS

1. const float fTAX_RATE = .065;
2. const char stMESSAGE1[] = "Please try again";
3. int

Variables

A data item frequently needs to be variable to allow the value of the data item to change during execution of the program or from one run of the program to the next. Variables may be one of several data types but are differentiated when they are declared.

The type of data that the variable can hold is specified when the variable is declared. Variables may be declared either inside or outside of a function.

DECLARING A VARIABLE

To declare a variable, the type of data is followed by the variable name.

```
float fAmount;
int iQuantity;
```

A semicolon follows the variable **declarations.** Remember, most C++ statements and declarations end with a semicolon (;).

The possible values for a data type depends on the compiler implementation. The data types on page 20 are used to declare the variables to the given ranges on a PC.

There are additional data types available as extensions to standard ANSI C on most compilers.

STRING VARIABLES

Strings are not really a separate type of variable but rather an array of characters terminated by a null character. To specify the maximum number of elements in an array, follow the variable name by the maximum number of characters in square brackets. To declare a field called name 20 characters long the declaration would be:

```
char stName[20];
```

This field should actually hold only 19 characters to allow for a null character. In the case of the string literal the machine supplies the null automatically. With a string variable it may be automatic in most cases but you must allow enough space in the array for it.

DECLARING MULTIPLE VARIABLES OF THE SAME TYPE

When declaring multiple variables of the same type, they may be declared with a single statement. Each of the variable names are separated by a comma.

```
float fAmount, fTotalAmount;
char cLetter, stName[20];
```

LOCATION OF DECLARATIONS

The location of the variable declaration within the program determines where the variable may be used. Variables declared outside of a function, usually before the main() function, are called **global** or external variables. Global variables may be used in any function after the point where they are declared, and any function may change the value of the variable. This is referred to as the **scope** or visibility of the variable. A global variable is visible to all functions after the line in which it is declared. The initial value of a global numeric variable is set to zero unless otherwise initialized. It is usually considered poor programming to use global variables. Although this chapter uses them in examples, they will be replaced when using classes in Chapter 3.

Variables that are declared inside a block are visible only to that block and can be changed only by statements in the block. These variables are said to be **local** or internal. Local variables are usually declared within the function or **block.** A block is a series of declarations and statements that are enclosed inside of braces. Local variables are not initialized automatically. When creating a function with local variables, those variables are known only within that function.

Example of Global Variable Declarations

```
int number;         // global variables
float amount;
void main()
{
}
```

Example of Local Variable Declarations

```
void main()
{
    int number;
    float amount;
}
```

■ SELF-TEST

1. Declare an integer variable called iNumberDays.
2. Are the following variable names valid? If not, why not?
   a. fSale.Amount
   b. f%OfSales
   c. void
   d. iValuable

3. In the following code, are the variables local or global?

   ```
   void main()
   {
       int   iIndex, iCount;
   }
   ```
4. Declare a variable that will hold a character address that may be up to 30 characters long.

■ ANSWERS

1. int iNumberDays;
2. a. invalid, cannot contain a period.
   b. invalid, the % sign is not a valid character.
   c. invalid, void is a reserved word.
   d. valid
3. The variables are both locals because they are defined inside of the function.
4. char stAddress[31];

INITIALIZING VARIABLES

Variables can be given a beginning value when they are declared. The following statement creates the integer variable called iNumber and assigns the value of 0 to the variable at the same time.

```
int iNumber = 0;
```

INITIALIZING STRING VARIABLES

Character arrays(global) can also be initialized with strings when they are declared. Technically, the initialization assigns a character to each position of the array.

```
char stWord[6] = {'H','e','l','l','o','\0'};
```

Fortunately, you do not need to assign each position individually. The following declaration and initialization works exactly the same.

```
char stWord[6] = "Hello";
```

Remember to put the string literal in double quotes and allow for the trailing null character.

If a string variable is initialized when it is declared, it is not necessary to specify the size of the array. The proper amount of storage is allocated according to the size of the assigned literal plus a null character.

```
char stWord[] = "Hello";
```

MULTIPLE VARIABLES AND INITIALIZATION

When declaring multiple variables with the same statement, the initial value applies only to the one to which it is assigned.

```
float fAmount, fTotalAmount = 100.0;
```

The value of 100.0 is stored in the variable called fTotalAmount. The value of fAmount depends on whether it is global(defaults to 0.0) or local(undefined).

```
float fAmount = 0.0, fTotalAmount = 0.0;
```

This statement causes two variables to be declared; both will be initialized to 0.0.

■ SELF-TEST

What, if anything, is wrong with the following:
1. int iNumber = 5.0;
2. int iNumber
3. char cLetter = "c";
4. char stLetters[5] = "abcde";
5. char cCode = '\n';

■ ANSWERS

1. The value 5.0 is not an integer. This will compile but causes a conversion to be performed.
2. The semicolon is missing.
3. A character constant is enclosed in single quotes.
4. There is no room left for the null character to terminate the string. The size should be 6 if it is being treated as a string.
5. Nothing.

ASSIGNING VALUES TO A VARIABLE

Variables may also be assigned values after they have been declared. As in the previous declaration and initialization, the symbol used for assignment is = (with the exception of string data). Let's repeat the earlier example, initializing the variable iNumber as it is declared and assigning a value to the variable amount separate from the declaration.

```
int iNumber = 0;
float fAmount;

void main()
{
    fAmount = 0.0;
}
```

One note to make in this example is that the type of data that is assigned to a variable should match the data type of the field. The integer is initialized with the value 0 while the float variable is assigned the value 0.0.

ASSIGNING A VALUE TO MULTIPLE VARIABLES

It is possible to assign the same value to several variables at the same time. The assignment is performed from the right to the left.

```
int iVariable1, iVariable2, iVariable3;

iVariable1 = iVariable2 = iVariable3 = 1;
```

The assignment statement assigns a 1 to iVariable3, then the value of iVariable3 is assigned to iVariable2, and finally the value of iVariable2 is assigned to iVariable1. The significance of the sequence of the assignments may not seem important at this time, but become very significant as more operators are introduced.

SELF-TEST

1. Declare a variable called fTotalPay as type float and initialize the variable to 0.0.
2. Assign a value of 0 to the field fTotalSales.
3. Declare the variables iMaleCount and iFemaleCount as integer and initialize them to a beginning value of 0.
4. Set the values of two integer variables, iTotalPossible and iTotalCorrect to 100, assume the fields have already been declared.

ANSWERS

1. float fTotalPay = 0.0;
2. fTotalSales = 0.0;
3. int iMaleCount = 0, iFemaleCount = 0;
4. iTotalPossible = iTotalCorrect − 100;

    or

    iTotalPossible = 100;

    iTotalCorrect = 100;

ASSIGNING VALUES TO A STRING VARIABLE

There is no data type in C for strings; they are an array of characters as you have already seen. Therefore the "string" or character array cannot use the assignment operators. The strings must be assigned values through the use of a string function such as strcpy(). The string functions require the inclusion of the string.h file.

The string copy can be used to copy the contents of one string variable to another or it may be used to assign a string constant to a string variable. Remember that string constants are placed inside of double quotes.

The format of the strcpy() function is:

```
strcpy( string1, string2);
```

where the value of string2 is placed into string1. String2 may be a variable or a constant but string1 must be a variable in order to provide a memory address for the copied string to be stored.

```
strcpy(stMessage,"Press Enter");
```

places the string "Press Enter" into the variable called stMessage.

```
strcpy(stCurrentName,stName);
```

places the value that is in the variable called stName into stCurrentName.

```
strcpy(stName,"Quit");
```

This statement copies the string quit to the string called stName. The null character is automatically placed at the end of stName. If there was a value in stName before the strcpy() it is replaced when the function is executed. Notice that the movement is from string 2 to string 1. **String1 must be large enough to contain string2 including a terminating null character.**

MOVING A PORTION OF A STRING

The strncpy() allows the number of characters to be moved from string 2 to string 1 to be specified. The format is:

> strncpy(string1, string2, number of characters);

A terminating null character is *not* added when the number of characters specified is less than the size of string2.

Assuming stName contains the value "Mary Lou":

```
strncpy(stAccount,stName,3);
```

The first 3 characters of the variable stName will be moved to the variable stAccount. The value of account is "Mar" without a null character.

■ SELF-TEST

1. Assign the string "Press any key to Continue" to the variable stMessage1.
2. What is wrong with the following?

    char stSalutation[10];

    ....

    strcpy("Hello",stSalutation);
3. Would it be possible to use the following statement?

    stAddress = "123 Main Street";
4. What will happen in the following?

    char stAbbrev[4], stMonth[10];

    ....

    strncpy(stAbbrev, stMonth,3);

■ ANSWERS

1. strcpy(stMessage1,"Press any key to Continue");
2. The first item inside of the parentheses for the strcpy() function must be a variable because it is the location where the second item will be copied to.
3. A string cannot use a numeric assignment symbol; the value must be copied into the variable using the strcpy().
4. The first three characters from the month string variable would be moved to the stAbbrev character array.

PRINTING VARIABLES

You can print variables using the output objects. Insertion operators separate each item on an output line. It is possible to combine both variable and constant data on the same output line. Be careful to place appropriate spaces within the constants to control proper spacing on the print line.

```
cout << "The amount is " << fAmount;
```

FORMATTING DATA

The output of the data can be controlled with features called **manipulators** The manipulators are contained in the iomanip.h file which must be included for their use. Some of the features controlled with the manipulators are: column width, justification, precision of decimal numbers, and the number of decimal places.

The manipulators are like switches in that they stay set once they have been defined with the exception of setting the width which only applies to the field following it. Therefore, the rest of the print settings may be set at the beginning of a print function and then only altered as necessary.

Column Width

The column width is controlled with the setw() manipulator. The setw() contains the number of characters in the column and is included in cout. This manipulator may be used for numeric or string fields and requires the use of an additional insertion operator. For example:

```
cout << setw(15) << stName;
```

The setw() may be used on either a cout or a printer output.

```
Printer << setw(15) << stName << setw(8) << fAmount;
```

Remember that the setw() only affects the field following it and must be repeated for each field. In the previous example the stName column is 15 wide and the fAmount column is 8 spaces.

Justification

The justification is set with what is known as an input/output flag using setiosflags(). The default justification of all fields is to the right. In order to set the field to the left, use an ios::left flag in the function, setiosflags(ios::left). The flags typically contain ios, referring to the input output stream, followed by double colons. The significance of the :: symbol will become clear in later chapters.

The manipulator is incorporated into the output statement.

```
cout << setiosflags(ios::left) << stName;
```

Avoiding Exponential Format of Numbers

The output of numeric fields may print in an "E" format if the number is large. Specify fixed format flag to avoid this. This is done with setiosflags(ios::fixed).

```
cout << setprecision(2) << setiosflags(ios::showpoint|ios::fixed) << fAmount;
```

Combining Multiple Flags and Manipulators

You can combine the flags and manipulators as desired for a specific output statement. They may vary by variable if desired. Note that the | operator (the piping symbol) is used to combine flags.

For example the following may be combined.

```
cout << setprecision(2) << setiosflags(ios::fixed|ios::showpoint) << fAmount;
```

Precision of Decimal Numbers

The rounding position for the accuracy in a decimal number is determined by the setprecision() manipulator. Note that this function does not specify the number of decimal places but the number of positions of accuracy for rounding. To work properly, the setprecision() function must be accompanied by the flags and fixed showpoint setiosflags(ios::showpoint) which control the number of decimal positions.

```
cout << setprecision(2) << setiosflags(ios::showpoint|ios::fixed) << fAmount;
```

Example Program

```
#include <iostream.h>
#include <iomanip.h>

void main()
{
  float fNumber = 5.25;
  char stName[] = "J. Jones";

  cout << setiosflags(ios::left) << setw(10) << stName;
  cout << setprecision(1) setiosflags(ios::showpoint|ios::fixed)
     << setw(10) << fNumber;
}
```

OUTPUT

```
J. Jones    5.2
```

```
#include <iostream.h>
#include <iomanip.h>

void main()
{
    float fNumber = 5.2;
    char stName[] = "J. Jones";
    cout << setiosflags(ios::left) << setw(10) << stName;
    cout << setprecision(2) << setw(10)
       << setiosflags(ios::showpoint|ios::fixed) << fNumber;
}
```

OUTPUT

```
J. Jones    5.20
```

Resetting Manipulators

If it becomes necessary to change a manipulator setting back to the original state, a resetiosflags() will be required. This will frequently be used for justification. To change justification back to right you must reset the left flag.

```
cout << resetiosflags (ios::left) << fAmount;
```

Setting the Manipulators Before the Print Line

The manipulators do not need to appear on the same cout used to print the data. Because they are flags that are being set to a specific setting, they may appear on a separate cout.

```
cout << setprecision(2) << setiosflags(ios::showpoint|ios::fixed);
cout << setiosflags(ios::left) << setw(25) << stName
     << resetiosflags(ios::left) << setw(10) << fAmount;
```

Notice that the print lines are split onto two lines, this makes the code easier to read. The terminating semicolon only exists on the final line.

SELF-TEST

What output will the following produce given:

```
int iNumber = 7;
float fAmount = 2.25;
char cLetter = 'c', stName[15] = "Jack Spratt";
```

1. `cout << setw(20) << setiosflags(ios::left) << stName << fAmount;`
2. `cout << fAmount << setw(20) << setiosflags(ios::left) << stName;`
3. `cout << setw(5) << stName << setw(4) << iNumber;`
4. `cout << "\n" << "\t" << cLetter;`
5. `cout << setw(25) << setiosflags(ios::left) << stName;`
   `cout << setw(10) << fAmount << setw(10) << iNumber;`

ANSWERS

1.
   Jack Spratt   2.25
2.
   2.25Jack Spratt
3. Only five characters will be printed from the string. The number will be right justified over 4 spaces.
   Jack   7
4. On a new line, one tab will be printed and then the character c.
   c
5. The name will be left justified and then followed by spaces for a total column width of 25 characters. The amount and number will be printed in columns 10 characters wide.
   Jack Spratt   2.25   7

ENTERING DATA

To obtain data values from the keyboard use cin. This object accepts data from the keyboard and places the value in the specified variable. The cin object uses the **extraction operator >>.** Use the cin object for numeric or single character data.

```
cin >> variable
```

```
float fAmount;
int iNumber;
cin >> fAmount;
cin >> iNumber;
```

When obtaining data for a string field one problem may be encountered. The cin function is terminated by any white space; this includes a return, a tab, or a blank. When entering a name, a blank space may be desired as part of the field value. To avoid termination of the data entry use the cin.getline() function. The format of the function is:

```
cin.getline(variable name, number of characters);
```

The number of characters must contain the field length of the variable which allows for the null which will terminate the string.

```
char stName[20];
cin.getline(stName,20);
```

The field length will control the number of characters that are placed in the character array. However, note that it DOES NOT FLUSH THE KEYBOARD BUFFER. This means that if too many characters are entered at the keyboard they will be held for the next input.

Solving the Skipped String Entry Problem

When a string field is input following a numeric field it is necessary to add a function to control the keyboard buffer. This makes sure that the string input function is not skipped. The statement cin.get() will precede the cin.getline() for string data or you may wish to create a function for clearing the buffer.

```
void ClearBuffer()
{
    cin.get();
}
```

Basically this function call will place an "input pointer" at the end of the previous input. Without this function you may find that the program does not stop for a field to be entered. This is true when an input for a string follows an input for a numeric field. The problem is more critical when using loops. (See Chapter 6.)

A safe solution is to place the ClearBuffer function before each input:

```
cout << "Please enter your name:    ";
ClearBuffer();
cin.getline(stName,20);
ClearBuffer();
cout << "Social Security Number    ";
cin.getline(stSocialSecNumber,12);
```

Prompts

Use of cin should be preceded by a cout statement that will **prompt** the user for specific data input. It is not possible to include a prompt or question as part of the cin. The printing of a question or prompt is separate from the input of a response.

Example 1

```
char stName[20];

cout << "Enter your name";
cin.getline(stName, 20);
```

Example 2

```
float fAcctNum;

cout << "Account Number:   ";
cin >> fAcctNum;
```

Sample Problem

Write a program that will ask the user to enter a name and balance. The information will then be output to the screen.

This will require two variables for each person—one for the name and one for the balance. The name variable will be a string (character array) and the balance can contain a balance so the data type should be float. It is up to the programmer to select names for the variables—you will call them stName and fBalance.

VARIABLE	DATA TYPE	NAME
Name	char array	stName
Balance	float	fBalance

FUNCTION	PURPOSE
ObtainData	Input name and balance
PrintInfo	Print out information

```
//Ch02Pr01
/*******************************************
Programmed by:    A Millspaugh
Date:             July 1997
Purpose:          Enter information from keyboard and
                  Print to screen
*********************************************/
#include <fstream.h>
#include <iomanip.h>

//Function Declarations
void ObtainData();
void PrintInfo();

//Variable Declarations
char stName[20];
//Remember that one space is for the null
float fBalance;

void main()
{
    ObtainData();
    PrintInfo();
}

void ObtainData()
{
    //Prompt for and obtain data
    cout << "Name:          ";
    cin.getline(stName, 20);

    cout << "Balance: ";
    cin >> fBalance;
}

void PrintInfo()
{
```

```
    //Send information to the screen
    cout << setiosflags(ios::left) << setw(25) << stName
      << setprecision(2) << setiosflags(ios::fixed| ios::showpoint)
      << fBalance;
}
```

SELF-TEST

1. Write the code to prompt and enter the following data:
   Last Name:
   First Name:
   Phone:

ANSWERS

1.
```
cout << "Last Name:";
cin.getline(stLastName,10);
cout << "First Name:";
cin.getline(stFirstName,10);
cout << "Phone:";
cin.getline(stPhone,9);
```

STRUCTURES

A structure allows us to combine several variables together and to treat them as a single unit. You might be familiar with the concept of a record containing several fields of data. You can then refer to the group of data by the record name or refer to an individual field. This is also true of structures. A structure may combine as few or as many fields as desired, and the fields may be of any type or combined types. The format for defining a structure is:

```
struct [tag]
{
field 1;
field 2;
...
} [variable_name1, variable_name2,...];
```

The structure tag is a name given to the new data type created by this definition: The tag is optional. The *tag does not reserve memory* for a variable but merely gives a name to the structure that may be referred to later in the program. The structure declaration may contain a variable name associated with this structure type: The *variable name does create a variable and reserves memory.*

If other variable names are to be declared to be of a structure type at a later point in the program then it is necessary to have a structure tag.

```
struct date
{
     int iYear;
     int iMonth;
     int iDay;
};


date dtHireDate, dtBirthDate, dtReviewDate;
```

The structure was given a tag date. Notice that this is used in the declaration as the data type for dtHireDate, dtBirthDate, and dtReviewDate.

```
struct name
{
     char stLastname[12];
     char cInitial;
     char stFirstname[10];
     float fAmount;
};
```

Use the reserved word struct to define the data in a structure. This structure contains four items: stLastname, cInitial, stFirstname, and fAmount. The **tag** is not a variable but merely a shorthand notation for the structure definition for use when declaring any variables to be of this type of structure.

A variable would be declared to be of this structure type as follows:

name nmEmployee;

Now there is a variable called nmEmployee of a structure type with the tag name. You may create a prefix appropriate for your new data type.

Structure Variables

There may be multiple variables of a given structure type. These may be declared when the structure is defined or declared later in the program.

```
struct
{
     int iYear;
     int iMonth;
     int iDay;
}dtHireDate, dtBirthDate, dtReviewDate;
```

This example does not have a tag, so additional variables may not be designated as this structure type later without redefining the structure. The dtHireDate, dtBirthDate, and dtReviewDate are all variables that contain three integers each.

Size of a Structure

The size of a structure is the sum of the size of all of its parts. The size is found by adding up the size of each of the component fields, but this may change from one type of machine to another. If any changes are made to the structure then the size will also change. A better way to determine the size is through the use of the sizeof operator. The sizeof may refer to the tag or the variable.

```
struct name
{
    char stLastname[12];
    char cInitial;
    char stFirstname[10];
};
```

In this example

```
sizeof(name)
```

would yield a 23, which is the sum of the two strings plus one byte for the character.

Referring to a Field within a Structure

To refer to the individual elements of a structure, combine the structure variable name with the field name, separated by a dot operator(.).

> structurevariable.fieldname

Use this notation anytime that a field within a structure is accessed, including printing, input, and calculations.

```
struct name
{
    char stLastname[12];
    char cInitial;
    char stFirstname[10];
}nmEmployee;
```

To assign the first name "Steve" it is necessary to use:

```
strcpy(nmEmployee.stFirstname, "Steve");
```

Similarly to input the initial, the field will be referred to as stEmployee.cInitial.

```
cin >> nmEmployee.cInitial;
```

■ SELF-TEST

1. Declare a structure called inventory that will contain a 25 character description, a quantity (integer), the current unit cost (float), and the last order date (9 characters).
2. Write a cin function to input the unit cost from the inventory structure.
3. Write a cout function that will print the description and the quantity from the inventory structure.

ANSWERS

1. ```
   struct
   {
        char stDescription[25];
        int iQuantity;
        float fUnitCost;
        char stLastOrderDate[9];
   } inventory;
   ```

2. `cin >> inventory.fUnitCost;`

3. `cout << inventory.stDescription << inventory.iQuantity;`

Structures within Structures

Structures may also be used as a data type within the definition of another structure. Name would be a common data type in many different applications.

```
struct name
{
     char stLastname[12];
     char cInitial;
     char stFirstname[10];
};

struct date
{
     int iYear;
     int iMonth;
     int iDay;
};

struct
{
     name nmEmployee;
     char stSocialSecurity[12];
     date dtHireDate;
}EmployeeRecord;
```

EmployeeRecord is a variable name for a structure that contains two other structures as well as a character array.

`cin.getline(EmployeeRecord.nmEmployee.stFirstname, 10);`
```

Structures 39

To enter data into the stFirstname field, stFirstname will be used with a period behind nmEmployee. nmEmployee is a component field of the structure variable EmployeeRecord so another period notation is required.

Example Program

Rewrite previous example using a structure.

```
//Ch02Pr02
/****************************************************
Programmed by:    A Millspaugh
Date:             July 1997
Purpose:          Enter information from keyboard and
                  Print to screen
****************************************************/
#include <fstream.h>
#include <iomanip.h>

//Function Declarations
void ObtainData();
void PrintInfo();

//Variable Declarations
struct
{
    char stName[20];
    float fBalance;
}Customer;

void main()
{
    ObtainData();
    PrintInfo();
}

void ObtainData()
{
    //Prompt for and obtain data
    cout << "Name:            ";
```

```cpp
    cin.getline(Customer.stName, 20);

    cout << "Balance: ";
    cin >> Customer.fBalance;
}

void PrintInfo()
{
    //Send information to the screen
    cout << setiosflags(ios::left) << setw(25) << Customer.stName
     << setprecision(2) << setiosflags(ios::fixed|ios::showpoint)
     << Customer.fBalance;
}
```

PROGRAMMING STYLE

Following the declaration of variables, leave a blank line to separate the declarations from the actual statements in the program. Although the program runs the same without the blank line, it improves in the readability of the program. Notice in the examples in this chapter that a blank line follows the preprocessor directives and another follows the declarations of the global variables prior to the main() function.

If the variables are declared inside a function, leave one blank line between the variables and the first instruction.

```cpp
#include <iostream.h>

void main()
{
    int number;
    cin >> number;
    cout << "The number entered was " << number;
}
```

Key Terms

block	identifier
constant	integer
data type	local variable
declaration	prompt
double	scope
escape sequence	string literal
float	symbolic constant
global variable	variable

Chapter Summary

The information or data used in a program can be variable or it can be constant. The basic types of data in C++ are integer, long integer, float, double, and character. Values may be assigned to variables as they are declared or through the use of assignment statements.

String data is stored as an array of character data, containing one or more characters. Character arrays are terminated by a null character. Strings use specific string functions rather than the assignment operators.

Variables and constants can be output using the cout and Printer objects. Formatting of the output can be accomplished through the use of flags and manipulators.

Data entry can be done with the cin. The cin will terminate at any white space. For string fields it is better to use cin.getline(). Both of these functions allow data to be obtained from the keyboard.

When obtaining data for related fields, the data can be grouped together through the use of a structure. The individual fields of the structure may be accessed individually.

Review Questions

1. Differentiate between a constant and a variable.
2. Name three data types available in C++.
3. What is a constant?
4. Name two ways that can be used for inputting data from the keyboard.
5. What is the purpose of the manipulators in a cout?
6. List the rules for naming variables.
7. What function should be used to input string data?
8. Why would it be desirable to create a structure?

Exercises

1. Write a program that will allow students to input their name, major, and current number of units or credit hours into a structure. Make the name and major fields string while units should be a floating point. Output the data in the following format:

   Name: xxxxxxxxxxxxxxxxxxxx
   Major: xxxxxxxxxxxxxxxxxxx
   Units: ##.#

2. Create an invoice heading for the Ace Paper Company. The program should prompt the user for their name and address. The billing heading should print as:

         Ace Paper Company
         111 Main Street
         Richville, California 99999-1111
   Bill To: XXXXXXXXXXXXXXXXXX
           XXXXXXXXXXXXXXXXXX
           XXXXXXXXXXXXXXXXXX

3. Write a program that will print the prompts for first name, last name, and phone number and enter the data into a structure. Print the information to the printer.

4. Write a program that will print out a mailing label. The input screen should be designed to prompt for the following.

   Name:

   Title:

   Street Address:

   City:

   State:

   ZIP Code:

   The label should print on four lines, with one blank line preceding the label and one blank line following it. It will be necessary to combine city, state, and ZIP Code on a single line, and to print the appropriate comma and spaces.

   Name

   Title

   Street Address

   City, State ZIP Code

5. Write a program that will create a cover sheet for any assignment.

   Input: Create a prompt screen that will ask for the author's name, course title, assignment number, and the date.

   Output: Center the appropriate information neatly on an 8½-by-11-inch sheet of paper.

6. Write a program that prompts for the responses in a program that requests patient information.

   Input: First Name

   Last Name

   Street

   City

   State

   ZIP Code

   Phone Number for Home

   Work Number

   Insurance Company

   Policy Number

   (Yes or No)

   Hospitalized during past 12 months

   Currently taking medication

   Family history of heart disease

   Family history of cancer

   Output: Print a neatly designed report of the information to the printer.

7. Write a program that inputs both numeric and character data(string) to print up a current price update. Use the cin.getline() for the string data and the cin for the numeric data.

Input: The input will include the product name, the model number, the new price, and the effective date of the increase.

Output: Create a memo sheet to the attention of the salesman giving the price update information.

Hayley Office Supplies

Using the data from the letterhead, create an invoice header. The invoice header will contain the company name and address for Hayley Office Supplies. It will also contain the name and address of the client. The client name and address will change on each invoice, so these fields will be input items. Use a structure for name, street address, city, state and ZIP Code. The date field may use an assign for now.

Be sure to create appropriate prompt screens for the entry of the data.

SAMPLE OUTPUT

Date: xx/xx/xx

                                                Hayley Office Supplies
                                                    1111 Main Street
                                                Chino, California 91710

Sold To:
Bob Smith
10252 Hale Ave.
West Somecity, CA 91111

CREATING OBJECTS

CHAPTER OBJECTIVES

By the end of this chapter you should be able to:
- Encapsulate properties (data members) and methods (member functions) into classes and structures.
- Understand the difference between a class and a structure.
- Select the appropriate access method, public and private.
- Initialize an object through a constructor.
- Pass values to a function.
- Use return values in functions.
- Pass arguments to a function.
- Overload functions.
- Create constructor and destructor functions.

CHAPTER OVERVIEW

In object oriented programming the data and the functions that manipulate that data are combined into a single unit using a structure or a class. Both structures and classes are capable of containing variable declarations as well as function prototypes. The public and private keywords determine access to the members.

You may use a constructor function to set initial values to the properties of an object. This chapter also covers functions that return values, requiring the return type to be specified and overloaded functions. The same function name may be overloaded (polymorphically used) if the argument list is different.

CREATING DATA TYPES CONTAINING FUNCTIONS

A fundamental component of object based programming is the ability to encapsulate data and functions together. In C++ this is done with a class or with a structure. Structures were introduced in the previous chapter and very closely resemble a class. The difference between the two is the default type of access to their contents, public or private, discussed later in the chapter.

A Structure with a Member Function

In addition to containing **data members,** a structure in C++ (this is not true of C) may also contain functions called **member functions.** The data members, variables, are often referred to as the **properties** of an object, while the member functions are known as **methods.** The methods (member functions) are declared inside of the structure. They may be defined within the structure or have a prototype declared within the structure and the function definition outside of the structure.

```
struct Invoice
{
        char stProduct[20];
        float fPrice, fAmtDue;
        int iQuantity;
        void ObtainData();
        void Print();
};
```

The Invoice structure contains three properties (data members): stProduct, fPrice, and iQuantity; and two methods(member functions): ObtainData() and Print(). Since the methods have only been declared within the structure, they must be defined at some other point.

Functions Defined Outside of the Structure Declaration

When defining a method outside of the structure it is necessary to use a **scope resolution operator ::** to associate the function with the appropriate structure. The format of the function header is:

> returntype structurename :: functionname(arguments)

The same function name may be used with various structures. In the following example, the ObtainData() function is associated with the Invoice structure with the scope resolution operator.

```
void Invoice::ObtainData()
{
        cout << "Description   ";
        cin.getline(stProduct,20);
        cout << "Price";
        cin >> fPrice;
        cout << "Quantity";
        cin >> iQuantity;
}
```

Use of Properties by Methods

The methods have access to all of the properties that are declared in the structure. Notice that the function need not define the variables because they are already known as "members" through the structure. They are accessed as stProduct, iQuantity, and fPrice without the dot notation required in non-methods.

Classes

A class is very similar to a structure, the difference is in the default access type of the variables and the functions. In a structure the contents are considered **public** by default and can be accessed by an object within a program as well as by the methods. In a class all members (data and functions) are **private** by default, limiting their access only to methods (member functions) of the class. In both a class and a structure the programmer can explicitly specify any property or method as public or private by using the keyword public or private. Some functions have to be public in order to be called from the program.

```
class Invoice

{
    char stProduct[20];
    float fPrice, fAmtDue;
    int iQuantity;
    void Calculate();
    void ObtainData();
    void Print();
public:
    void Run();
};
```

Notice that a colon follows the word public. In this class the variables and the first three functions are private by default but the remaining function is declared as public. Only the public methods can be accessed by objects defined in the program. The private members are known only to the class members. All methods have access to all of the class properties. In a structure the word private may be used in the same manner to specify member data or functions as private.

When you declare an object in a program it only needs access to the Run() function which must be public to be called by the object. The Run() function can then call any private method or use any private property.

This method of giving limited access to the class provides a greater level of data integrity. The object can only modify class members that it is granted access to.

Objects

Declaring a class or struct creates a new data type that can be used in variable declarations similar to existing data types such as int. The declaration specifies the members of the data type but does not allocate any memory. The memory allocation occurs when a variable is declared to be of a specific data type.

The term **object** refers to the actual variable that is associated with a struct or class and its encapsulated properties and methods. Sometimes an object is referred to as an **instance**. Any object declared in a program to be of a struct or class type has access using a dot operator to only the properties and the methods that have been made public. Only other members of the class or struct may access the private properties and methods.

The following variable declaration uses the called invoice data type to create an object called grocery and allocates memory for the storage of data for the grocery object.

```
Invoice Grocery;
```

To call a public method or property the object must use the dot (.) notation along with the function or data names (same as the structure.variable in the last chapter). The function calls use the object name (not the data type) and therefore will be:

```
Grocery.Run()
```

Remember that cin is an input object, cin.getline() calls the method getline().

CONSTRUCTORS

A **constructor** is a specialized function that automatically executes when an object is created. The constructor name is the same as the structure or class to which it belongs. The constructor function does not have any return type. It can be used to initialize beginning values or perform other "housekeeping" activities.

```
class Invoice
{
    char stProduct[20];
    float fPrice, fAmtDue, fTaxRate;
    int iQuantity;
    void Calculate();
    void ObtainData();
    void Print();
public:
    Invoice();      //this is a constructor
    void Run();
};


Invoice::Invoice()
{
    fTaxRate = .0875;    //sets initial value of a property
}
```

The variable fTaxRate is set to .0875 when the constructor is executed. Since the constructor function is automatically executed when an object is declared to be of the class type:

```
Invoice grocery;
```

automatically causes the Invoice::Invoice() function to be called when the object grocery is created. After the object is created, there is a variable grocery.fTaxRate with a value of .0875.

■ SELF TEST

1. Write a class called InterestPmt that contains the variables of principal, rate, time, and interest along with a function to calculate the interest.
2. Write the function for calculating the interest. Use * to represent multiplication.

■ ANSWERS

1.
```
class InterestPmt
{
    float fPrincipal;
    float fRate;
    float fTime;
    float fInterest;
    void CalcInterest();
}
```

2.
```
void InterestPmt::CalcInterest()
{
        fInterest = fPrincipal * fRate * fTime;
}
```

Inline Functions

Functions that are defined inside of the struct or class declaration are considered to be **inline.** These function definitions are placed in a "symbol table"(memory space permitting). This means that the functions are treated different from other functions in that the object code compiled from the function statements is substituted into the program rather than being "linked" to the calling location(s) in the program. An inline function has its statements placed in the code at every location that calls the function. The result is that the object code is longer but the execution time is faster.

```
class Invoice
{
    char stProduct[20];
    float fPrice, fAmtDue, fTaxRate;
    int iQuantity;
    void Calculate();
    void ObtainData();
    void Print();
```

```
public:
   Invoice()
   {
      // This function is inline because the definition
      // of the function is within class declaration
      fTaxRate = .0875;
   }
   void Run(); //Declaration only, definition is outside of class declaration
};
```

Notice that there is no semicolon after the function header Invoice(). This is not a prototype, it is the actual function header and the function definition. A prototype is needed only for the functions that are not defined within the class itself. Any of the functions within the class could have been defined inline within the class declaration.

DATA TYPES FOR FUNCTIONS

A function may return one value to the location from which the function is called. The return value of a function is integer by default, meaning that if no return type is specified the compiler expects return of an integer value. Most of the time you have been using a return type of void that means there is no return value.

To find the extended price in the invoice program the return value would need to be of type float. The function may be declared to be of type float in the variable declaration area, which is referred to as a prototype. The format for a prototype is:

```
return-type name-of-function();
```

The return type indicates the data type for the value that will be returned from the function back to any location from which the function is called. The return type may be any data type.

```
class Invoice
{
   char stProduct[20];
   float fPrice;
   int iQuantity;
   float Calculate();    // prototype for return type float
   void ObtainData();    // prototype for no return (void)
   void Print();         // prototype for no return
public:
   Invoice();            // no return type for a constructor
   void Run();
};
```

The return type is specified again when the function is defined.

```
float Invoice::Calculate()
{
   return fPrice * iQuantity;
}
```

A function may only return one value. Functions may return any data type, including programmer defined types. Arrays and functions may not be returned. Since the extended price is returned directly to the Print() function, there is no need for the fAmtdue variable used in the previous examples.

Returning a Value from a Function

In order for a function to return a value to a calling function the reserved word return must be used. The return statement may contain a value or an expression. The value or the result of the expression will be sent back to the location where the function was called.

```
float Invoice::Calculate()
{
   return fPrice * iQuantity;
}


void Invoice::Print()
{
      ofstream Printer("PRN");
      Printer << setprecision(2) << setiosflags(ios::showpoint);
      Printer << "\n";
      Printer << stProduct << "      " ;
      Printer << Calculate() << "\f";   //returns a float value
}
```

The return statement causes the answer of the calculation to be sent back to the requesting location in the program. In this case, the requesting location was the call to Calculate() in the Invoice::Print() function.

Using the Return Value from a Function

The value that is returned from a function may be used in a print statement as it was earlier or as an assignment within another function. Many variations are possible.

Example Program

Write a program using a class that produces an invoice. The input will obtain the product description, the price, and the quantity. The input information will be output along with the total due.

PROPERTY	DATA TYPE	NAME
Product Description	char array	stProduct
Price	float	fPrice
Quantity	int	iQuantity
Amount Due	float	fAmtDue

METHOD	PURPOSE
ObtainData	Prompt and input product, price, and quantity.
Calculate	Multiply the price by the quantity.
Print	Output amount due.

```
//Ch03Pr01
#include <fstream.h>
#include <iomanip.h>

const char FORMFEED = '\f';
class Invoice
{
      char   stProduct[20];
      float fPrice, fAmtdue;
      int    iQuantity;
      void ObtainData();
      void Calculate();
      void Print();
public:
      void Run();
};

void Invoice::Run()
{
  ObtainData();
  Calculate();
  Print();
}

void Invoice::ObtainData()
{
      cout << "Description ";
```

```
        cin.getline(stProduct,20);
        cout << "Price ";
        cin >> fPrice;
        cout << "Quantity ";
        cin >> iQuantity;
}

void Invoice::Calculate()
{
        fAmtdue = fPrice * iQuantity;
}

void Invoice::Print()
{
        ofstream Printer("PRN");
        Printer << setprecision(2)<< setiosflags(ios::showpoint|ios::fixed);
        Printer << "Amount due is " << fAmtdue << "FORMFEED";
}

void main()
{
        Invoice grocery;

        grocery.Run();
}
```

■ SELF-TEST

1. Write a function that uses the length and the width of a rectangle class (in feet) and will return the square footage.
2. Write a function that will calculate merchandise turnover rate, using the formula:

    Turnover = average inventory/cost of goods sold

    Assume beginning inventory, ending inventory, and cost of goods are properties of a merchandise class. Create a local variable called turnover. Return the turnover as integer.

■ ANSWERS

1.
```
float Rectangle::SquareFeet()
{
        return fLength * fWidth;
}
```

2.
```
int Merchandise::FindTurnover()
{
    int iTurnover;
    iTurnover = ((iBeginInventory + iEndInventory)/2)/ iCost;
    return iTurnover;
}
```

CONSTRUCTORS WITH ARGUMENTS

In addition to returning values, a function may have values passed to it when the function is called. This is not usually necessary within the members of a class since they have access to the other members. However, when a constructor is called from within the program, you may send a value to be used in the initialization. Recall that the constructor function is automatically called when an object is created. The initial values for the object may not be known when the class is created but only when the object is actually declared.

```
class Invoice
{
    char stProduct[20];
    float fPrice, fAmtDue, fTaxRate;
    int iQuantity;
    void Screen();
    float Calculate();
    void ObtainData();
    void Print();
public:
    Invoice(float fTax)
    {
        fTaxRate = fTax;
    }
    void Run();
};
```

When called from within the program a value may be directly sent to the constructor or a variable may be passed. Either a variable or a value should match the data type expected. In the example the constructor is expecting a float data item. The statement that creates the object called grocery could be either of the following:

```
Invoice Grocery(.0875);
```

or

```
fTaxRate = .0875;
Invoice Grocery(fTaxRate);
```

OVERLOADING CONSTRUCTORS

The **polymorphism** feature of an object-oriented language allows the programmer to provide multiple definitions for an operator or for a function. Another term used to refer to polymorphism is **overloading.**

More than one function may have the same name, if the argument list is different. When the program is compiled the appropriate occurrence of the function will be linked based on the data type that is used in the call to the function.

Therefore it is possible to have multiple constructor functions within a single class.

```
class Invoice
{
    char stProduct[20];
    float fPrice, fAmtDue, fTaxRate;
    int iQuantity;
    void Calculate();
    void ObtainData();
    void Print();
    public:
    Invoice()  // a constructor with no arguments
    {
        fTaxRate = .0875;
    }
    Invoice(float fTax) // a constructor with one float argument
    (
    fTaxRate = fTax;
    }
    void Run();
};
```

Notice that both constructor functions have the same name Invoice(), the difference is within the parentheses. When an object is declared, the contents of the parentheses determine which function is called. (It is possible to postpone determining which function until execution time; this is called late binding and will be covered later.)

```
Invoice grocery;
//Declaration calls the constructor with no argument because
//no value is passed
Invoice grocery(.05);
//Calls the constructor with the argument
float fTaxRate = .06;
Invoice grocery(fTaxRate);
//Calls the constructor with the argument
```

There may also be multiple functions with arguments but the arguments are of different types or with different numbers of arguments for overloaded functions.

```
Invoice();
Invoice(float);
Invoice(int);
Invoice(float, int);
Invoice(int, float);
```

All of the above are different and could be used within a single class or independently of classes. A function may be redefined with different argument lists using the same function name. It is possible to have different return types. However, the return types cannot be the only differing factor in the function declarations because the compiler would not be able to distinguish between the two functions at the point of the function call.

```
class Customer
{
    char stLastName[20];
    float fBalance;
public:
    Customer();              //constructor with no parameters
    Customer(char [], float);    //constructor with parameters
};

Customer::Customer()
{
    strcpy(stLastName,"");
    fBalance = 0.0;
}

Customer::Customer(char stName[], float fBal)
{
    strcpy(stLastName,stName);
    fBalance = fBal;
}
```

The object declaration could be:

```
Customer Customer1();                     //Creates a generic Customer
Customer Customer2("Mills",500.00); //Assigns initial values
```

Default Values

When using arguments on the constructor, it is also possible to set default values in the prototype. If no value is passed, the default value is used.

```
Customer(char [], float fBal = 0.0);        //Constructor with parameters
Customer Customer3("Lee");  //Create an object with balance set to default value
```

OVERLOADING OPERATORS

An operator can be overloaded (redefined) using the keyword **operator** preceding the operator that is being overloaded, such as "operator <<." The ostream class already defines the << operator for use with cout. However, you can redefine the operator to work with your own classes and structures. This helps to eliminate the cryptic look of the output within the report function. If you have an object called BowlerData, simply say cout << BowlerData and have it formatted the way you want.

Assume the following structure and object have been defined:

```
struct Bowler
{
    char stFirstName[10];
    char stLastName[10];
    char stTeamName[20];
    int iHighGame;
    int iHighSeries;
    float fAverage;
}
Bowler BowlerData;
```

In order to overload the operator << set up two variables for use by the function giving the new definition. The cout object already has the << operator overloaded for many data types including integer, float, character, and character arrays. Below you see detail line that refers to the output stream and b which refers to our structure. The & operator is discussed later; it is required here as a result of the way in which the associated items have been defined.

```
ostream& operator << (ostream& DetailLine, Bowler& b)
{
    DetailLine << setw(20) << setiosflags(ios::left) << b.stFirstName
        << " " << b.stLastName << setw(20) << b.stTeamName
        << setw(4) << setprecision(0) << iHighGame
        << highseries << setprecision(1) << fAverage << '\n';
    return DetailLine;
}
```

In your program function for print report your detail line print will is:

```
cout << BowlerData;
```

Because of the operator overload, the entire print line is produced and formatted as indicated in the definition of how to deal with a variable of bowler data type.

DESTRUCTORS

Another type of special function that is associated with a class or structure is the destructor. A **destructor** function is automatically executed when an object goes "out of scope." This usually occurs at the end of the function in which the object was declared. At that time, the destructor function, if one exists, is called without any explicit action by the programmer. A destructor may not have any arguments and therefore, could never be overloaded.

Naming a Destructor Function

The destructor function is the same name as the structure or the class within which it is defined or declared. To differentiate it from a constructor, the destructor function is preceded by a ~ (tilde), usually located above the tab key on the keyboard.

```
class Invoice
{
public:
      Invoice();   // Constructor function
      ~Invoice(); // Destructor function
)


Invoice::~Invoice()
{
      //Define the destructor outside or inline
}
```

Contents of a Destructor

Just as a constructor is used to set initial values, a destructor is used for "cleanup" purposes. This includes closing data files or releasing memory that has been dynamically allocated by the programmer. These topics are beyond the scope of this text at this point.

PROGRAMMING HINT

Some optional features you may want to try are creating header files. Your own header file is an easy way to store functions and classes that are reused in multiple projects. You can also shorten your object declaration by using an implied object.

Creating Header Files

The class declarations and function declarations may be stored in a header file. To create your own header file, save the desired code using a .h extension. Do not include the main() function in the header file. Every program can have only one main() function and it will be in the .CPP file.

If the header file is not included in the \INCLUDE or other specified include folder where C++ is installed, the path may be declared on the #include directive. The <> around the header file name were used to indicate that the file was in the standard location. To specify a path, place the header file in quotes.

```
#include "a:my.h"

#include "c:\MyFiles\Ch01.h"
```

Example

Rewrite the previous program using a header file to contain the class definition and the function definitions for the class.

```
//Header file for Ch03Pr02

class Invoice
{
        char    stProduct[20];
        float   fPrice, fAmtdue;
        int     iQuantity;
        void ObtainData();
        void Calculate();
        void Print();
public:
        void Run();
};

void Invoice::Run()
{
  ObtainData();
  Calculate();
  Print();
}

void Invoice::ObtainData()
{
        cout << "Description ";
        cin.getline(stProduct,20);
```

```cpp
        cout << "Price ";
        cin >> fPrice;
        cout << "Quantity ";
        cin >> iQuantity;
}

void Invoice::Calculate()
{
        fAmtdue = fPrice * iQuantity;
}

void Invoice::Print()
{
        ofstream Printer("PRN");
        Printer << setprecision(2)<< setiosflags(ios::showpoint|ios::fixed);
        Printer << "Amount due is " << fAmtdue << "FORMFEED";
}


//Ch03Pr02
#include <fstream.h>
#include <iomanip.h>
#include "a:Ch03Pr02.h"

const char FORMFEED = '\f';

void main()
{
        Invoice().Run();
}
```

Implied Object

Since the invoice object is never used in main except to call the run function you do not need to specify a name for it. The main function in the preceding program contains an implied object.

```
Invoice().Run();
```

executes exactly the same as the two statements:

```
Invoice grocery;
grocery.Run();
```

Note that you must place parentheses behind the class name (Invoice()).

Key Terms

constructor
data member
destructor
instance
member function
method

object
private
property
prototype
public
scope resolution operator

Chapter Summary

A structure or a class may contain data items as well as methods. These items may be public or private. All methods have access to the data items and to the other methods. An object declared to be of the structure or class type and be given access to the data items and to the methods.

Functions may return values to the calling locations. The default return type is integer when no return type is specified. Other data types may be specified in the declaration and the definition of the function. The keyword void denotes that there will be no return value.

Multiple objects or instances may be declared to be of the same class type.

Review Questions

1. Differentiate between a structure and a class.
2. What is an object?
3. Describe the relationship between the properties in a class and the methods of that class.
4. How and where are the contents of a method defined if they are not defined within the declaration of the class or the structure?
5. What is a constructor, how is it named, and what types of statements would it contain?
6. What does the return type indicate?
7. How is a value returned from a function?
8. How many values can be used on a return from a single function?
9. What would be contained in a "Run()" function?
10. How would a class declaration be placed in a header file? What would the actual program using the class look like?
11. What is a destructor?
12. Give an example of when a destructor may be used.

Exercises

1. Rewrite any assignment out of Chapter 2 using a class that encapsulates the data and the methods. Create an object in the main() function to use the class or structure.
2. Write a program using objects that enter employee information and prints a completed "application."

Sample Input Data:

Last Name:	Smith
First Name:	Connie
Street:	1100 Main Street
City:	Atascadero
State:	California
Birthdate:	April 1, 1955

Printer Output:

Connie Smith

1100 Main Street

Atascadero, California

Date of Birth: April 1, 1955

3. Write a program using objects that creates an optical patient class with a name and appointment date and time. Print a reminder slip for the patient containing the office name "V. Rasner, Optician" and the appointment information.

Sample Output:

A reminder notice from V. Rasner, Optician

    to: Carol Jones

Appointment Date: January 5, 1999

    Time: 3:30

4. Write a program for a travel agency that includes the travel information and creates an itinerary for the customer listing travel departure and arrival times for a round trip. It must include the city of departure and the flight number. Assume that all travel is by air and nonstop.

Hayley Office Supplies

Create a customer class that contains the company name, the contact person name and company address. The name should be broken down into first name and last name while the address should consist of street, city, state (2 letter abbreviation), and ZIP Code.

    The customer class must also contain a function to create the data entry screen and obtain the data.

    Make the variables private and the functions public.

    Test the class by writing a program that creates an object called client. Call the functions to enter the data and then print a

BILL TO:

heading for an invoice.

PROCESSING DATA: CALCULATIONS

CHAPTER 4

CHAPTER OBJECTIVES

By the end of this chapter you should be able to:
- Calculate using binary and unary operators.
- Implement increment and decrement operators in both prefix and postfix modes.
- Know how to assign values with operators.
- Understand the importance and effect of precedence.

CHAPTER OVERVIEW

Having learned how to declare variables and assign values, it is now important to find out how to perform calculations on those values. This provides you with the ability to process the data and calculate the results of financial and mathematical formulas.

C++ has a multitude of operator for performing calculations. In addition to the normal arithmetic operators, the language allows math operations to be combined with assignment operations. The calculation statement may be embedded within another expression. The use of prefix and postfix positioning of the operators determines the sequence in which the expression is evaluated.

ARITHMETIC OPERATORS

As with other languages, C++ has arithmetic operators for performing calculations. The operators for calculations are either unary or binary. A **unary operator** has only one factor or **operand** on which the operation is performed. A **binary operator** has two factors or operands.

Binary Operators

The binary operators are as follows:

OPERATOR	PURPOSE
+	Addition
-	Subtraction
*	Multiplication
/	Division
%	Modulus or remainder.

Using the assignment operator, you might write a C++ statement as follows:

```
fTax = fTaxRate * fAmountOfPurchase;
fAmountDue =  fAmountOfPurchase + fTax;
```

These statements call for a calculation to be performed and the result to be assigned to the variable on the left of the assignment operator.

Multiple operators may be used in a single calculation statement but then attention must be paid to the **precedence** of the operators, that is the sequence in which the operators will combine with the operands. The operators follow the normal mathematical order of precedence when more than one operator is used in an expression.

Precedence of Operators

The order of precedence is multiplicative operators from left to right, followed by additive operators from left to right.

MULTIPLICATIVE OPERATORS	
*	Multiplication
/	Division
%	Modulus

ADDITIVE OPERATORS	
+	Addition
-	Subtraction

Of course, the order of precedence can be altered through the use of parentheses to indicate the desired sequence of calculations. Anything inside of parentheses will be calculated first.

The following program shows several calculation statements and the use of parentheses with calculations.

```
#include <iostream.h>

void main()
{
    int iAnswer = 0,  iNum = 5;

    //Add 2 to the variable iNum
    iAnswer = iNum + 2;
    cout << iAnswer<<"\n";

    //Multiply 2 times the variable iNum
    iAnswer = 2 * iNum;
    cout << iAnswer<<"\n";
```

```
//Multiply 2 times iNum then adds iNum
//   the value of iNum does not change
iAnswer = iNum + 2 * iNum;
cout << iAnswer<<"\n";


//Use parentheses to have iNum added to 2
//     before multiplying by iNum
iAnswer = (iNum + 2) * iNum;
cout << iAnswer<<"\n";


// Use the modulus function to divide iNum by 2
//     and store the remainder in iAnswer
iAnswer = iNum % 2;
cout << iAnswer<<"\n";
}
```

OUTPUT

```
7
10
15
35
1
```

Notice the difference in answers with and without the parentheses. When there are no parentheses in the calculation, the precedence is determined by default. In this case, multiplication has a higher precedence and is, therefore, performed before the addition. The parentheses, however, caused the addition to be performed first on the next calculation.

Modulus

The **modulus** operator is used to find a remainder. It performs a division and then returns the remainder as the result of the operation. This operator is very handy when doing conversions that are not in base 10. When converting minutes to hours, any remainder will become a fraction of 60. Therefore, a decimal remainder is not easily understandable because it would relate to 10ths or 100ths.

If you wish to convert minutes to hours, you can divide the number of minutes by 60 and then use the modulus to determine the remaining number of minutes.

```
iHours = iMinutes/60;

iMinutes = iMinutes % 60;
```

In the first calculation, the whole number of hours is placed in iHours (assuming minutes is an integer field), the remaining minutes are placed into iMinutes.

■ SELF-TEST

What will be the results of the following calculations if int iNum1 = 5, iNum2 = 2, iNum3 = 7;

1. iNum1 * iNum2 - iNum3

2. (iNum1 * iNum2) - iNum3
3. iNum1 % iNum2
4. iNum1 * 4 / iNum2
5. iNum1 * 4 % iNum2

ANSWERS

1. 3
2. 3
3. 1
4. 10
5. 0

UNARY OPERATORS

C++ contains increment and decrement operators that will increase or decrease the value of an integer variable by one. The unary **increment operator** is ++ while the **decrement operator** is --.

Increment Operator

The expression iCount++ is the same as the binary calculation iCount = iCount + 1. The increment operator performs and addition operation and an assignment, increasing the value of the variable by 1.

Binary Operator	Unary Increment Operator
iCount = iCount + 1;	iCount++;

Both statements perform the same operation.

Decrement Operator

Similarly the following statements are equivalent:

Binary Operator	Unary Increment Operator
iCount = iCount - 1;	iCount--;

The result of both statements will be to reduce the count by 1.

Prefix versus Postfix

The increment and decrement operators may be used as a part of another expression. It is important to determine exactly when the addition or subtraction operation takes effect in relation to the evaluation of the rest of the expression. The increment and decrement operators may be used either as a prefix or as a postfix. This means that the increment may be expressed as iCount++ or ++iCount.

iCount++ is a postfix increment while ++iCount is prefix increment. The placement of the operator determines the timing of the calculation. With a **prefix** increment the addition is done prior to the evaluation of the remainder of the expression or statement, while a **postfix** operator evaluates the expression and then increments the variable.

Assume that iCount is 5.

```
x = iCount++;
```

The postfix operator will assign iCount to x and then increment iCount. Therefore, x will be 5.

```
x = ++iCount;
```

The prefix operator performs the increment first and then proceeds with the remainder of the expression or statement. In this case, iCount will be incremented to 6 and then will be assigned to x, leaving x with a value of 6.

The decrement operator may also be used as a prefix or a postfix, as in

```
--iCount or iCount--
```

If iCount is 5, then

```
x = iCount--;
```

assigns 5 to x then decrements iCount to 4, whereas

```
x = --iCount;
```

decreases iCount to 4 and then assigns the value of iCount to x, leaving x with a value of 4.

Another Look at Precedence

The increment and decrement operators have a higher order of precedence than the binary operators that you have already considered. Be careful when evaluating expressions to understand the impact of this precedence.

```
#include <iostream.h>

void main()
{
        int iAnswer=0, iCount=0, iNum = 5;

        //Postfix incrementer
        iAnswer = iNum + iCount++;
        cout << iAnswer<<"\n";

        //Prefix incrementer
        iAnswer = iNum + ++iCount;
        cout << iAnswer<<"\f";
}
```

OUTPUT

```
5
7
```

With the postfix incrementer iCount was 0 at the time that iCount was added to iNum. After that calculation, iCount was then incremented to 1. The prefix incrementer caused iCount to be increased from 1 (previous increment) to 2. After the increment, iCount was added to iNum giving a result of 7.

■ SELF-TEST

What will the results of the following calculations be, given that:

```
int iCount = 0, iNum = 5;
```

Note: Assume that each problem is a unique situation and iCount will be 0 and iNum is 5 before each problem.

1. `iCount-- + iNum`
2. `iCount++ -- iNum`
3. `--iCount + iNum`
4. `iNum % ++iCount`
5. `iNum++ / iCount--`

■ ANSWERS

1. 5
2. -5
3. 4
4. 0
5. Division by 0, which is an error.

ASSIGNMENT OPERATORS

Another category of operators in C++ is the assignment operators. These allow us to shortcut the writing of our code as the increment and decrement did. In fact, the unary increment and decrement operators are frequently considered to be assignment operators.

The **assignment operator** =, which assigns the value of the expression on the right of the = operator to the variable on the left, is already familiar. In addition, there are +=, -=, *=, /=, and %=. These also require a variable on the left of the operator for the result of the operation to be stored in.

The expression x+=5 is equivalent to writing the assignment

```
x = x + 5.
```

Similarly, the other calculation operators can be combined with an assignment operator to produce a shortcut method of doing a calculation on a variable and then storing the value back into the same variable.

ASSIGNMENT OPERATORS

=	Simple assignment
+=	Addition assignment
-=	Subtraction assignment
*=	Multiplication assignment
/=	Division assignment
%=	Modulus assignment
++	Unary increment
--	Unary decrement

Some examples of the use of these assignment operators are:

```
fTotal += fSales;                    //Add sales to the total
iGrade -= iWronganswers;   //Subtract the incorrect answers from the grade
iMinutes %= 90;            //Find the minutes remainder
```

The next program uses the assignment operators to change the value of an integer called iNum.

```
#include <iostream.h>

void main()
{
    int iNum = 0;

    iNum += 5;
    cout << iNum<<"\n";

    iNum = 1;
    iNum *= 5;
    cout << iNum<<"\n";

    iNum = 1;
    iNum -= 5;
    cout << iNum<<"\n";

    iNum = 10;
    iNum /= 5;
    cout << iNum<<"\n";
```

```
        iNum = 10;
        iNum %= 3;
        cout << iNum<<"\f";
}
```

OUTPUT

```
5
5
-4
2
1
```

Precedence

The assignment operators, with the exception of the increment and decrement, have a lower order of precedence than the binary operators. This means, of course, that the binary operations will be performed first and then the assignment.

```
int iNumber = 5;
iNumber *= 2 + 10;
cout << iNumber;
```

The value of number that will be printed is 60. The 2+10 yields 12, which is then multiplied by 5 and assigned to number.

■ SELF-TEST

1. What values will be printed?
   ```
   int iNumber1 = 10, iNumber2;
   iNumber1 *= iNumber2 = 4;
   cout << iNumber1 << "\t" << iNumber2;
   ```
2. What is the value of x?
   ```
   int x=3;
   x*=5-2;
   ```

■ ANSWERS

1. 40 4
2. x = 9

Mixing Data Types in Calculations

The binary arithmetic operators may cause a conversion of the data type depending on the operator and on the type of the operands. This conversion is known as an **arithmetic conversion.**

Most operators will make all operands the same type. If an operand is of type char or short it is converted to int. Basically, if two fields of different types are used, the compiler will "promote" the type of the operand from the less accurate data type to the more accurate type.

Assignment Operators

If there are mixed data types in your calculation statement you may be surprised by the results.

```
int iNum, iAnswer ;
float fNum, fAnswer;

fNum = 3.5;
iNum = 2;
fAnswer = fNum/iNum;
iAnswer  = fNum/iNum;
cout << "float = " << fAnswer << ", ";
cout << "integer = " << iAnswer << "\n";

fAnswer = fNum + iNum;
iAnswer  = fNum + iNum;
cout << "float = " << fAnswer<< ", ",
cout << "integer = " << iAnswer<< "\n";
```

OUTPUT

```
float = 1.750000, integer = 1
float = 5.500000, integer = 5
```

(Note: trailing zeroes may not appear.) The data type of the integer was promoted or converted to type float because there are mixed types in the calculation. The operation evaluates as 3.5/2.0. The assignment to an integer variable truncates the answer to an integer. Notice that the floating-point number is not rounded to the nearest integer. Rather, the decimal portion simply truncates. The result of the division is not rounded, only the integer portion is retained, which in this case is 1.

Similarly, in the addition, the floating-point calculation retains the decimal portion during the calculation and in the answer while the integer calculation truncates the decimal portion.

■ SELF-TEST

What is the result of the following calculations given that
```
    int iNum = 1, iAnswer;
    float fNum = 7.5, fAnswer;
  1. fAnswer = fNum - iNum;
  2. fAnswer = iNum + iNum;
  3. iAnswer = fNum;
  4. fNum += iNum;
  5. iNum *= fNum;
  6. fAnswer = iNum/2;
```

■ ANSWERS

1. 6.500000
2. 2.000000

3. 7
4. 8.500000
5. 7
6. 0

THE sizeof OPERATOR

One operator in C++ is a word rather than a symbol. The **sizeof** operator is used to determine the number of bytes that are occupied by a given data element. It can be used to determine the size of a variable or of a data type.

> sizeof(data element);

Using the sizeof operator, it is possible to determine how many bytes of storage are used by a specific computer and compiler. This can aid in the portability of a C++ program.

```
sizeof(int);
```

In addition, this operator may be used on a variable or an array.

```
sizeof(stName);
```

The sizeof a character array determines the number of bytes of memory allocated to the array. This is different than strlen(), covered in Chapter 5, which tells the number of occupied positions within a character array.

EXPONENTIATION

There is not an operator in C++ for raising a value to a power. This does not require an operator because exponentiation can be achieved by multiplying the number by itself the specified number of times. Rather than writing the code to do this, the ANSI function pow() may be used. The format for the pow() function is:

> pow(the value to be raised, the power);

It is illegal for both the value and the power to be equal to zero, and if the value is negative, then the power must be an integer. In order to use this function it is necessary to include the math.h file.

```
#include <iostream.h>

#include <math.h>


void main()
{
        int x=2, y=3, z;
        z = pow(x,y);
        // z will be 2 raised to the power of 3
        cout << 2 << endl;
}
```

SELF-TEST

1. Write the statement to find 2 to the power of 10 and assign the answer to K.
2. Write the monthly compound amount formula in C++.
    Compound amount = loan amount X (1+rate/12)^(number years X 12)

ANSWERS

1. K = pow(2,10);
2. fCompoundAmount = fLoan*pow((1+fRate/12),iNumYears*12);

    or

    fValue = fLoan*1+fRate/12;
    fPower = iNumYears * 12;
    fCompoundAmount = fLoan*pow(fValue, fPower);

USING CALCULATIONS IN A METHOD

Using calculations in a method is no different than in any other calculation. The variables need not be defined if they come from the class definition.

```
struct Item
{
    char stDesc[20];
    float fPrice;
    int iQuantity;
    float fCalculate();
};


float Item::fCalculate()
{
    return fPrice * iQuantity;
}
```

The fCalculate() function directly uses the fPrice and the iQuantity from the structure in which fCalculate() is declared as a method.

MANIPULATING STRING DATA

In Chapter 2, you found that string fields could not be assigned the same as numeric fields. The same is true about manipulating the data.

Combining String Fields-Concatenation

Combining two string fields is known as **concatenation.** In this case a longer string is formed, which is the combination of string 1 and string 2.

```
strcat(string1, string2);
```

It might be necessary to have several successive strcat() functions.

`strcat(stLastName, stFirstName);`

The previous example does not put a space between the first and last names. It would be better to say:

`strcpy(stFullName,stFirstName);`

`strcat(stFullName, " ");`

`strcat(stFullName, stLastName);`

String 1 must be large enough to hold all of the parts. If it is not you may have very unpredictable results. When C++ prints a string, it starts at the first character of the string and prints until it encounters a null. If the field does not have a null, it will print on through the next items in memory, whatever they may be, until a null is found.

Concatenating the Beginning of a String

A partial string may be concatenated to a string by using the strncat() function, which has the format:

| strncat(string1, string2, number of characters); |

The specified number of characters from string 2 will be concatenated to string1.

To combine the last name with the first initial of the first name, the strcpy() would be used along with the strncat().

`strcpy(stName, stLastName);`

`strcat(stName, ", ");`

`strncat(stName, stFirstName,1);`

■ **SELF-TEST:**

1. Code the statement(s) that will concatenate the address fields to combine the variables city, state, and ZIP so that the field address will contain the city followed by a comma and a space, which will then be followed by the state, one space and then the ZIP Code.

2. What will the following print:

   `stWord1[] = "Programming";`

   `char stWord2[] = "Ready";`

   `char stCombined[20];`

   `.............`

   `strcpy(stCombined, stWord2);`

   `strcat(stCombined, " to ");`

   `strncat(stCombined, stWord1, 7);`

   `cout << stCombined;`

3. Write the statement to concatenate the first five characters os stWord1 with stWord2.

■ **ANSWERS:**

1. strcpy(stAddress, stCity);

   strcat(stAddress, ", ");

```
strcat(stAddress, stState);
strcat(stAddress, " ");
strcat(stAddress, stZip);
```
2. Ready to Program
3. `strncat(stWord2, stWord1, 5);`

Complete Example

Write a program to calculate subtotal, total, and tax for an invoice. The user will input the product description, price, and the quantity. Use a tax rate of 8.75%.

PLANNING

PROPERTIES	DATA TYPE	NAME
Description	char array	stDescription
Price	float	fPrice
Quantity	integer	iQuantity
Subtotal	float	fSubtotal
Tax	float	fTax
Total	float	fTotal

METHOD	PURPOSE
Constructor	Intialize totals.
Run	Control execution.
ObtainData	Prompt and input description, price, and quantity.
Calculate	Find subtotal, tax, and total.
PrintInvoice	Create formatted report.

```cpp
//Ch04Pr01.cpp
/***************************************************
Programmer:    A. Millspaugh
Date:          Dec 1997
Description:   Input a price and quantity, calculate
               and print subtotal, tax, and total
***************************************************/
#include <fstream.h>
#include <iomanip.h>

float const TAXRATE = .0875;
```

```cpp
           char   const FORMFEED = '\f';

           class Invoice
           {
              char stDesc[20];
              float fPrice;
              int iQuantity;
              float fSubtotal;
              float fTax;
              float fTotal;
              void ObtainData();
              void Calculate();
              void PrintInvoice();
           public:
              Invoice();
              void Run();
           };

           Invoice::Invoice()
           {
              fSubtotal = fTotal = 0;
           }

           void Invoice::ObtainData()
           {
              //Obtain Data from the keyboard
              cout << "Description ";
                 cin.getline(stDesc,20);
              cout << "Price       ";
              cin >> fPrice;
              cout << "Quantity    ";
              cin >> iQuantity;
           }

           void Invoice::Calculate()
           {
              fSubtotal = fPrice * iQuantity;
```

```cpp
      fTax = TAXRATE * fSubtotal;
      fTotal = fSubtotal + fTax;
}


   void Invoice::PrintInvoice()
{
 ofstream Printer("CON");
 // titles
 Printer << setw(35) << "ABC Inc." << "\n\n";
 Printer << setw(15) << "Description"
            << setw(10) << "Price"
            << setw(10) << "Quantity"
            << setw(10) << "Subtotal"
            << setw(8)  << "Tax"
            << setw(10) << "Total"
            << "\n\n";
 //detail
 Printer << setprecision(2) << setiosflags(ios::showpoint|ios::fixed);
 Printer << setw(20) << setiosflags(ios::left) << stDesc
      << setw(10) << fPrice
      << setw(10) << iQuantity
      << setw(10) << fSubtotal
      << setw(10) << fTax
      << setw(10) << fTotal
      << endl << FORMFEED;
}

void Invoice::Run()
{
   ObtainData();
   Calculate();
   PrintInvoice();
}

void main()
{
   Invoice().Run();
}
```

Key Terms

arithmetic conversion
assignment operator
binary operator
bind
decrement
increment
modulus

operand
operator
postfix
precedence
prefix
unary operator

Chapter Summary

There are a large number of operators in C++. For calculations, you have both unary and binary operators. When using the operators, it is extremely important to understand the priority of each of the operators.

Data can be manipulated using the arithmetic operators. Variables can be changed using the assignment operators. String data still requires the use of string functions.

Review Questions

1. Name the operator necessary for the following operations:
   a. Postfix increment
   b. Modulus
   c. Multiplication
   d. Multiplication assignment
   e. Division
2. What will be the result of the following if x = 5 at the beginning of each problem?
   a. `++x;`
   b. `x -= 2;`
   c. `x++ *= 2;`
3. What importance is the precedence of operators to calculation results?
4. How can the order of the precedence be altered in a calculation statement?
5. How can a portion of a string be appended to another string?

Exercises

1. Write a program that will determine the number of packages of strip paneling required to do each wall in a room, if each package contains 13 square feet of paneling. The walls to be covered are 8 feet high, input the length of the wall.
   Preprocessor Constant: HEIGHT
   Input: Client last name:
        Client first name:
        North wall size:
        South wall size:
        East wall size:
        West wall size:

Processing:	Calculate the number of packages for each wall
Print:	Neatly formatted list including customer name. Specify wall and number of packages for each wall.

2. Calendari Publications is having a special promotion for its sales staff. A commission rate of 10% is paid on the sales. Write a program that inputs the amount of sales and the salesperson's name, and calculates the normal commission rate and the bonus rate. Print out a statement that includes the company name, the salesman's name, the amount of sales, the commission, and the bonus.

Input:	Salesperson's last name:
	Salesperson's first name:
	Amount of sales:
Processing:	Find total commission for each salesperson.
Output:	
Heading:	Use appropriate titles and column headings.
Detail:	Print out the salesperson's name (concatenated with first initial and last name), the amount of sales, and the commission.

Sample Output (three runs):

Calendari Publications

Sales Commission Report

Name	Sales	Commission
J. Jon	1700.00	170.00

Calendari Publications

Sales Commission Report

Name	Sales	Commission
F. Hong	2655.00	265.50

Calendari Publications

Sales Commission Report

Name	Sales	Commission
C. Marquez	2000.00	200.00

3. Write a report program that will determine that rate of straight-line depreciation for each asset item within a company.

Input:	The program must prompt the user to enter the asset name, the asset cost, the life in years, and the salvage value. Create an appropriate input screen for the input prompts.
Processing:	The formula for the annual rate for straight-line depreciation is:
	$$\frac{\text{Cost - salvage value}}{\text{Life in years}}$$
Output:	Send an output report to the printer that contains the necessary information as follows:

Whatever Corporation Depreciation Schedule

Description of Asset	Cost basis	Salvage Value	Life	Depreciation
XXXXXXXXXXXXXXXXXX	XXXX.XX	XXXX.XX	XX	XXXX.XX

Sample Data: Use the following item to test your program. Try others of your own.

Description	Cost	Life	Salvage
Office Furniture - Desk	842.12	10	25

(If your calculations are correct, the result will be 81.71.)

4. Write a program to calculate a grade report for a class of students. The prompts should ask for the student's name, two test scores, and three program grades. The tests are worth 40% of the grade and the programs are worth 60% of the grade.

   Input: Student name:

   Two test scores:

   Three program grades:

   Processing: Find the average by taking 40% of the sum of the tests divided by 2, and add that to 60% of the sum of the programs divided by 3.

   Output:

   Heading: Course Title and appropriate headings

   Detail: Student name, test scores, program grades, average

5. Write a program to produce a mailing label for magazines. The labels will contain four lines; the account number on line 1 will be printed to the right. Names will be printed first name and then last. You may wish to concatenate the city, state, and ZIP Code to eliminate extra spaces.

   Input: Last Name:

   First Name:

   Street Address:

   City:

   State:

   ZIP Code:

   Expiration Date:

   Processing:

   Detail: Concatenate the name and address fields as necessary.

   Create the account number as the first two characters of the last name, the first three digits of the ZIP Code, and the expiration date.

   Output:

   Label:

   Sample Output:

   B191711/95

   Tim Black
   1115 Second Avenue
   Montclair, CA   91763

Hayley Office Supplies

Write a program to calculate the merchandise turnover rate and the average inventory. The average inventory is found by finding the average of the beginning inventory and the ending inventory. The merchandise turnover rate can be determined by dividing the cost of the goods sold by the average inventory amount. Assume that Hayley Office Supplies had a beginning inventory of 27,000 and an ending inventory of 32,500. The cost of goods sold is 14,867.

DECISIONS

CHAPTER 5

CHAPTER OBJECTIVES

By the end of this chapter you should be able to:
- Be familiar with the relational operators.
- Code decision statements using the if/else statement.
- Find the highest and lowest values from a series.
- Use string functions for comparisons.
- Understand the precedence of relational operators in conjunction with arithmetic operators.

CHAPTER OVERVIEW

Relational and logical operators are used to compare values in variables and constants. Conditional expressions may contain relational operators or may have an implied condition.

The processing of data often requires the use of an **if** statement to decide if the calculation or another operation should be performed, or to select a particular option to be performed. The if statement is introduced in this chapter, along with a discussion on how to find the highest and lowest value in a series.

Relational operators can be used in conditional statements to determine whether or not a block will be executed. Statements that will be executed only if certain criteria are met can be coded using the if statement.

MAKING COMPARISONS USING RELATIONAL OPERATORS

Relational operators are used to compare data items. It is possible to compare two variables or a variable and a constant. The comparison determines the relationship between the two fields.

The relational operators in C++ are shown in the table below:

RELATIONAL OPERATOR	PURPOSE
<	Less Than
>	Greater Than
==	Equal To
!=	Not Equal To
<=	Less Than Or Equal To
>=	Greater Than Or Equal To

It is important to note that the comparison for equality in C++ is denoted by the operator ==. If a single = is used, the result will be an assignment, not a comparison.

The not operator ! may be used to find the logical not of a conditional expression.

Examples of Conditions

```
fHours == 40.00     //Compare hours and 40 for equality
iBonus != 1   //Check if bonus is NOT equal to 1
```

The relational operators may be used on character or numeric data. You may not use the operators on an array of characters. Comparisons of strings require the use of string functions.

Comparing Numeric Data

```
int iCount;
iCount == 0


float fNumber;
fNumber < 2000.00
```

The comparisons are **expressions** that will become a part of a statement. A semicolon does not follow the expression because it is not a complete statement.

Numeric comparisons of data are determined to be true or false based upon the actual value of one number compared to the numerical value of the second operand.

Comparing Character Data

CODE	VALUE	CODE	VALUE	CODE	VALUE
0	NULL	38	&	60	<
8	Backspace	39	'	61	=
9	Tab	40	(	62	>
10	Linefeed	41	)	63	?
12	Formfeed	42	*	64	@
13	Carriage Return	43	+	65-90	A-Z
27	Escape	44	,	91	[
32	Space	45	-	92	\
33	!	46	.	93	]
34	"	47	/	94	^
35	#	48-57	0-9	95	_
36	$	58	:	96	`
37	%	59	;	97-122	a-z

```
cItem == 'x'
cItem != '\0'        //Check for non-null character
cItem == '4'         //Compares with the digit 4
cItem == 4           //Compares with the ASCII code 4
```

To determine if the character condition is true or false, compare the value of the character as it is positioned in the ASCII code table (for DOS machines). This means that numeric characters would come before uppercase characters, which are then followed by lowercase characters.

Examples:

```
char cLetter1 = 'A';
char cLetter2 = 'a';


cLetter2 > cLetter1
```

is true because the ASCII code of 'A' is 65 while the code for 'a' is 97.

```
char cSymbol1 = '?';
char cSymbol2 = '!';


cSymbol1 > cSymbol2
```

is TRUE because the ASCII code for ? is 63 while the ASCII code for ! is 33.

```
x = 0
```

will be false. 0 is assigned to x, not compared to it. The value of x is then 0 that evaluates to false.

■ SELF-TEST

Are the following expressions true or false?

1. ```
   float fNum1 = 5.00;
   int iNum2 = 5;
   fNum1 == iNum2
   ```

2. ```
   char cLetter1 = 'A';
   char cLetter2 = 'C';
   cLetter1 > cLetter2
   ```

3. ```
   char cLetter1 = 'A';
   char cLetter2 = ' ';
   cLetter1 > cLetter2;
   ```
   ```

4. Are the following conditions true or false given that:

   ```
   int   iCount = 0;
   float fNumber = 15.75;
   char  cLetter = 'x';
   ```

   a. iCount < 10

   b. fNumber == 0

   c. cLetter = 'x'

   d. iCount !=0

▪ ANSWERS

1. True, the values are both equivalent; the int will be converted to a float.
2. False, C comes after A in the alphabet, which makes C greater than A
3. True, the space comes before the letter A in the ASCII code.
4. a. True, iCount (0) is less than 10.
   b. False, fNumber is not equal to 0.
   c. Careful, this assigns x to cLetter, rather than testing equality. C++ will still determine that this is true, as will be explained next.
   d. False; iCount is equal to 0.

Implied Conditions—True or False

Following Boolean logic, a condition will be considered to be true if it returns a nonzero value, a 0 will evaluate to false. This allows us to imply conditions in a sense.

```
iAmount != 0
```

If this condition is true, the computer will return a value of 1 while a 0 will be returned if the condition is false. Therefore, it would be possible to say:

```
iAmount     //True if amount is not equal to 0
```

This will be true as long as iAmount is not equal to 0, because if the value of iAmount is not 0 it is the same as a true, while a value of 0 is equivalent to a false.

This means that in C++, anything could be used as a condition, whether or not it contains a relational operator.

THE LOGICAL OPERATORS

To test for multiple conditions, the relational operators may be combined together. The logical operators for combining conditions are:

LOGICAL OPERATOR	PURPOSE
&&	And
||	Or

The && operator requires that both conditions be true for the condition to evaluate to true. With the || operator, only one condition needs to be true, but both may be true.

```
iAmount == 0 || fNumber == 3.0
```

This condition will test if iAmount is equal to 0 or if fNumber is equal to 3. The condition will be true if either iAmount is 0 or if fNumber is 3. It would, of course, be true if both iAmount and fNumber are equal to 0 and 3 respectively. Conditions combined with || or && are frequently referred to as **compound conditions.**

Precedence of And and Or in Compound Conditions

The && and || operators may be used together in the same expression if more than two conditions are to be tested. In this situation, it is necessary to understand the precedence of operators to determine the results of the relational test. The && operator is of a higher precedence and the conditions around the && will be tested first to see if both are true.

The "smart" compiler will not continue the evaluation of a condition once it has been determined to be false.

The order of precedence can be overridden with the use of parentheses.

Examples

Assume that:
iNum1 is 5, iNum2 is 6, and iNum3 is 7

CONDITION	EVALUATES
(iNum1 < 5)	False
(iNum2 == 6)	True
(iNum1 < 5 || iNum2 == 6)	True
(iNum1 < 5 && iNum2 == 6)	False
(iNum3 < 10)	True
(iNum1 < 5 || iNum2 == 6 && iNum3 < 10)	True
(iNum1 < 5 && iNum2 == 6 || iNum3 < 10)	True
(iNum1 < 5 && iNum2 == 6 && iNum3 < 10)	False

■ SELF-TEST

Will the following conditions be true or false given that:
```
int iAmount = 0;
float fNumber = 3.0;
```
1. iAmount == 0 || fNumber == 0.0
2. iAmount != fNumber && iAmount == 0
3. iAmount > fNumber && fNumber < 10.0
4. iAmount = 0
5. iAmount == 0 && fNumber < 10.0 || iAmount > fNumber

ANSWERS

1. True, iAmount is equal to 0.
2. True, iAmount is not equal to fNumber and iAmount is equal to 0.
3. False, iAmount is not greater than fNumber. For an && to be true, both conditions must be true.
4. False, this assigns the value 0 to iAmount, and as a value 0 is false.
5. True, both && conditions are true, iAmount is 0 and fNumber is less than 10. Since the && is evaluated first, it does not matter what the second condition on the or is, you already have one true for the or.

STRING COMPARISONS

As already indicated, you cannot compare strings using the relational operators. Instead they require the use of special functions designed for handling string data. The basic function used to compare strings is strcmp().

The format of strcmp() is:

```
strcmp(string1, string2)
```

The strings may be variables or literals. The function returns an integer greater than 0 if string 1 is greater than string 2, 0 if the strings are equal, or a negative integer if string 1 is less than string 2.

```
strcmp(fSalaryStatus,"Salary") == 0
```

Notice that the test for equality checks for a 0. If you wish to test if two items are not equal the condition would be:

```
strcmp(stString1,stString2) != 0
```

The return value from the string comparison functions is:

EVALUATION	RETURN VALUE
string 1 less than string 2	negative value
string 1 equal to string 2	0
string 1 greater than string 2	positive value

Comparing a Specified Number of Characters

It is also possible to compare a specified number of characters from each string with the strncmp() function. The format is:

```
strncmp(string1, string2, number of characters)
```

The expression

```
(strncmp(item,"A11",3) == 0)
```

compares the first 3 characters of the variable item with the characters A11.

Comparing Strings and Ignoring the Case

C++ provides a function that compares the contents of two strings without regard to the case of the two strings. When ignoring the case, the character 'A' would be considered to be equivalent to the character 'a'. This function is the stricmp() function. The form is the same as the *strcmp()* function, which has two strings as the parameters.

> stricmp(string1, string2)

where string1 and string2 may be string variables or string literals.

Example

```
char stWord[] = "Almost";

stricmp(stWord,"ALMOST") = = 0
```

is True.

Finding the Length of a String

Sometimes it is necessary to know how long a string is. Remember that the size set in the declaration is the maximum size of the array. The actual string value is terminated by a null character. The **string length** is the number of characters up to but not including the null character. To determine the actual string length use strlen(). The format is:

> strlen(string1)

The only parameter required by this function is the name of the string. It may be used as part of an assignment or part of a condition. The following example assigns the number of characters in the stName to the variable iStringSize.

```
iStringSize = strlen(stName);
```

The strlen() returns an integer, the length in bytes. Therefore, you can use the assignment operator to store this value in an integer variable, if desired.

You could also use the strlen() function in a condition to determine if a string contained a specific number of characters.

```
strlen(stName) != 0;
```

This condition checks to see if stName contains a value. If stName is empty it only contains the null and the strlen() function would return a count of 0, which would make this condition false.

■ SELF-TEST

1. Is the following statement true or false?
   ```
   char stName[] = "Mary Lou";
   ..........
      strcmp(stName, "quit") != 0
   ```
2. Code a condition that will be true if enter is pressed for the name prompt.
3. Write an expression that will compare the array stName, with the string "END" and return a match regardless of the case of the text that is entered into stName.

ANSWERS

1. True, stName is not equal to quit.
2. a. strcmp(stName,"") != 0
   b. strlen(stName) == 0
3. stricmp(stName,"END")

DECISIONS—THE IF STATEMENT

Sometimes it is necessary to execute certain commands or statements only when certain criteria (conditions) are met. One of the ways this decision making can be accomplished in C++ is with the if statement. The statement takes the following format:

```
if(condition)
statement;
[else
statement;]
```

An if statement only allows us to have one statement executed when the condition is true. If you wish to have more than one statement you must use braces{ } to enclose a block of statements. It is good practice to always use the braces.

The else is optional as indicated by the placement of the else in the square brackets. Not every if statement requires an else. If there is no else then the execution will begin with the next statement whenever the result of the condition is false. When an else is used, one or more statements will be executed when the resultant value of the condition is false. However, to have multiple statements for the false condition, you must once again use the braces to enclose the block.

The conditions used with an if are the same as those that are used in the loop conditions using the relational operators, <, >, ==...

```
if(iHours > 40)
{
    OverTime();
}
```

The OverTime function is to be performed only if iHours exceeds 40. If iHours is less than or equal to 40 execution will continue with the statement following the semicolon.

Any C++ statement or function may be executed when the condition is true including input, output, your functions, or another if.

Note that the condition is enclosed in parentheses and that there is no semicolon after the condition. If a semicolon is placed after the condition it is interpreted in C++ that there are no statements to be executed when the condition is true. This will not cause a syntax error in C++, it simply executes as a null statement and does not control the execution of any statements.

When the else clause is used, instruction(s) will be given that are to be performed if the condition is false. Remember, that the else is optional. The else clause may also be followed by any instruction, including another if.

```
if(iGrade >= 70)
{
      cout << "Pass";
}
else
{
      cout << "No Pass";
}
```

In this example, there is a semicolon after both couts.

Sample Program Using an if

```
#include <iostream.h>

void main()
{
      int iNum = 10;

      if(iNum > 10)
      ++iNum;
      cout << iNum;            //Not part of the if
}
```

OUTPUT

```
10
```

In this example the condition is false, iNum is NOT greater than 10. Therefore, the variable iNum is not incremented. Notice that the cout is not part of the if because there are no braces. The only statement that executes when the condition is true is ++iNum. Since the statement is false, iNum is not incremented and the execution continues with the statement following the if, which is the cout.

```
#include <iostream.h>

void main()
{
      int iNum = 10;
      if(iNum > 10)
      {
            ++iNum;
            cout << iNum;      //Part of if block
      }
}
```

In this example, the cout will never be executed because the cout is part of the if, which will only be executed when the condition is true. Since iNum is not greater than 10, neither the increment nor the cout are executed.

Once again, it's always better to use the braces when coding an if or an if with an else. The braces will make certain that all statements that are intended to be a part of the if are blocked with it.

■ SELF-TEST

What will the output be:

1. ```
   iNum = 5;
   if(iNum++ < 10)
   {
           cout << "Increment is after comparison";
   }
   ```

2. ```
   iNum = 5;
   if(iNum-- < 5)
   {
           cout << "less than 5";
   }
   else
   {
           cout << "not less than 5";
   }
   ```

3. ```
   if('c' == 'd')
   {
           cout << "The letters are equal";
   }
   ```

4. ```
   iBalance = 1000;
   if( iBalance <= 0);
   {
           cout << "It's all gone";
   }
   ```

■ ANSWERS

1. Increment is after comparison. The value of iNum at 5 is compared to 10, the condition is true, then the increment is made.
2. Not less than 5. The comparison is made first and 5 is not less than 5, iNum is then decremented to 4. The else will be executed because the statement is false.

3. Nothing will print.
4. It will print the statement. It does not matter what the balance is equal to because the condition has a semicolon after it, leaving an if with no statements belonging to it. The print function is therefore not dependent upon the outcome of the condition.

Using if in a Member Function

Consider the previous invoice example with items that may or may not be taxable. You will use a character field to contain a y or n to indicate if an item is taxable.

```
struct Item
{
    char stDesc[20];
    float fPrice, fTax;
    int iQuantity;
    char cTaxable;      //Contains a y or n
    void Calculate();
};
```

Now the calculations must take this question of taxability into consideration.

```
void Item::Calculate()
{
    if(cTaxable == 'Y' || cTaxable == 'y')
    {
        fTax = fPrice *iQuantity * TAXRATE;
    }
}
```

Nested if Statements

An if inside of an if is called a **nested** if and is used when more than one condition is to be tested. The second condition will be tested only if the first condition is true in the following example.

```
if(cSalaryStatus == 'h')
    if(iHours > 40)
        OverTime();
```

The OverTime() function will only be called if the first condition, cSalaryStatus equals h, is true; and the second condition, iHours greater than 40, is also true.

A condition may be nested within the if or the else portion of the if statement.

```
if(cSexCode == 'm')
    if(iAge < 21)
        iMinorMale++;
```

```
     else
       if(cSexCode == 'f')
           if(iAge< 21)
               iMinorFemale++;
```

When nesting an if, the else belongs to the last unmatched (no else) if regardless of indentation. In the previous code, the test for female will only be performed if it is a male, but not a minor. The best way to correct this example would be to use braces and indentation to clearly delineate what if statement the else belongs to.

```
       if(cSexCode == 'm')
       {
       if(iAge < 21)
       {
           iMinorMale++;
       }
       }
       else
       {
       if(cSexCode == 'f')
       {
           if(iAge< 21)
           {
               iMinorFemale++;
           }
       }
       else
       {
           cout << stErrorMsg;
       }
       }
```

Compound Conditions

Another way of testing multiple conditions would be to use the logical operators && or ||.

```
if(cSalaryStatus == 'h' && iHoursWorked > 40)
Overtime();
```

In this conditional statement both conditions must be true because of the && operator. If the salary status is hourly and the hours worked is greater than 40 then the OverTime() function will be called.

An && requires that both conditions be true, while an || only requires one to be true. Also recall that the && has a higher precedence than the ||.

Example

```
int x,y,z;
x=y=z=1;
if(x > 0 && y == 1 || z = 0)
cout << "True";
```

This will print out true because the operators will bind as follows:

```
(x>0 && y == 1) || z=0
```

After binding, the evaluation of the condition is from left to right. Once the solution is known the evaluation will end. Since x is greater than 0 and y is equal to 1, the first condition is true. The || condition will never be tested because the final solution must be true at this point because one of the conditions in an || is true.

■ SELF-TEST

1. Write a conditional statement using nested conditions that checks to see if an item is on the depreciation list (the char variable depreciate will contain a value of 'y'). If it is on the depreciation list, check if the depreciation type is straight-line (the char variable type will contain the value 's'). If both conditions are true, give the instruction to execute the depreciation() function.

2. Answer the previous question using compound conditions.

3. Modify question number 1 to use string variables.

4. What will print in the following?

   ```
   int a,b,c;

       a=b=0;
       c = 5;


   if(c<10 || a == 0 && b != 0)
   {
       cout << "True";
   {
   else
   {
   cout << "False";
   }
   ```

ANSWERS

1. ```
   if(depreciate == 'y')
   {
           if(type == 's')
           {
                   depreciation();
           }
   }
   ```

2. ```
   if(depreciate == 'y' && type == 's')
   {
           depreciation();
   }
   ```

3. ```
   if(strcmp(depreciate, "y") == 0)
   {
           if(strcmp(type, "s") == 0)
           {
                   depreciation();
           }
   }
   ```

4. True, the binding is c<10 || (a = 0 && b!=0). The evaluation begins at the left, and after c < 10 is determined to be true, the evaluation will end.

Conditional Operator

C++ provides a **conditional operator** that will express an entire conditional in a single statement. It is a ternary operator, meaning that it requires three operands: the condition, the action if true, and the action if false.

```
condition ? true : false
```

The assignment statement

```
a = x < 5 ? b : c;
```

can be read as

if x is less than 5 then a = b else a = c.

In this case the result of the condition is assigned to the variable a. If the condition is true then the value of b is assigned to a; otherwise, the value of c will be assigned to a.
```

The conditional operator is the only ternary operator in C. Remember, there must be three parts to the operation: condition, action if true, and action if false. The first part is followed by a question mark and the other two parts are separated by a colon.

■ SELF-TEST

1. Using the conditional operator, assign a 0 to iCount if balance is less than 1000, otherwise iCount should be assigned 1.
2. Read the following condition:
   fCommission = FSales < 50000 ? .05: .06;

■ ANSWERS

1. iCount = balance < 1000 ? 0 : 1;
2. If the fSales is less than 50,000, the commission rate will be .05, otherwise commission is .06.

Example:

Write a banking program that finds a new balance of deposits and withdrawals to a noninterest-bearing account. The program will use screen entry for the transaction type and for the amount.

INPUT	PROCESSING	OUTPUT
Transaction type:	Balance	Transaction Desc:
d for deposit	Add deposit	Amount
w for withdraw	Subtract withdraw	Balance
Amount of transaction	Message if invalid	

PLANNING

PROPERTIES	DATA TYPE	NAME
Amount	float	fAmount
Trans type	char	cType
Trans desc	char array	stDescription
Balance	float	fBalance

METHOD	PURPOSE
Constructor	Intialize balance.
Run	Control execution.
ObtainData	Prompt and input transaction type and amount.
Calculate	Find subtotal, tax, and total.
PrintReport	Create formatted report.

```
//Ch05Pr01
/***********************************************
Programmed By:         A. Millspaugh
Date:                  Dec 1997
Purpose:   Maintain an account balance providing for
    deposit and withdrawal transactions.  Use a decision
    statement to determine appropriate transaction.
***********************************************/


/*    include header files as needed      */
#include <fstream.h>
#include <iomanip.h>
#include <conio.h>
#include <string.h>

void Pause();

class Account
{
        float fAmount;
        char cType;
        char stDescription[9];
        float fBalance;
        void ObtainData();
        void Calculate();
        void PrintReport();
public:
        Account();
        void Run();
};


Account::Account()
{
        cout << "Initial Balance";
        cin >> fBalance;
}


void Account::PrintReport()
```

```cpp
{
    ofstream Printer ("CON");
    Printer << setiosflags(ios::showpoint| ios::fixed)
         << setprecision(2);
    Printer << "\n\t                    Transaction Report\n\n";
    Printer << "       Description           Amount      Balance    \n";
    Printer << "\t" << setw(25) << setiosflags(ios::left)
    << stDescription
    << setw(10) << fAmount
       << setw(10) << fBalance << endl;
    Pause();
}


void Account::ObtainData()
{
    cout << "Transaction Entry Screen\n";
    cout << "Enter the transaction type:\n";
    cout << "d) deposit  w) withdrawal\n ";
    cin >> cType;
    cout << "Amount of Transaction    ";
    cin >> fAmount;
}


void Account::Calculate()
{
    if(cType == 'd'|| cType == 'D')
    {
        strcpy(stDescription, "Deposit");
        fBalance += fAmount;
    }
    else
    if(cType == 'w' || cType == 'W')
    {
        strcpy(stDescription,"Withdrawal");
        fBalance -= fAmount;
    }
    else
```

```
    {
        strcpy(stDescription,"Invalid");
        cout << "Invalid transaction type";
        Pause();
    }
}

void Pause()
{
    cout << "Please Press Any Key to Continue to Next Transaction";
    getche();
}

void Account::Run()
{
    ObtainData();
    Calculate();
    PrintReport();
}

void main()
{
    Account().Run();
}
```

PRECEDENCE OF ASSIGNMENT, LOGICAL, AND RELATIONAL OPERATORS

Expressions can be combined in C++ to make very complex statements. This fact makes it necessary for the programmer to understand the way in which operators will **bind** (combine according to precedence) and how expressions will be evaluated.

All operators on the same line have equal precedence and will be evaluated according to the appropriate association.

The following examples are not realistic and demonstrate poor programming practice. However, they are designed as an exercise in understanding the underlying significance of the precedence of operators.

Combining logical operators and assignment operators:

```
#include <iostream.h>

void main()
{
```

Precedence of Assignment, Logical, and Relational Operators

PRECEDENCE OF OPERATORS
(all on same line are same precedence evaluated by association)

OPERATOR	ASSOCIATION
() [] . -> ++ -- sizeof * / %	left to right*
+ -	left to right
< > <= >=	left to right
== !=	left to right
&&	left to right
||	left to right
?:	right to left
= *= += /= %= -=	right to left

*except unary operators, which are right to left

```
int iNum1, iNum2, iNum3, iAnswer;

iNum1 = iNum2 = iNum3 = 0;
iAnswer = iNum1 || iNum2 && !iNum3;
cout << iAnswer;
}
```

OUTPUT

```
0
```

First:

`iNum1 || (iNum2 && (!iNum3))`

The && is FALSE   (False(0) and True(not zero))

Second:

`0 || False`

The || is FALSE   (False or False)

Third: Since the expression evaluates to false, it has a value of 0, which is assigned to iAnswer.

Combining Assignment and Increment Operators:

```
#include <iostream.h>

void main()
```

```
{
    int iNum1, iNum2, iAnswer;

    iNum1 = iNum2 = iAnswer = 5;
    iAnswer += -iNum1++ - ++iNum2;
    cout << iNum1 << iNum2 << iAnswer;
}
```

OUTPUT

6 6 -6

First:

iAnswer += -(iNum1++) - (++iNum2)

5+= -(5) - 6

5+= -11

iAnswer = -6

iNum1 = 6 (note the - is a unary operator)

iNum2 = 6

Combining Increment and Logical Operators

```
#include <iostream.h>

void main()
{
    int iNum1, iNum2, iNum3;

    iNum1 = iNum2 = iNum3 = 5;
    iNum1++ || ++iNum2 && iNum3++;
    cout << iNum1 << iNum2 << iNum3;
}
```

OUTPUT

6 5 5

First: (iNum1++) || ((++iNum2) && (iNum3++))
         iNum1 is 5 which is True

Since the statement can be evaluated at this point to definitely be TRUE because of the ||, the iNum2 and iNum3 will not be evaluated.

iNum1 becomes 6
iNum2 and iNum3 remain 5

After these examples, you may ask yourself, "Who would write a statement or expression like these examples?" C++ provides the ability to nest functions, operations, and expressions within each other. The important thing is to understand exactly how these will be evaluated. It is feasible that an increment may be used with a relational operator. If so, what happens?

Take a look at the next realistic application.

```
if(iRemainder %= iHoursPerPerson > 0)

++iPeopleNeeded;
```

This statement attempts to find if any partial (remainder) of a person was needed, rounding up if even a fraction remains. Unfortunately, the relational operator has a higher precedence than the assignment operator, which means that the expression will be evaluated as follows:

First: iHoursPerPerson > 0 is probably true, which results in a value of 1 being used with the modulus.

Second: Dividing by 1, there will be no remainder, assigning a value of 0 to remainder.

Finally: The expression will evaluate to 0, which will be considered false. The increment will never take place.

To Solve: if((iRemainder %= iHoursPerPerson) > 0)
++iPeopleNeeded;

Use parentheses to override the precedence, or, better yet—do not mix assignments with conditionals.

```
iRemainder %= iHourPerPerson;
        if(iRemainder > 0)
            {
              ++iPeopleNeeded;
            }
```

■ SELF-TEST

1. What will the value of iNum1, iNum2, and iNum3 be?
   int iNum1,iNum2 = 0, iNum3 = 1;
   iNum1 = iNum2++ == iNum3;

2. What will be the value of iNum1, iNum2, and iNum3?
   int iNum1,iNum2,iNum3;
   iNum1=iNum2=iNum3=0;
   iNum1 *= iNum2 == iNum3 ? iNum2++ : iNum3++;

■ ANSWERS

1. iNum2 = 1 , but not at the time of the comparison
   iNum3 = 1
   iNum1 = 0 because == causes an equality test which is false

2. iNum1 = 0 because 0*=1
   iNum2 = 1, incrementing after the assignment
   iNum3 = 0, since condition is FALSE iNum3 does not change

PROGRAMMING STYLE

When working with the arithmetic operators, the computer will follow the order of precedence. However, the use of white space will make it easier for the programmer to read and may affect the interpretation of the operators. Consider the following example:

```
iAnswer=iAmount+++iBalance;
```

The three plus signs represent an increment and an addition operator. But there is still a question as to whether this means there is a postfix increment on amount or a prefix increment on balance. It could be written as:

```
iAnswer = iAmount++ + iBalance;
```

or

```
iAnswer = iAmount + ++iBalance;
```

Without the whitespaces, it will be interpreted with the increment attached to amount.

```
#include <iostream.h>

void main()
{
        int iAmount = 0 , iBalance = 5, iAnswer;

        iAnswer=iAmount+++iBalance;
        cout << "answer " << iAnswer << "\n";
        cout << "amount " << iAmount << "\n";
        cout << "balance "  << iBalance;
}
```

OUTPUT

```
answer 5
amount 1
balance 5
```

From this output, you can conclude that the fbalance of 5 was added to the amount of 0 and stored in answer. After that amount was incremented to 1. Now try the same program with whitespaces.

```
#include <iostream.h>

void main()
{
        int iAmount = 0, iBalance = 5;
        int iAnswer;

        iAnswer = iAmount + ++iBalance;
```

```
        cout << "answer " << iAnswer << "\n";
        cout << "amount " << iAmount << "\n";
        cout << "balance "  << iBalance;
}
```

OUTPUT

```
answer 6
amount 0
balance 6
```

The answers changed because now the increment operator belongs to balance. In this instance, balance was incremented to 6 and was then added to amount. The value of amount never changed.

Because of the interpretation issue as well as to improve the readability of the code leave a space before and after each arithmetic and assignment operator.

Key Terms

compound condition
concatenation
conditional operator
expression

nested if
relational operator
string length

Chapter Summary

Relational operators provide the ability to create conditions. Using conditions to determine what action is to be taken is an important factor in processing data. The if statement provides this capability. The conditional if may be combined with an else as needed. Multiple conditions may be tested using compound conditionals or through the use of nested if statements. One application of the conditional statements is the determination of a maximum or minimum value in a range of data.

In addition to the if statement, C++ also contains an operator for doing conditions. The conditional operator is the only one that contains three operands.

Review Questions

1. What is the purpose of the operators && and || ?
2. When two conditions are combined with an &&, when will the entire condition be considered true?
3. What is meant by a nested if? A compound if?
4. Why must the processing for a high-low comparison be performed during the detail portion of the processing?
5. What will the output be?

   ```
   void main()
   {
           int iNum1, iNum2, iNum3;
           iNum1 = iNum2 = iNum3 = 5;
   ```

```
            iNum1++ || ++iNum2 && iNum3++;
            cout << iNum1 << iNum2 << iNum3;
      }
```

6. What is the significance of uppercase and lowercase in string comparisons?

Exercises

1. Calendari Publications is having a special promotion for its sales staff. A bonus of 5% will be paid for all sales over $2000.00, in addition to the normal commission rate of 10%. Write a program that will input the amount of sales and the salesperson's name, and that will calculate the normal commission rate and the bonus rate. Print out a statement that includes the company name, the salesman's name, the amount of sales, the commission, and the bonus.

   Input: Salesperson's last name:
                    Salesperson's first name:
                    Amount of sales:

   Processing: Determine if a bonus is to be paid.
                    Find total commission for each salesperson.

   Output:
   Heading: Use appropriate titles and column headings.
   Detail: Print out the salesperson's name (concatenated with first initial and last name), the amount of sales, amount of bonus, the commission, and the total compensation.

   Sample Output:

   Calendari Publications
   Sales Commission Report

Name	Sales	Commission	Bonus	Total
J. Jon	1700.00	170.00	0.00	170.00

   Calendari Publications
   Sales Commission Report

Name	Sales	Commission	Bonus	Total
F. Hong	2655.00	265.50	132.75	398.25

   Calendari Publications
   Sales Commission Report

Name	Sales	Commission	Bonus	Total
C. Marquez	2000.00	200.00	0.00	200.00

2. Write a program to determine bowling averages, handicaps, and the high game for the bowler.

   Input: Bowler's name
   Score for game 1
   Score for game 2
   Score for game 3

   Processing: Find the bowler's average for the three games.
   Find a handicap of 80% of 200 by subtracting the average from 200 and multiplying by 80%.
   Find the highest game for this bowler.

   Output:
   Heading: Use appropriate titles and column headings.
   Detail: Print out the bowler's name, three scores, average score, high game, and handicap.

3. Write a program to determine overtime hours based on an 8 hour day.

   Input: Employee Name
   Start time
   End time

   Processing: Find the number of regular hours, the overtime hours, and the total hours.

   Output:
   Heading: Use appropriate titles and column headings.
   Detail: The detail line will include the employee name, regular hours, the overtime hours, and the total hours.

4. The elementary school PTA is having a fund-raiser selling chocolate bars. The students will receive bonus gifts based on the number of cases of candy that they sell.

   Input: For each student, input the student's name, the number of cases sold, and the room number.

   Processing: The first two cases receive 10 points toward the prize list, while the third through fifth case will earn 15 points. All cases beyond 5 will receive 20 points each.

   Output:
   Heading: Use appropriate titles and column headings.
   Detail: Print out a detail line that contains the name and the number of points earned.

   Test Data: (three runs)

Name	Cases Sold	Room #
Annie Ace	3	5
Barney Boy	5	2
Clara Cool	1	5
Danny Dare	20	6
Eric Early	7	5

5. Modify the grade report from Chapter 4 to print out a numeric average and an alphabetic grade.

   Input: The input will include the name, two test scores, and three program grades.

   Processing: The grading scale will be:

   90-100 A   80-89 B   70-79 C   60-69 D   <60 F

   Output:
   Heading: The report will contain appropriate title and headings.
   Detail: Include the student name, numeric average, and the letter grade.

Hayley Office Supplies

Create a screen that displays the codes for the various departments.

Software	S
Hardware	H
Paper Goods	PG
Furniture	F
Snacks	NT

Prompt for the user to enter a department code, the product description, the price, and the quantity. Calculate a 10% discount on software items. Charge a 9% sales tax on everything except snack items.

LOOPS AND ARRAYS

CHAPTER OBJECTIVES

By the end of this chapter you should be able to:
- Create loops with the while statement
- Recognize the significance of comparisons of strings that may contain upper or lowercase characters
- Obtain loops with exit conditions using the do loop
- Code for loops
- Find highest or lowest value using an if
- Understand the concepts behind creating an array in C++
- Access individual elements within an array
- Create a report program

CHAPTER OVERVIEW

All of the programs to this point have been sequentially executed or used a decision structure. In this chapter, the concept of iteration will be introduced, allowing statements to be executed multiple times.

Relational operators may be used to create loops that use conditions to exit. The looping process allows for conditions at the beginning or the ending of the loop. Loops may be terminated with a condition (the do or while) or may be controlled by a counter (for).

Arrays are used to store multiple values for a variable. They can be used with an object when a list of items or names is required as an element within the class or structure.

Using loops, you will be able to produce a report complete with heading, body of the report, and a summary.

LOOPS

To make our programs more useful, it is necessary to create a **loop** so that the instructions in the program can be repeated as many times as necessary to complete the job. If you were processing data for just one transaction, you probably would not need a computer or a program. In business applications you almost always need to repeat the program instructions numerous times.

Two of the loop constructs in C++ are the do loop and the while loop. Both of these loop constructs will continue executing the loop instructions until a condition is met.

A while tests the condition at the beginning of the loop, and a do tests the condition at the end of the loop. In other words, the while has an **entry condition** and the do has an exit condition.

With an **exit condition,** the condition to determine when to terminate the loop is at the end of the loop. The statements in a do loop will always be executed at least once before the condition is tested at the end of the loop.

The while loop will test the condition before the loop is entered, so it is possible that the statements in a while loop will never be executed.

The while Loop

The while loop is the loop form in C++ that has an entry condition. This means that the condition will be tested prior to the loop being performed. If the condition is true, the body of the loop will be executed. Otherwise, the program will continue execution at the statement after the loop.

Format of the unblocked while loop:

```
while(condition)
    statement;
```

This form of the while loop will *ONLY EXECUTE ONE STATEMENT.* As a statement, the loop consists of only one statement prior to the semicolon.

Usually, the body of the loop will contain more than one statement. If more than one statement is to belong to the body of the loop, the statements must be blocked. Braces { } will be required to form the block around the body of the loop.

```
:while(condition)
{
    statement;
    statement;....
}
```

It is an excellent technique always to use braces around the body of the loop. This will assure that the braces are not forgotten when more than one statement is intended to be included within the loop.

Do not place a semicolon after the while (condition) or the loop terminates at the semicolon. Then you would have an empty loop. If the condition is continually met, it will be an infinite loop because there is no way for it to end.

```
while(condition);   // the loop contains no statements
{
    statement;
}
```

INFINITE LOOPS

You must be sure that there is some way for the condition to end inside the loop or any loop could become infinite.

Example of Possible Infinite Loop

```
int iNumber;
cin >> iNumber;
```

```
// an infinite loop
while(iNumber != 5)
{
    cout << iNumber;
}
```

This code will cause an infinite loop if 5 is not the number entered, because the cin is not part of the loop and will only be executed one time.

To solve this problem you could create a block containing the cin. This would appear as follows:

```
while(iNumber != 5)
{
    cin >> iNumber;
    cout << iNumber;
}
```

However, this will print the 5 because the number 5 will be printed before it loops back to the while where the relational test is made. This may not be what was intended.

This problem will be even more apparent with a test for a string condition.

```
while((stricmp(stName,"quit")!=0)
{
    cin.getline(stName,21);
    cout << stName;
}
```

Once again, the condition is tested after the cout has been executed so "quit" will print before the loop is terminated.

Priming Input

A better alternative is to use a **priming input** and to put the input as the last statement in the loop. This means that the cin at the end of the block of the loop will be the last statement to be executed before the condition is tested by the while condition. By obtaining input just before the end of the loop you can terminate execution of the loop as soon as the user enters the value you are testing for. (Note: the cin.gef() will be needed in Microsoft projects, but not in Borland.)

```
char stName[20];
cin.getline(stName,21);      //Priming input
while(stricmp(stName,"quit")!=0)
{
    cout << stName;
    cin.get()  //make sure next input gets executed
    cin.getline(stName,20);  //inputs next name
}
```

This code gets a name from the keyboard and prints it on the screen. The program will loop until the name is equal to "quit."

```
char stName[20];
cin.getline(stName,20);      //Priming input
while(strlen(stName)!=0)
{
    cout <<stName;
    cin.get() //prepare for input
    cin.getline(stName,20); //inputs next name
}
```

If no name is entered, the string length of the name field will be 0, causing this loop to terminate.

■ SELF-TEST

1. Code a while loop that will obtain and print a number until 999 is entered.
2. What will the following print?

   ```
   cin.getline(stWord,10);
   while(stricmp(stWord,"End")!=0)
   {
       cout <<"Hello";
       cin.get();
       cin.getline(stWord,10);
   }
   ```

3. Write a loop that will input a name and print the name until the Enter key is pressed.

■ ANSWERS

1. ```
   cout << "Type in a number or 999 to quit";
   cin >> iNumber;
   while(iNumber != 999)
   {
       cout << iNumber;
       cout << "Type in a number or 999 to quit";
       cin >> iNumber;
   }
   ```

2. Hello will print until End is typed regardless of case. (END would also terminate the loop.)

3. ```
   char stName[20];
       cout << "Enter a name ";
       cin.getline(stName,20);
   ```

```
while(strlen(stName)!=0)
{
    cout <<  stName << endl;
    cout << "Enter a name or type Enter to quit";
    cin.get();
    cin.getline(stName,20);
}
```

The do loop

The do loop provides a loop format in C++ containing an exit condition. Since the condition of the loop is tested after the body of the loop, the loop will always be executed at least one time. Therefore, even if the condition is false the body of the loop will be executed. This type of loop will be handy when you create menu programs. In most other situations, you will want to use an entry condition so that the user has a way out in case they do not want to execute this portion of the program.

The format for the do loop is:

```
do
{
}while(condition)
```

Example

```
float fBalance = 0.0;
do
{
    cout << fBalance;
}while(fBalance > 0.0);
```

OUTPUT

0.00

The loop is executed one time because the condition is not tested until after the balance has been printed. If a while had been used in this instance, the loop would never have been executed.

```
float fBalance = 0.0;
while(fBalance > 0.0)
{
    cout << fBalance;
}
```

OUTPUT

Nothing prints because the condition is false, not allowing the body of the loop to be executed.

SELF-TEST

1. What will the output be in the following:

   ```
   do
   {
           iCount = 0;
           cout << "The count is " << iCount << "\n";
   }while( iCount < 10);
   ```

2. What will the output be?

   ```
   iCount = 0;
   do
   {
           cout << "The count is " << iCount << "\n";
   }while(++iCount < 10);
   ```

ANSWERS

1. 0 is printed infinitely.
2.
   ```
   The count is 0
   The count is 1
   The count is 2
   The count is 3
   The count is 4
   The count is 5
   The count is 6
   The count is 7
   The count is 8
   The count is 9
   ```

The for Loop

There is a third type of loop available in C++ that is used primarily with a counter when the number of times the loop is to be executed is known. Since we have not yet discussed calculations, the first look at for loops will contain string functions.

A for loop consists of initialization, a condition, and an incrementation. The format is:

```
for(initialization; condition; action-increment)
statement;
```

Semicolons separate the three parts. All three parts are not required, but the semicolons must be there to distinguish the function of each part.

If you need to execute a print statement 10 times you could use:

THE PARTS OF THE FOR ARE:	
Initialization	int i= 0;
Condition	i < 10;
Action	i++;

```
for(int i = 0; i < 10; i++)
{
    cout << "print line # " << i << endl;
}
```

OUTPUT

```
print line # 0
print line # 1
print line # 2
print line # 3
print line # 4
print line # 5
print line # 6
print line # 7
print line # 8
print line # 9
```

The following example is nonsensical but demonstrates that any function can be used in the parts of the for statement making it different from this form of statement in other languages.

```
//A program combining a for loop and string functions
#include <iostream.h>
#include <string.h>
char stName[20],stMsg[10];

void main()
{
    cout << "Enter a name";
    cin.getline(stName,21);
    for(strcpy(stMsg,"Hello");strlen(stName)!=0;strcpy(stMsg,"And again" ))
    {
        cout << stMsg << stName;
        cout << "Enter another name or press ENTER to quit: \n";
```

```
        cin.get();
        cin.getline(stName,21);
    }
}
```

The for statement in this example is:

```
for(strcpy(stMsg,"Hello");strlen(stName)!=0;strcpy(stMsg,"And Again"))
{
}
```

THE PARTS OF THE FOR ARE:	
Initialization	strcpy(stMsg,"Hello");
Condition	strlen(stName)!=0;
Action	strcpy(stMsg,"And Again");

The loop will initially set msg to "Hello" and the condition will be tested to see if there is a name (length of the name not equal to 0). If the condition is met, the loop will be entered, and then msg will be changed to "And Again."

Note: Similar to the do and the while loops, the for loop will contain only one statement if the braces are not used. Had the braces been omitted from the previous example, only the cout for the name and the message would have been part of the loop. This would have caused an infinite loop.

MULTIPLE INITIALIZATION, CONDITION, OR ACTION

The for statement allows compound conditions. The other parts—initialization and action (usually increment)—may have multiple statements. Multiple statements within a part are separated by commas, while the three parts are still separated by semicolons.

```
for(int i = 0, int n = 10; i < 5 && n > 5;  i++, n--)
{
    cout << i << n << "\n";
}
```

THE PARTS OF THE FOR ARE:	
Initialization	The value of i is set to 0 and n to 10
Condition	compound condition with And
Action	increment i and decrement n

■ SELF-TEST

1. Write a for loop that will print the even numbers from 0 to 100, using a loop variable called n.

2. What is wrong with the following loop?

   ```
   for(int i = 0, i < 10, i++)
   {
           cout << "Hello";
   {
   ```

3. What is wrong with the following loop?

   ```
   for(int x = 5; x < 25; x ++);
   {
           cout << x;
   }
   ```

4. What will the output be in the following?

   ```
   for(int iNum = 5; iNum > 0; iNum--)
   {
           cout << iNum;
   }
   ```

5. What will the loop do?

   ```
   for(;;;)
   {
           cout << "Let's loop";
   }
   ```

ANSWERS

1. ```
   for(int n = 0; n <= 100; n+=2)
   {
           cout << n;
   }
   ```

2. The parts of the loop should be separated by semicolons not commas. The compiler will interpret this to mean that there were three things for initialization but nothing for the condition or the action, a syntax error.

3. The semicolon after the for means that there are no statements inside of the loop. The cout will only be executed one time after the loop is complete. The value of x at the time that the cout is executed will be 25.

4. 54321

5. The loop will print "Let's loop" forever. This is a legal loop since not all parts are required on the loop. However, there is no condition to exit the loop causing an infinite loop.
   ```

NESTED LOOPS

Sometimes it will be desirable to nest loops, placing a second loop inside of another. The following example places one for loop inside of another.

```
for(int i=0; i< 3; i++)
{
   for(int j=0; j<2; j++)
   {
       cout << i << j << "\n";
   }
}
```

OUTPUT

```
0 0
0 1
1 0
1 1
2 0
2 1
```

In this case the value of i is set to 0 and the condition i less than 3 is tested. The second loop is executed setting the initial value of j to 0, which is less than 2. Therefore, the body of the loop is executed printing the current value of i and j (both 0).

The next step that will be taken is to increment j. The inner loop must be completed before control will be returned to the outer loop. In this case, j becomes 1 and the loop is executed printing i, still with a value of 0 and j with its value of 1. As j is incremented to 2, the condition of the inner loop becomes false and control is returned to the outer loop where i is incremented to 1.

When the inner loop is executed, it starts over again, so j is once again initialized to a value of 0. This time the inner loop will print two lines with i = 1 both times while j = 1 and then j = 2.

The outer loop will execute a third time when i is incremented to 2, causing the inner loop to once again restart and be executed twice. This prints the next two lines where i = 2.

When i is incremented again to a value of 3 the condition on the outer loop becomes false and the loop will not be executed again.

■ SELF-TEST

1. What will the output be in the following?

```
for(int a = 5; a < 10; a + = 3)
{
    for(int b = 1; b < 3; b++)
    {
        cout << a << b << "\n";
    }
}
```

2. What will the output be:

   ```
   for(int i = 0; i < 3;i ++)
   {
           cout << "Outer Loop << i << "\n";
           for(int j = 0; j < 2; j++)
           {
                   cout << i << j << "\n";
           }
   }
   ```

3. Write a nested loop that will produce the following output:

   1 2

   1 3

   1 4

   2 2

   2 3

   2 4

ANSWERS

1.
   5 1

   5 2

   8 1

   8 2

2.
   ```
   Outer loop 04
   0 0
   0 1
   Outer loop 1
   1 0
   1 1
   Outer loop 2
   2 0
   2 1
   ```

3.
   ```
   for(int x = 1; x < 3; x++)
           for(int y = 2; y < 5; y++)
   ```

HIGHEST/LOWEST LOGIC USING THE IF

Sometimes you need to find the largest or the smallest value from a group of data that has been entered or processed. Since the values of the variables change each time you process a new record in the detail processing loop, it would be impossible to wait until after the loop to determine the smallest or largest value.

By the time you reach the summary or totals portion of our report program, the only values left in memory are from the last record that was input and processed. Therefore, if you want to perform a comparison to find the maximum and minimum value it must be done during the loop process.

To find the maximum value you need to compare each time through the loop to determine if this record contains the highest value so far. If you keep track of the highest value "so far," when you reach the end of the detail loop, you will have found the maximum value—whether it was in the first record, the last record, or any one in between.

```
if (fGrade > fMaxGrade)
    fMaxGrade = fGrade;
```

You need to store this highest value and then use it in the comparison each time through the loop. To make sure that you are comparing to a small value, you normally need to initialize the variable for the highest value to 0, assuming all values to be compared are positive. If the highest value begins at 0, you can be certain that the first record to be processed will become the highest so far. Likewise, the variable to hold the smallest value must be initialized to a large value to be sure that the records being processed will actually contain a smaller value than where the variable started. Another alternative would be to initialize both the highest and the lowest comparison variable to the value in the first record because it definitely the highest and lowest value at the time that the first record is processed.

Let's look at the detail processing to find the highest, lowest, and average grade on an exam. The input will contain the student name and the exam grade. You will also print out the name of the individual with the highest grade.

Assume that:

```
float fMaxGrade = 0; fMinGrade = 999;
char stName[20]; stMaxName[20];


void Calculations()
{
    if(fGrade > fMaxGrade)
    {
        fMaxGrade = fGrade;
        strcpy(stMaxName, stName);
    }
    if(fGrade < fMinGrade)
    }
        fMinGrade = fGrade;
    {
```

```
        iCount++;              //   accumulate grade, iCount
        fTotalGrade += fGrade;
}
```

The comparison for the small grade cannot be an else of the first condition. Just because a grade is not the largest it does not meant that it would automatically be the smallest, which is what an else implies. Most of the grades being processed will probably not be the smallest or the largest so far.

The summary function for this grade example might be coded as:

```
Summary()
{
        fAaverage = fTotalGrade/iCount;
        cout << "Average: " << fAverage;
        cout << "Highest Grade:    " << iMaxGrade;
        cout << " by              " << stMaxName;
        cout << "Lowest Grade:    " << fMinGrade;
}
```

This logic does not account for two names both having the highest grade. The way it is written, the first record processed that contains the highest grade will have the name stored in stMaxName. If anyone else has an equal score it would not be greater and would not do anything. You will not attempt to solve this issue right now.

■ SELF-TEST

1. Write the decision statement to find the name of the person with the highest amount of sales, given the following variables:

    ```
    char stName[20], stHighName[20];
    float fSales, fHighSales;
    ```

■ ANSWERS

1.
    ```
    if (fSales > fHighSales)
    {
            fHighSales = fSales;
            strcpy(stHighName, stName);
    }
    ```

SINGLE DIMENSION ARRAYS

An **array** is a data structure that can hold a list of values as opposed to the variables, which, so far, have contained one value at a time. An exception to this has been string data, which is an array of characters. With an array it is possible to store an entire list of values at one time. One data name is assigned along with the maximum number of elements that the variable will contain. Each **element** of an array contains a separate value.

| P | r | o | g | r | a | m | \0 |

```
char stString[8] = "Program";
```

is the same as:

```
char stString[] = {'P','r','o','g','r','a','m',NULL};
```

The square brackets [] used to give the length of a string field are the notation for an array. In the declaration the brackets may contain the maximum number of elements in the array.

Declaring an Array

Arrays may be string or they may be of any numeric data type or data structure. A numeric array is defined similarly to the way that strings have been defined. An integer array called number with 10 elements would be defined as:

```
int iNumber[10];
```

Initializing an Array

An array can be initialized at the time it is declared by enclosing the list of elements inside of braces. If the items are string or character, they must also contain quotes.

```
int iNumber[5] = {1,2,3,4,5};
char stLetters[6] = {'a','b','c','d','e', NULL};
```
or
```
char stLetters[6] = {"abcde"}; // Automatically adds a null
```

If the char arrays are to be accessed as a string they must allow one extra position for the null character as previously covered. When the character array is initialized using the double quotes "" around the string, a null will automatically be placed at the end of the string.

If the array is to be a local variable and to be initialized as it is declared, some compilers require it to be of storage type **static.** (The keyword static has other uses not related to the discussion at this point.)

```
static int iQuantity[5] = {77,54,88,92,7};
```

Initializing an Array of Unspecified Size

When an array is being initialized as it is being declared it is not necessary to specify the size of the array if it does not need to be larger than the number of elements being initialized.

```
int iNumber[] = {1,2,3,4,5};
```

At run time the size of the array will be determined to be five elements.

```
char stMsg[] = "Press Any Key to Continue";
```

This stMsg will be allocated the appropriate number of elements and will allow a position for a null character.

Partially Filled Array

An array does not need to be filled, so more elements may be specified than are actually used. It would be legal to say:

```
int iNumber[5] = {1,2,3};
```

There is now room for two more elements. This feature will be very important when an array needs to be declared and the size is unknown. One technique would be to use a symbolic constant for the maximum number of elements and then declare the array using the symbolic constant.

```
const int iMAXITEMS = 100;

float fAccountBalance[MAXITEMS];
```

SUBSCRIPTS

When a single value within the array is to be accessed, the position of the element must be specified. The position number of the element is called a **subscript** and is the offset (distance in values) from the beginning of the array. Since the subscript points to a position within the array, the subscript must be an integer value. The subscript is also placed in [].

Given the declaration:

int iNumber[9]={10,20,30,40,50,60,70,80,90};

10	20	30	40	50	60	70	80	90
[0]	[1]	[2]	[3]	[4]	[5]	[6]	[7]	[8]

The actual elements in the array are numbered from 0 to 8. C++ always starts arrays at a base element position of 0. If you wanted to access the third position in the array number, you would use a subscript of 2.

```
cout << iNumber[2];
```

would print 30.

The first element is at subscript 0, the second at subscript 1, and the third at subscript 2.

■ SELF-TEST

1. Given the following array, what is the value of iNum[3]?
   int iNum[5] = {2,4,6,8,10};

2. What is the subscript for the last element in the array iNum[5]?

3. Declare a char array called stZipCode that can contain an extended ZIP code with 9 characters and a hyphen.

■ ANSWERS

1. 8
2. 4
3. char stZipCode[11];   // Don't forget a space for the null

FOR LOOPS AND ARRAYS

When accessing an array, a loop is frequently required that will increment the subscript position each time through the loop. The subscript, an integer variable, will change for each iteration of the loop. This can be handled easily with a for loop.

A loop would be appropriate for entering data into the array, finding a total of all of the elements in the array, or outputting each position in the array. These tasks all call for repeated access to the array, changing the subscript each time.

To print every element in an array of 10 integers, the following loop could be used.

```
int i, iNumber[10] = {2,4,6,8,1,3,5,7,9,0};
for(i=0; i<10; i++)
{
    cout << iNumber[i] << endl;
}
```

OUTPUT

```
2
4
6
8
1
3
5
7
9
0
```

The value of i is first initialized to 0, the condition is tested, and since i is less than 10 the loop will be executed. After the loop statement is executed, the value of i is incremented, and the condition is once again tested. The loop will continue to be executed until the condition is false.

The previous loop example works well with arrays in C++. First, set the subscript variable to 0, which, of course, will point to the first element in the array. Since the elements in the array are numbered from 0, the last element is actually one less than the size of the array. As a result, the condition is tested as less than the size of the array that assures us that the loop will terminate when the end of the array has been reached. Notice that the condition is not == or <=, which would cause the loop to access one location in memory beyond the array.

```
int iNumbers[10];
for(i = 0; i < 10; i++)
{  process the array };
```

Both numeric and character arrays can be accessed one character at a time.

```
const int iMAXITEMS = 100;
int i;
float fAccountBalance[MAXITEMS];

//Find the total for account_balance
```

```
for(i=0; i< iMAXITEMS; i++)
{
    fTotal += fAccountBalance[i];
}
```

Actually this could be condensed but it would become more difficult to read:

```
//Find the total for account_balance
for(i=0; i < iMAXITEMS; fTotal += fAccountBalance[i],i++);
```

Remember that the character array contains a null character at the end, which allows us to access the entire array by using the array name as a string expression. This cannot be done with numeric arrays. If you accessed the numeric array by its name you would get the address of the first position of the array. We will discuss the reason for this in a later chapter.

```
void main()
{
    int iNum[5] = {1,2,3,4,5}, i;
    char stLetters[6] = {'a','b','c','d','e','\0'};
    char stWord[6] = {"abcde"};

    // Print out array elements
    for(i=0; i<5; i++)
    {
        cout<<iNum[i]<<stLetters[i]<<stWord[i]<<endl;
    }
    //Try to print entire array
    cout << iNum << stLetters <<stWord;
}
```

OUTPUT

```
1 a a
2 b b
3 c c
4 d d
5 e e
3792 abcde abcde
```

Notice that both character arrays act the same whether they were initialized as individual characters or as a string. The 3792 on the last line of output is the address of the array iNum and may differ if the program is executed again.

Using a for Loop on Partially Filled Arrays

Sometimes all of the elements in the array may not be filled. In this case you would need two conditions: one to test the size of the array and another to determine if you have reached the number of elements that are being used.

```cpp
#include <iostream.h>

void main()
{
        char stCity[15];
        int i;

        cout << "Enter City:    ";
        cin.getline(stCity,15);

        //Test for end of array or last character

        for(i=0; i < 15 && stCity[i] != NULL; i++)
        cout << stCity[i] << endl;
}
```

OUTPUT

Enter City: Chicago
C
h
i
c
a
g
o

In the first example, the loop continues until it reaches a null. If more than 15 characters are typed for the city name, the loop would terminate when the end of the array is reached. The s at the end of Hacienda Heights is never printed.

```cpp
#include <iostream.h>

void main()
{
        char stCity[15];
        int i;

        cout << "Enter City:    ";
        cin >> stCity;

        //    test for end of array or last character

        for(i=0; i < 15 && stCity[i] != NULL; i++)
```

```
        cout << stCity[i] << endl;
}
```

OUTPUT

```
Enter City:   Hacienda Heights
H
a
c
i
e
n
d
a
```

The blank space terminates the output. A string longer than 15 characters will create an infinite loop.

■ SELF-TEST

1. Write the loop that will print out each of the elements in the array:
   `int iGrade[10];`
2. Write the loop that will find the average of all of the elements in the array:
   `int iGrade[10];`
3. What will the following print?
   ```
   #include <iostream.h>

   void main()
   {
           static char stCity[] ="Chino";
           int i;

           //     test for end of array or last character

           for(i=0; i < 15 && stCity[i] != NULL; i++)
           cout << stCity[i] << endl;
   }
   ```

■ ANSWERS

1. ```
   int i;
   for(i=0; i < 10; i++)
   {
           cout << iGrade[i];
   }
   ```
   ```

2. ```
   int i;

   for(i = 0; i < 10; i++)
   {
       fTotal += iGrade[i];
   }
   cout << fTotal/10;
   ```

3. Chino

A REPORT PROGRAM

You now have the statements necessary to create a program to produce a report. This is one of the most common applications, since most business systems need several different reports.

Let's begin by considering the parts of a report. A report can be broken down into the heading, the body of the report, and the summary. The heading portion may contain a title and possibly column headings. The title may contain the date and page number.

The main body of the report is also called the detail portion. The detail portion of the report would contain an output line for each transaction. Although the titles would be only required once for each page, the detail lines will be repeated over and over. Therefore, the heading will precede the loop while the detail processing will be inside the loop.

The summary portion of the report contains items, such as totals, averages, and item counts. The summary portion is optional depending on the needs of the particular situation. A report may also be a summary report that does not contain any detail lines but merely the summary information.

Calculations for totals must be performed during the detail loop while the information is available. Since each time that new data is entered into a variable the old value is lost, accumulations are done during the detail processing.

The detail portion of the report will process each record using a loop. This is the part of the program that will have the transaction input and processing. The information may be printed immediately or retrieved later from the array to print the report.

Example Program

Using the invoice example from the previous chapter, you will create an invoice that has multiple products purchased. The invoice will be printed after all purchases are processed.
   ```

PLANNING

PROPERTIES	DATA TYPE	NAME
Description	char array	stDescription
Price	float	fPrice
Quantity	integer	iQuantity
Subtotal	float	fSubtotal
Tax	float	fTax
Total	float	fTotal

METHOD	PURPOSE
Constructor	Intialize totals
Run	Control execution
ObtainData	Prompt and input description, price, and quantity
Calculate	Find subtotal, tax, and total
Print	Create formatted report

```
//Ch06Pr01
#include <fstream.h>    //io objects
#include <iomanip.h>    //formatting
#include <string.h>     //string functions

void ExitMessage();

struct Item
{
      char stDescription[20];
      float fPrice;
      int iQuantity;
};

class Invoice
{
      Item Product[50];
      int iNumItems;
      void ObtainData();
```

```cpp
        void Print();
public:
        Invoice();
        void Run();
};

Invoice::Invoice()
{
        iNumItems = 0;
}

void Invoice::ObtainData()
{
        int i = 0;
        cout << "Description: ";
        cin.getline(Product[i].stDescription, 20);     //Priming input
        while(stricmp(Product[i].stDescription,"Q")!=0)
        {
                cout << "Price: ";
                cin >> Product[i].fPrice;
                cout << "Quantity: ";
                cin >> Product[i].iQuantity;
                ExitMessage();
                cin.ignore();
                cout << "Description: ";
                cin.getline(Product[++i].stDescription, 20); //Next Desc.
        }
        iNumItems = i;    //Number of products entered
}

void Invoice::Print()
{
        ofstream Printer("CON");
        Printer << endl;
        Printer << setprecision(2) << setiosflags(ios::showpoint|ios::fixed);
        // the character data will be right aligned in headings
        Printer << setw(45) << "ABC Inc." << "\n\n";
```

```
        Printer << setw(25) << "Description    " << setw(15) << "  Price"
                << setw(20) << "Amount Due" << "\n\n";


        for(int i = 0; i < iNumItems; i++)
        {
            Printer << "          ";  //10 spaces at left margin
            Printer << setw(15)
                    << setiosflags(ios::left) << Product[i].stDescription
                    << setw(15) << Product[i].fPrice << resetiosflags(ios::left)
                    << setw(15) << Product[i].fPrice * Product[i].iQuantity << endl;
        }
        Printer << endl;
        Printer << "Number of Records Processed  " << iNumItems ;
}


void Invoice::Run()
{
        ObtainData();
        Print();
}


void ExitMessage()
{
        ofstream Screen("CON");
        Screen << "\nType Q for description to quit\n\n";
}


void main()
{
        Invoice().Run();
}
```

Key Terms

compound condition
concatenation
detail
entry condition
exit condition
expression
loop
priming input
relational operator
string length

Chapter Summary

A loop is a logic construct that allows for a statement or block of statements to be repeated. By using a condition, the programmer can determine when the loop statements will be executed and when the loop will terminate. The condition may be placed at the beginning of the loop (entry condition) using the reserved word while. In a while loop, it is possible that the loop will never be executed because the condition is tested before the loop is entered.

With a do loop, the condition is at the end of the loop (exit condition). Since the loop is not tested until the end of the loop, the statements in the loop will always be executed at least one time. A for loop contains three parts; the initialization, the exit condition, and the action for each iteration. A do or while is typically used when the number of iterations is not known and is determined by a test. The for loop works best when the number of repetitions is known.

An array is a type of data structure that can contain multiple values at the same time. Another way to think of an array is as a variable that contains a list of values. Each value is called an element within the array. In order to specify which element you are referring to, every access to the array must include a subscript. A subscript is an index to a position within the array. The subscript must evaluate as an integer value but it may be a constant, a variable, or an expression. A for loop can be used to access an array using the subscript as a variable.

A report program typically will contain three major parts: the heading, the detail body, and a summary. Some reports may not contain a summary, while a summary report contains no detail lines. These parts can be used to form the basis of the structure of a report program.

Review Questions

1. What is a loop?
2. What is the difference between a loop with an entry condition and a loop with an exit condition?
3. How many times will an exit condition loop be executed?
4. What are the primary parts of a report?
5. What does detail line mean?
6. In what part of the program—heading, detail, or summary—would you expect to find a loop?
7. How many times should a loop be executed?
8. What is an array?
9. Define the term subscript.
10. What constitutes a legal value for a subscript?
11. Why is the for loop a natural for accessing array elements as opposed to a while loop or a do loop?
12. Given an array declared as int iQuantity[10]:
    a. What is the subscript of the first element?
    b. What is the subscript of the last element?
13. What happens if a processing loop attempts to access a subscript larger than the size of the array?
14. What will the termination test be for a for loop to access a 25-element array, assuming the loop starts with i = 0?

What will the output be in questions 15–18:

15. ```
    while(int iNum < 10)
    {
         cout << iNum << endl;
         iNum++;
    }
    ```

16. ```
    char cLetter;
    while(cLetter != 'a')
         cout << cLetter;
    ```

17. ```
    while(int iNum < 10);
    {
         cout << iNum << endl;
         iNum++;
    }
    ```

18. ```
    char cLetter;
    do
    {
         cin >> cLetter;
         cout << cLetter;
    }
    while(cLetter != NULL);
    ```

Exercises

1. Write a program to produce a report of the total labor costs for FIXIT Construction.

   Input: Description of task

   The number of hours

   Cost per hour.

   Processing:

   Detail: Calculate the total cost for each task.

   Summary: Accumulate the total labor cost.

   Output:

   Headings: Include appropriate titles and column headings.

   Detail: Must contain the description, the number of hours, the cost per hour, and the cost for that line.

   Summary: At the end of the report, print out the total labor cost for all jobs.

2. Write a program to produce a billing report.

   Input: First name
   Last name
   Account number
   Amount billed

   Processing:
   Detail: Concatenate the first and last names.
   Summary: Accumulate the total amount billed and the number of customers.
   Output:
   Heading: Include appropriate titles and column headings.
   Detail: Must contain the full customer name (concatenated together), the account number, and the amount billed.
   Summary: At the end of the report, print the total billing, the number of customers, and the average amount billed.

   Sample Data:

FIRST NAME	LAST NAME	ACCOUNT NUMBER	AMOUNT BILLED
Jane	Seemore	11821	28.31
Michael	Miller	12061	320.00
Jennifer	Longchamp	10932	102.50
Edward	Catllin	12390	96.52

3. Write a program to produce a roster for the computer club that contains names and phone numbers, and a summary containing the number of members.

   Input: Last name
   First name
   Phone number

   Processing:
   Detail: Concatenate the first and last name as last name, followed by a comma and space, and then followed by the first name.
   Summary: Count the number of members.
   Output:
   Heading: Use appropriate titles and column headings.
   Detail: Full name and phone number; the concatenated name.
   Summary: Print a line specifying the number of members.

   Sample Output:

   ```
                       The Computer Club
                       Membership Roster


   Name    Phone Number
   Ace, Annie                                               111-1111
   Brown, Billy                                             222-2222
   Cook, Crystal                                            333-3333

   Number of members               3
   ```

4. Write a program to generate and produce a report of subscription account numbers for a magazine. Each account number will consist of the first two letters of the last name, the first three digits of the ZIP Code, and the expiration date.

Input: Last Name:

First Name:

ZIP Code:

Expiration Date:

Hint: Make the ZIP code type char[].

The expiration date may be in the form of 07/92 or Jul-92, whichever you prefer.

Processing:

Detail: Determine the account number by concatenating together the first two letters of the last name, the first three characters in the ZIP code, and the expiration date.

Summary: Count the number of accounts as they are processed.

Output:

Heading: Use appropriate titles and column headings.

Detail: Name and account number, the name will be the last name concatenated with a comma and a space and then concatenated with the first name.

Summary: Print a line containing the number of records processed.

Sample Data:

LAST NAME	FIRST NAME	ZIP CODE	EXP. DATE
Doe	Sam	11232	12/94
Smith	Carol	84567	08/94
Winters	Sharon	34571	08/95
Black	Tim	91763	11/95

Sample Output:

```
                    Micro Magazine
                  Subscription Report


Name                              Account Number
Doe, Sam                          Do11212/94
Smith, Carol                      Sm84508/94
Winters, Sharon                   Wi34508/95
Black, Tim                        Bl91711/95


Number of accounts processed   4
```

Hint: Since the strncpy() function does not insert a null it will be necessary to force a null after the first two letters (ie. stAccount[2] = NULL;)

5. Write a program to produce an invoice report for Widget Mfg. Company.

   Input: Product Description:

   Quantity:

   Cost:

   Processing:

   Detail: Calculate the extended price (unit price times quantity)

   Summary: Accumulate the total extended price

   At summary time, use a sales tax of 8% on the total price and add the sales tax to produce the total amount due.

   Output:

   Headings: Use appropriate titles and column headings.

   Detail: The detail line will include the description, the cost, the quantity, and the extended price.

   Summary: Print out the total of the extended prices, the sales tax, and the total amount due.

   Sample Data:

PRODUCT DESCRIPTION	QUANTITY	COST
Blue widgets	1.45	17
Miniwidgets	.87	25
Gray widgets	1.40	18

6. Modify the invoice example from the chapter so that it has a class for customer information. Create the loops to allow invoices to be prepared for multiple customers.

Hayley Office Supplies

Using the invoice header created in Chapter 2, create individual customer invoices for sales for Hayley Office Supplies. Set up a loop that will input the appropriate information for a customer and then use a second loop to enter individual product information.

Input:

Customer: Last Name (loop until Q is pressed)
First Name
Address: Street, City, State, and ZIP Code

Product: Description (loop until enter is pressed)
Unit price
Quantity

Processing: Find the extended price by multiplying the price by the quantity.
Accumulate the total amount due.

Output:

Heading: For each customer, print the invoice header.

Detail: Each detail line will include the product description, the quantity, the cost, and the extended price.

Summary: At the end of each invoice, print the total amount due.

CREATING MENU PROGRAMS USING THE SWITCH STATEMENT

CHAPTER OBJECTIVES

By the end of this chapter you should be able to:
- Use a switch statement as an alternative to the if.
- Create menus through the use of the switch statement.
- Access other executable programs and return to the menu program.
- Generate a general class for menus.

CHAPTER OVERVIEW

Another alternative to the if statement for determining whether or not selected statements are executed is a switch statement. The switch statement allows for different "cases" to be tested; switch and the case will be covered as well as the break statement.

This chapter introduces programs that are controlled by a menu. Although the if statement can be used to determine which option is selected, the switch statement provides an easier approach. An additional advantage of the switch is the ability to do some automatic validity checking with a default statement.

THE SWITCH STATEMENT

Another decision-making tool in C++ is the switch statement. This statement allows a variable to be tested for several various possible values called cases. There also is a built-in error-checking factor, called default, that may be used when none of the cases have been met. Each case may contain statements that are to be executed when a condition is met. These statements could involve calling other functions, providing a method of performing a conditional branch.

The format of the case statement is:

```
switch (expression or variable)
{
case value:
        statement(s);
case value:
        statement(s)

[default:
        statement(s);]
}
```

Break

A **break** statement must be used to indicate the end of the statement(s) for each case, or the execution of the program continues to flow through the remaining cases without testing the case conditions. When a break is encountered, execution continues with the statement following the closing brace of the switch statement.

The default case is executed if none of the other cases produce a match with the expression.

Suppose that you have a variable called cChoice that determines which function to execute. If the value of cChoice is A then the AddRecord() function is executed, a D causes the DeleteRecord() function to be performed and E causes the EditRecord() function to execute. All other entries are invalid.

```
switch (cChoice)

{

case 'A':

        AddRecord();

        break;

case 'D':

        DeleteRecord();

        break;

case 'E':

        EditRecord();

        break;

default:

        ErrorRtn();

}
```

Notice that the default statement is ErrorRtn(). It is executed if a choice other than A, D, or E is selected.

More than One Alternative for a Case

It is possible to have more than one value allowed for each case. Perhaps the AddRecord function could also be accessed with a lowercase 'a' or the number 1. Then we could change the code to:

```
case 'A': case 'a': case '1':

AddRecord();

break;
```

All of the values for choice must be enclosed in single quotes presuming that choice is of type char.

The switch statement may also be used on numeric variables. The value following the word case must then be numeric constants of type float or integer depending on the type of variable that is being tested. A range of numbers cannot be tested with the case, only individual values.

SELF-TEST

1. What, if anything, is wrong with the following?

   ```
   switch(cAnswer)
   case 'y'
   {
           iYcount++;
           cout << "Yes";
   }
   case 'n'
   {
           iNcount++;
           cout << "No";
   }
   ```

2. What will print in the following?

   ```
   int iCount = 0;
   while(iCount++ < 3)
   {
   switch(iCount)
   {
           case 1:
                   cout << "1";
           case 2:
                   cout << "2";
           case 3:
                   cout << "3";
           case 4:
                   cout << "4";
           default:
                   cout << "Oops\n";
   }
   }
   ```

3. What prints in the following?

   ```
   int iCount = 0;
   while(++iCount < 3)
   {
   ```

```
switch(iCount)
{
    case 1:
        cout << "1";
    case 2:
        cout << "2";
    case 3:
        cout << "3";
    case 4:
        cout << "4";
    default:
        cout << "Oops\n";
}
}
```

4. What prints in the following?

```
int iCount = 0;
while(iCount < 3)
{
switch(++iCount)
{
    case 1:
        cout << "1";
    case 2:
        cout << "2";
    case 3:
        cout << "3";
    case 4:
        cout << "4";
    default:
        cout << "Oops\n";
}
}
```

5. What prints?

```
int iCount = 0;
while(iCount < 3)
```

The switch Statement

```
{
switch(iCount++)
{
    case 1:
        cout << "1";
    case 2:
        cout << "2";
    case 3:
        cout << "3";
    case 4:
        cout << "4";
    default:
        cout << "Oops\n";
}
}
```

■ ANSWERS

1. There should be a set of braces around all of the cases. The open brace should follow the switch statement before the first case and the closing should be at the end of the set of cases or after the default (if there is one, default is not required). There should be a colon after the value for each case.

   `case 'y':`

   The statements for each case need not be in braces but there should be a break statement. The execution continues until a break is found.

2.
   ```
   Oops
   1234Oops
   234Oops
   34Oops
   ```

   There is no break so it falls through every statement after it is true. Count starts with a value of 1 because it was incremented after the condition on the while.

3.
   ```
   1234Oops
   234Oops
   ```

   In this instance, count is incremented before it tests the condition on the loop so the switch is only executed two times.

4.

    1234Oops

    234Oops

    34Oops

5.

    Oops

    1234Oops

    234Oops

Notice that, in this case, the value of Oops is printed because count has a value of 0; the first time that the switch statement is executed, count will be incremented after the test is made.

Example Program

Write the transaction balance program for deposits and withdrawals from a noninterest-bearing account using the switch statement. The planning remains the same as last chapter but a switch is used instead of the if in the Calculate() function.

INPUT	PROCESSING	OUTPUT
Transaction type	Balance:	Transaction Desc.
d for deposit	Add if deposit	Amount
w for withdraw	Subtract withdraw	Balance
Amount of transaction	Message if invalid	

The processing function becomes:

```
Calculate()
{
//Select action depending on transaction
switch(cType)
{
        case 'd':
        case 'D':
                strcpy(stDescription,"Deposit");
                iNumberDeposits++;
                fBalance += fAmount;
                break;
        case 'w':
        case 'W':
                strcpy(stDescription,"Withdrawal");
```

```
            iNumberWithdrawals++;
            fBalance -= fAmount;
            break;
        default:
            strcpy(stDescription,"Invalid");
            cout << Invalid transaction type";
            Pause();
    }
}
```

SELF-TEST

1. Write a switch statement that prints "Hello World" to the printer or to the screen.

ANSWER

1. char cOption;

```
cout << "Printer/Screen, enter a P or an S";
cin >> cOption;
switch(cOption)
{
case 'S': case 's':
    cout << "Hello World\n";
case 'P': case 'p':
    ofstream cprn("PRN");
    cprn << "Hello World\n";
}
```

Using the switch for a Range of Values

The switch statement is not designed to use for a range of values using relational operators. Multiple values need to be listed as we did earlier. This does not help in situations using floating-point numbers where we need to test a continuous range. The if would, of course, be available. However, in some situations a little manipulation makes the switch feasible.

Consider the example of converting numeric grades to a letter grade using percents. If everything between 90 and 100 is an 'A', we could list each integer. This solution would require a lot of code but it still does not work for a value such as 95.4. If the grade is divided by 10, then the first digit could be used in the cases.

```
/*------------------------
Determine the letter grade from a numeric grade
using the scale:
    90-100  A
    80-89   B
```

```
                    70-79   C
                    60-69   D
                    < 60    F
            ------------------------- */
float fGrade;
int iGrade;
char cGrade;

cout <<  "Enter numeric grade";
cin >> fGrade;
//Divide the grade by 10 to get first digit
iGrade = fGrade/10;
switch (iGrade)
{
case  9:
case 10:
      cGrade = 'A';
      break;
case 8:
      cGrade = 'B';
      break;
case 7:
      cGrade = 'C';
      break;
case 6:
      cGrade = 'D';
      break;
default:
      cGrade = 'F';
}
cout << fGrade << cGrade;
```

OUTPUT

```
Enter numeric grade
76
76C
```

SELF-TEST

1. Write the statement to evaluate the pay rate for the following piecemeal pay rate system. The pay per unit is determined by the number of units produced. Once the number of units produced is determined that rate applies to all units for that individual.

# UNITS	RATE PER UNIT
Less than 200	.40
201-499	.50
Over 500	.65

ANSWER

1.

```
fUnits /= 100;
switch (fUnits)
{
    case 0: case 1:
        rate = .4;
        break;
    case 2: case 3: case 4:
        rate = .5;
        break;
    default:
        rate = .65;
}
```

MENU PROGRAMS

One of the most useful applications of a switch statement can be the creation of a menu routine. A **menu** is a program that displays several different options that may be selected. In an earlier example, a variable called cChoice was tested to determine what function should be performed. This is an example of a menu.

```
switch (cChoice)
{
case 'A':
    AddRecord();
    break;
case 'D':
    DeleteRecord();
    break;
```

```
case 'E':
        EditRecord();
        break;
default:
        ErrorRtn();
}
```

Notice that if the case matches an A that the AddRecord() function is performed followed by a break. This results in the switch statement being exited after the appropriate action has been taken. The default ErrorRtn() function will only be performed if choice is not an 'A', 'D', or 'E'.

Structure of a Menu Program

In creating a menu program, the menu must be displayed, an option will be selected and the proper function executed, and then the program returns to the menu until the user elects to quit.

The Run() function for this type of program differs from the report program structure that has been used in the previous programs. The Run() must contain a loop that will not be exited until the user selects the quit option.

```
void Run()
{
while(cChoice != '0')
{
        PrintMenu();
        GetChoice();
}
}
```

The PrintMenu() function clears the screen and displays all of the options. The GetChoice() allows the user to enter a selection and then executes a switch statement.

After any option from the menu is executed, the control of the program returns back to the Run() function because of the loop. The menu continues to print until the loop is terminated by the selection of the "quit" option on the menu.

Sample Program

Write a menu program to allow the user to either find the average of a series of numbers or to find the square of a number.

PROPERTIES	DATA TYPE	NAME
Menu option selection	character	cChoice

METHOD	PURPOSE
PrintMenu	Draw the menu screen
SelectChoice	Select appropriate function using a switch
Run	Loop until quit is selected

```cpp
//Ch07Pr01
#include <fstream.h>
#include <conio.h>

void Average(), Square();
void PauseMessage(), Pause();

class Menu
{
    char cChoice;
    void PrintMenu();
    void SelectChoice();
public:
    void Run();
};

void Menu::Run()
{
do
{
    PrintMenu();
    SelectChoice();
}while(cChoice != '0');
}
void Menu::PrintMenu()
{
    cout <<"\n\n         Sample Menu\n\n";
    cout << "    1. Find Average of two numbers\n";
    cout << "    2. Find Square of a number\n";
    cout << "    0. Quit\n";
    cout << "    Enter your Choice (0-2)\n";
    cin >> cChoice;
}

void Menu::SelectChoice()
{
    switch (cChoice)
    {
```

```cpp
        case '1':
            Average();
            Pause();
            break;
    case '2':
            Square();
            Pause();
            break;
    case '0':
             // Quit option should not fall to default
            break;
    default:
            cout << "You must enter a NUMBER (0-2)\n";
    }
}


void Average()
{
        float fNum1, fNum2;

        cout << "Enter first number    ";
        cin >> fNum1;
        cout <<"Now the second number ";
        cin >> fNum2;
        cout << "The average is " << (fNum1+fNum2)/2 << endl;
}


void Square()
{
        float fNum1;

        cout << "Enter a number    ";
        cin >> fNum1;
        cout << "The square of " << fNum1 << " is "
             << fNum1*fNum1 << endl;
}


void Pause()
```

```
{
    PauseMessage();
    getche();
}


void PauseMessage()
{
    ofstream Screen("CON");
    Screen << "Press any key to continue";
}




void main()
{
    Menu().Run();
}
```

OUTPUT

```
Sample Menu
1 Average of two numbers
2 Find Square of a number
0 Quit
Enter Your Choice =======>_
```

Using Letters or Numbers for Menu Options

Menus are often created that allow the user their choice of entering a letter or a number to make a selection. This can be done by declaring the option variable as character and then using a list of multiple cases for the switch statement.

```
switch (cOption)
{
    case '1':
    case 'A':
    case 'a':
        Average();
        break;
    case '2':
    case 'S':
    case 's':
        Square();
        break;
```

```
        case '0':
        case 'Q':
        case 'q':
                cChoice = '0';  // To exit the run() loop
                break;
default:
        cout << "You must enter a NUMBER or LETTER";
}
```

To make it clearer to the user that the A is an option, the letter could be capitalized, placed in parentheses, displayed in bold, italics, or in a different color. To use bold or italics see the programming tip at the end of this chapter.

Sample Menu

```
1 A)verage of two numbers
2 F)ind Square of a number
0 Q)uit
Enter Your Choice =======>_
```

SELF-TEST

1. Write the switch statement for the following menu:

   ```
   Trimet Auto Inc.


   1 E)nter a sale transaction


   2 D)isplay daily report


   3 P)rint weekly report


   0 Q)uit


   Enter your option =====>_
   ```

2. Why does the Run() contain a loop printing the menu?
3. If the loop terminates with an option of 0, what happens if someone types Q to quit?
4. Why is the pause() used at the end of each module that displays to the screen?

ANSWERS

1. ```
   switch (cChoice)
   {
        case '1':
   ```
   ```

```
            case 'E':
            case 'e':
                    EnterSale();
                    break;
            case '2':
            case 'D':
            case 'd':
                    DisplayDaily();
                    break;
            case '3':
            case 'P':
            case 'p':
                    PrintWeekly();
                    break;
            case '0':
                    case 'Q':
            case 'q':
                    cChoice = '0';  //   to exit the run() loop
                    break;
            default:
                    cout << "You must enter a NUMBER or LETTER";
    }
```

2. The only way to exit a menu program should be through the menu or an assigned function key that terminates the program. Until that time, the menu should be reprinted and another option selected.
3. The condition in the loop in Run() must contain compound conditions or the '0' can be assigned to the option variable in the switch statement.
4. Since the function returns to the loop that reprints the menu, any data that is printed on the screen will be cleared. The Pause() function allows the user to determine when to go back to the menu.

MENU HINTS

It is better to use a character type for the selection variable even if the options are all numbers. The default prints messages for any invalid characters. Even if the menu only lists numerical option, some user may attempt to type a letter, which would cause strange results when the variable is numeric.

The quit option should be consistent from one menu to another. If a menu has multiple levels, they should be connected with an option to return to the previous menu. This menu option should also always be consistent. When using numbers for the options, consider using an option of zero (0) for the quit and return to previous menu options.

SELF-TEST

1. Write the switch statement for the following menu:

   ```
   E)nter Production Orders

   P)rint Daily Schedule

   B)illing Information

   W)eekly Report

   Q)uit
   ```

2. What could be done in the previous example if a second item began with the same letter, for example:

   Produce Weekly Report

3. Why does the quit option require a case in the switch statement when there is no function to be executed?

ANSWERS

1.  ```
    switch(cChoice)
    {
            case 'E':
                    Production();
                    break();
            case 'P':
                    Schedule();
                    break;
            case 'B':
                    Billing();
                    break;
            case 'W':
                    Report();
                    break();
            case 'Q':
                    //Must have q option to avoid getting default
                    break;
            default:
                    ErrorRtn();
    }
    ```
    ```

2. Highlight any letter within a word to indicate that the option may be selected with that choice.
3. If the case was not included for the quit option, the program would execute the default routine when the quit was selected.

CREATING A MORE GENERIC MENU CLASS

The goal in object oriented programming should be towards reusable code. Menus are used in many circumstances. It is desirable to code the class so that many parts could be reused and functions are overloaded as needed. The following program demonstrates loading the menu items into a table and then displaying them on the screen. In the next chapter, the corresponding functions are placed in a second array.

STRUCTURE

PROPERTIES	DATA TYPE	NAME
Caption for screen	character array	stMenuCaption

PROPERTIES	DATA TYPE	NAME
Menu option selection	character	cChoice
Number menu options	integer	iNumOptions
Menu item	array of MenuItem structure	MenuOptions[]

METHOD	PURPOSE
PrintMenu	Draw the menu screen
SelectChoice	Select appropriate function using a switch
Run	Loop until quit is selected

```
//Ch07Pr02
//   An object oriented menu program
#include <iostream.h>
#include <string.h>

void option1(),option2(),option3(),option4();

struct MenuItem
{
     char MenuCaption[20];
};

class Menu
```

```cpp
{
    MenuItem MenuOptions[4];
    int iNumOptions;
    char cChoice;
    void PrintMenu();
    void SelectOption();
public:
    Menu(int, char MenuOptions[4][20]);
    void Run();
};

void Menu::PrintMenu()
{
    cout << "     Menu Selections\n\n";
    for(int i = 1; i < iNumOptions + 1; i++)
    {
        cout << i << ". "
             << MenuOptions[i-1].MenuCaption
             << endl;
    }
    cout << "0. Quit \n";
    cout << "Your selection ======> ";
    cin >> cChoice;
}

void Menu::SelectOption()
{
switch(cChoice)
{
    case '1':
        option1();
        break;
    case '2':
        option2();
        break;
    case '3':
        option3();
```

```cpp
                break;
        case '4':
                option4();
        case '0':
                break;
        default:
        cout << "Enter a Number";
    }
}
void Menu::Run()
{
do
{
    PrintMenu();
    SelectOption();
}while(cChoice != '0');
}


Menu::Menu(int iNumberItems, char MenuItems[4][20])
{
    // constructor loads the items in the array
    iNumOptions = iNumberItems;
    for(int i = 0; i < iNumOptions; i++)
    {
    strcpy(MenuOptions[i].MenuCaption, MenuItems[i]);
    }
}

void main()
{
    char MenuItems[4][20] = {"Add","List","Edit"};
    // this array is passed to constructor
    Menu(3,MenuItems).Run();
}

void option1()
{
```

```
        cout << "option 1\n";
        // Call the add routine here
}

void option2()
{
        cout << "option 2\n"; // Call list routine
}

void option3()
{
        cout << "option 3\n"; // Call edit routine
}.

void option4()
{
        cout << "option 4\n";
}
```

RUNNING EXECUTABLE FILES OR DOS COMMANDS FROM THE MENU

The C++ program can "shell" out to the operating system using the system() function. The program can be requested to run another program (an .EXE, .BAT, or .COM file) or to perform a DOS command. (This command is portable to UNIX machines, but, of course, they will not understand DOS commands. To make the switch it would be necessary to substitute, for example, ls for DIR.)

The system() function uses the following format:

system("string instruction to operating system");

The string must be enclosed in quotes, and may contain the name of an EXE, BAT, or COM file or a DOS command.

```
system("CH5EX6");
```

```
system("CLS");
```

One problem that you may encounter with the system command is that it does not work from within the editor environment. The program containing the system() function call will compile and link without errors. However, in order for the system() call to be performed, the program must be called from the DOS prompt.

Running Executable Files or DOS Commands from the Menu

```
/*
Programmer: A. Millspaugh
Date:
Purpose:  Demonstrate the ANSI C code to "shell"
  out to the operating system (DOS)     */

#include <iostream.h>
#include <stdlib.h>
#include <process.h>   //  for UNIX portability

void main()
{
      cout << "Hello to you from C";        //  print from C++
      system("dir a:/w");                         //  print from DOS
      cout << "...and back to C";           //  print from C++
}
```

After creating a file called dosdemo.exe:

`C:> dosdemo`

OUTPUT

```
Hello to you from C
Volume in Drive A has no label
Volume Serial Number is 2A4F-16CA
Directory of A:\

RETURN  BAT       NAMES            FUNCTION WK3   EXER1B
README            LETTERS
6 file(s)    769,362 bytes free
0 dirs       686,500 bytes free
...and back to C
```

This function may be used to make a menu program "tie together" several individual programs. At this point, you could create a menu that would run any of the previous programs that have been written for this course.

Clearing the Screen

Another advantage of this command is to improve the appearance of the previous menus by clearing the screen between options. When drawing the menu and in the screens for the individual options insert system("CLS");.

```
void Menu::PrintMenu()
{
      system("CLS");
      cout << "       Menu Selections\n\n";
```

```
            for(int i = 1; i < iNumOptions + 1; i++)
            {
            cout << i << ". "
                    << MenuOptions[i-1].MenuCaption
                    << endl;
            }
            cout << "0. Quit \n";
            cout << "Your selection ======> ";
            cin >> cChoice;
}
```

USING MENU BARS

Another type of menu allows the user to select from a list by using cursor keys and the enter key. This is referred to as a highlighted menu bar. To highlight the "selected" line is placed in one color (the "on" color) while the remaining options are in a different color (the "off" color). The colors used to indicate on and off may be specified in the constructor function. This may not work on all operating systems.

To test for the up key, the down key, and the enter key; the ASCII code is used in the test. A scan code may also be included. The codes are as follows:

ASCII CODE	VALUE
72	Up key
80	Down key
13	Enter key

```
//Ch07Pr04
/////////////////////////////////////////////////////////
//      Programmer:
//      Date:
//      Description:Uses a highlighted menu bar for making
//                      selections
/////////////////////////////////////////////////////////
#include <conio.h>
#include <stdlib.h>
#include <iostream.h>

void ColorOn()
{
```

```cpp
        cout << "\033[7m";
}

void ColorOff()
{
        cout << "\033[0m";
}

const bool FALSE = 0;
const bool TRUE = 1;

char MenuItem[5][20] = {"Wordprocessing",
                "Spreadsheets",
                "Database",
                "Graphics",
                "Quit"};
class Menu
{
        void Choice(), Validate(), DisplayMenu();
        int iSelection, iValidExit, iValidChoice;
        int iNumberOptions;
public:
        Menu(int iNumber);
        void Run();
};

void main()
{
        Menu(5).Run();
}

Menu::Menu(int iNumber)
{
        iNumberOptions = iNumber;
        iSelection = 0; iValidExit = FALSE; iValidChoice = FALSE;
}

void Menu::Run()
```

```cpp
    {
    while(!iValidExit)
    {
        DisplayMenu();
        Choice();
        Validate();
    };
    }

    void Menu::DisplayMenu()
    {
    system("CLS");
    cout << "Application Menu\n\n";
    for(int x = 0; x < iNumberOptions; x++)
    {
        if(iSelection == x)
            ColorOn();
        else
            ColorOff();
        cout << MenuItem[x];
        ColorOff();
        cout << endl;
    }
    }

    void Menu::Choice()
    {
    char cKey;
    cKey = getche();
    switch(cKey)
    {
        case 72: //up arrow
            iSelection--;
            break;
        case 80: //down arrow
            iSelection++;
            break;
```

```
                case 13:
                        iValidChoice = TRUE;
        }
}


void Menu::Validate()
{
        if(iSelection < 0) iSelection = iNumberOptions - 1;
        if(iSelection > iNumberOptions - 1) iSelection = 0;
        while(iValidChoice)
        {
                switch(iSelection)
                {
                        case 0: case 1: case 2: case 3:
                                cout << "Not yet available";
                                break;
                        case 4:
                                iValidExit = TRUE;
                }
                iValidChoice = FALSE;
        }
}
```

PROGRAMMING/DEBUGGING HINT

Reverse Video

Another way to accentuate options or prompts is to incorporate reverse video (sometimes called reverse image). The reverse video works on DOS system monitors. To do this you can incorporate the reverse video escape sequence within the print line to the screen or use a definition of an inline function.

To place the 1 and the A in reverse image for the line

1. Average

we could use the following cout.

```
cout << "\033[7m1. A\033[0mverage";
```

This statement turns on reverse video before the 1 and sets the print back to normal after the A. This might be clearer if we break it down as follows:

```
void Reverse()
{   cout << "\033[7m";}
void Normal()
```

```
{ cout << "\033[0m"; }
```

```
Reverse();
cout << "1. A";
Normal();
cout << "verage";
```

Printers

All of the escape sequences are for screen use only, they do not affect printed output. There are sets of codes that may be found in some printer manuals that can control the style, font, and size of a character, as well as the orientation (portrait or landscape).

Key Terms

break	menu
case	switch
default	system

Chapter Summary

In situations where a variable needs to be tested for several different values, the variable may be tested using a switch statement. The switch statement contains possible values that may be contained in the variable, each of which is called a case. In the case that none of the actual values tested for were met, a default may be specified.

Once the condition has been met, all of the following statements are executed without further testing, until a break statement is encountered.

A menu program can be written easily through the use of a switch statement. The values in the switch correspond to the possible selections from the menu. The statements or functions to be executed is determined by the value selected.

Using the system() function in C++ allows a program to temporarily "shell" to the operating system. The program may then execute another program or perform an operating system command.

The ANSI codes provide the capability of using colors, or reverse video on the screen.

Review Questions

1. When would a switch statement be preferable over an if statement?
2. Can a compound condition be used with a switch?
3. Why is the option of 0 suggested for the quit in a menu?
4. Why is the break statement necessary inside of the switch statement?
5. What would the Run() function of a menu program consist of?
6. A menu program executes one of various options. How will the program be terminated?
7. What statement easily allows the function for the correct option to be selected and executed?

8. Why would it be necessary to pause execution of a program?
9. What code can be used to pause the execution of the program?
10. How can a menu option contain another menu?

Exercises

1. Write a menu program to list your favorite movies by category. The menu should contain at least comedy, romance, and musical categories and an option to exit. When the choice is made a function executes that displays the appropriate information neatly on the screen. If exit is chosen, clear the screen before leaving the program.

    Use a pause function or macro before returning back to the menu from each display function.

2. Write a menu program that displays a company's current assets and liabilities. The menu will offer the choices of displaying assets, displaying liabilities, or of exiting.

    Use the following information in creating your display screens. Be sure to pause before returning to the menu.

    Assets:

        Cash

        Accounts receivable

        Building

        Office furniture

        Office supplies

    Liabilities:

        Accounts payable

        Building loan

        Office expenses

        Utility expenses

3. Create a menu program that displays a list of resort destinations along with an option to exit. For each resort, create a display screen that includes suggested hotel, dining recommendations, activities, and the approximate price range for each.

4. Create a menu program with at least three options and an exit that displays information on each screen about your favorite hobby or interest.

5. Write a landscape program that displays a menu of plants appropriate for: shade, sun, drought, freeze. Each option should list the names of flowers, shrubs, vegetables, or trees appropriate to the specified conditions.

6. Write a menu program that displays the meeting time and date for the following clubs. Be sure to add an option to exit.

    Computer Club

        First and third Tuesdays

        11:00-12:00

        Building 26D-4

Alpha Gamma Sigma
> Second and fourth Wednesdays
> Noon
> Third Thursday evening
> 7:00 p.m.
> Student center

Forensics
> Every Wednesday
> 1:00
> Department offices

7. Write a program that calculates and print a report for monthly utility bills for the Genie Electric Company. The rates for usage are on an escalating scale depending on the units used.

   Rates: Up to 300 Kilowatt Hours = 10.151 cents per KWH

               301 to 500 = 14.11 cents per KWH

               over 500 = 16.80 cents per KWH

   Input: Customer last name:

               Customer first name:

               Starting reading:

               Ending reading:

   Output: Appropriate title and column headings for name and amount due.

               Detail lines to include customer name and amount due

               Summary—average usage, total billings.

8. Write a menu program that runs the programs that you have written for the previous chapters.

9. Write a program that allows the user to:
   a. Format a low density diskette.
   b. Format a high density diskette.
   c. Copy Files.
   d. Display Disk Directory.
   e. Quit.

   Submenus:

       Option 1, 2, and 4:   Allow an option for Drive A, Drive B, or Drive C, and return to previous menu

       Option 3:   Allow options for all files or for a specific file. Also allow an option to return to the previous menu.

Hayley Office Supply

Write a menu program that allows letterhead to be printed (Chapter 1 Case Study), customer invoices to be prepared (Chapter 4 Case Study), or merchandise turnover to be calculated (Chapter 5 Case Study).

    The menu must contain an appropriate title. Use an option of 0 to exit the menu. Each option should allow the user to type in a letter or a number to select the option. If color is available, use different colors for the characters that can be used to select from the menu. If no color is available, use boldface print, or use low-intensity white and high-intensity white.

CHAPTER 8

POINTERS

CHAPTER OBJECTIVES

By the end of this chapter you should be able to:
- Understand the pointer operators for declaring variables to store addresses and for referring to values stored at those addresses.
- Avoid indirection errors through an understanding of levels of indirection.
- Use pointers to return and pass addresses to a function.
- Modify the general menu program to contain a pointer to the appropriate function.
- Use inheritance to add a title to the menu class.

CHAPTER OVERVIEW

The true power and flexibility of C++ comes through the use of pointers to access memory locations. This chapter introduces the use of pointers to store addresses of variables and functions.

Pointers are used to pass addresses to a function. The address may be of a variable or of a function. The menu program from last chapter can be improved by adding a pointer to the proper function with each menu item.

The address of an array may be returned from a function through the use of pointers. This data validation occurs as the data is entered. The address of the "validated" data may then be returned to a function for storage.

POINTER VARIABLES

One of the greatest advantages of C++ is the ability to use pointers. A **pointer** is a variable that contains an **address**, a location in memory. The address may be of a variable, a function, or another pointer.

There are many reasons for using pointers. The primary ones are:
1. Efficiency
2. Allow other functions to know the location of a local variable so that the actual value may be altered
3. To pass arrays as parameters to a function
4. Manipulation of arrays

The ability to pass arrays provides the capability of passing and "returning" strings. If a pointer variable contains the address where the string begins, that address may be referred to in other parts of the program.

Pointer Operators

Two symbols are used with pointers, the asterisk * and the ampersand &. Each of these symbols serves two different purposes in different circumstances. The * is used when declaring a pointer. The **indirection operator** (*) is also used when referring to the contents (value) stored at the location being pointed to (the **indirect value** of the pointer). The & is the **address of operator** and is read as "the address of" and as the "pass by reference" operator.

Declaring a Pointer

To declare a pointer, the * operator must be placed before the variable name, and it must be declared to be of the data type for the address which it contains. This takes the format:

```
data_type *pointer_name;
```

Thus,

```
char *cPtr;
```

declares a pointer that contains the address of (point to) type character. The character it will have the address of has not yet been assigned, but a pointer variable has been created. The pointer must be assigned to a character variable or to a function returning a character.

```
float *fPtr;
int *iPtr;
```

The variable fPtr contains the address of a float variable and iPtr contains the address of an integer variable.

```
char cLetter, *cPtr;
```

Even though cLetter and the pointer to a character have been declared, there is nothing yet that associates the two of these together. If the intention is to have the pointer cPtr hold the address of cLetter then it is necessary to assign the address of the variable to the pointer. This action may be performed with an assignment statement.

Assigning a Pointer to the Address of a Variable

Given the following declaration:

```
char cLetter, *cPtr;
```

The assignment may be made by :

```
cPtr = &cLetter;
```

This reads as the address of cLetter is assigned to the pointer cPtr.

cLetter	cPtr
	1002

ADDRESS	
1002	1004

Notice that when assigning an address to a pointer it is not necessary to use a pointer operand on cPtr. At this point, cPtr is a variable, which is being assigned the address of the variable cLetter. Further, assign a value to cLetter:

```
cLetter = 'a';
```

cLetter	cPtr
a	
	1002

ADDRESS	
1002	1004

Therefore,

VALUE	REFERENCE	MEANING
1002	cPtr	Address of cLetter
a	*cPtr	Indirect value (value at address indicated in cPtr)
1002	&cLetter	Address of cLetter
1004	&cPtr	Address of cPtr
a	cLetter	Value of cLetter

COMBINING DECLARATION AND ASSIGNMENT OF POINTERS

The declaration and assignment may be made in one step by coding:

```
char cLetter, *cPtr = &cLetter;
```

Note that the * was necessary in this case to designate that cPtr is a pointer when it is declared.

Now, what about declaring a variable of type character, initializing the variable, declaring a pointer to the variable and assigning the address at one time?

```
char cLetter = 'a', *cPtr = &cLetter;
```

STATEMENT	RESULT
`cLetter = 'a;'`	The contents of cLetter is 'a'
`*cPtr = 'a';`	The indirect value of cPtr is 'a'
`cPtr = &cLetter;`	The pointer variable contains the address of cLetter.

SELF TEST

```
int iQuantity, *iQuantityPtr;
char cLetter, *cLetterPtr;
```

1. Assign a 10 to iQuantity and then assign the address of iQuantity to iQuantityPtr;
2. Assign a 'C' to cLetter and then assign the address of cLetter to cLetterPtr;
3. Could the address of iQuantity be assigned to cLetterPtr?

ANSWERS

1. `iQuantity = 10;`

   `iQuantityPtr = &iQuantity;`

2. `cLetter = 'C';`

   `cLetterPtr = &cLetterPtr;`

3. No, the data type of the pointer must match the data type of the value whose address is stored in the pointer variable.

Dereferencing a Pointer Variable

The indirect value of a pointer variable is the value that is stored at the address that is contained in the pointer variable. If fPtr contains the address of fAmount, then the indirect value of fPtr is the value of fAmount. The indirect value of a pointer variable can be found with the dereference operator *. Yes, it is the same operator used to declare a pointer variable but it is a different meaning. After the declaration, the * operator is used to derive the indirect value.

```
float fAmount = 10.25, *fPtr = &fAmount;
cout << fAmount << endl;
cout << *fPtr << endl;
```

OUTPUT

```
10.250000
10.250000
```

The dereference operator can be used to get the indirect value in a print operation, but it could also be used in other situations such as an assignment or a calculation.

```
x = *fPtr;     // assign the indirect value of fPtr to x
y = 2 * *fPtr; // multiply the indirect value of fPtr by 2
```

A Pointer Contains an Integer

A pointer variable contains a memory address so it always contains an integer, however, the pointer must be declared as the type to which it will be pointing. This makes sense if you consider incrementing an address location to look at the next item in memory. The type of data that it is determines the number of bytes of memory that are occupied by each value. Therefore, if a pointer is used to reference character data that only occupies

1 byte, the address of the next character will only be one byte away. However, if the data being pointed to is of type float, each item occupies four bytes, and the beginning of the following data item address would be four bytes higher than the first one.

```
float *fPtrNum1, *fPtrNum2, fNum1, fNum2;
fPtrNum1 = &fNum1;
fPtrNum2 = &fNum2;
```

ADDRESS	VARIABLE	VALUE
1000	fPtrNum1	1008
1004	fPtrNum2	1012
1008	fNum1	
1012	fNum2	

The address of fPtrNum2 is 4 bytes beyond fPtrNum1 (since pointer values are stored as long integers). Each of the floating point variables occupies 4 bytes.

■ SELF-TEST

Complete the exercises given the following:

float fAmount, *fAmountPtr;

1. Code the statement to assign the address of fAmount to the pointer fAmountPtr.
2. Using the pointer, assign the value 10.24 to fAmount.
3. If #1 and #2 have been executed, what is the value of the following?
    a. fAmount
    b. *fAmountPtr
    c. &fAmount
    d. &fAmountPtr
    e. fAmountPtr

■ ANSWERS

1. fAmountPtr = &fAmount;

    The asterisk is not required because we are assigning the address of fAmount to the variable called fAmountPtr. The fAmountPtr variable is expecting to contain an address because it was defined with an * making it a pointer.

2. *fAmountPtr = 10.24;

    The indirection operator is used in this instance because we are assigning a value not into fAmountPtr but into the address location that is indicated by the number stored in fAmountPtr and which is actually the address of fAmount.

3. a. 10.24
    b. 10.24
    c. The address of fAmount.
    d. The address of fAmountPtr.
    e. The address of fAmount, which has been stored in fAmountPtr.

SUMMARY OF POINTER CHARACTERISTICS

From the discussion to this point, three characteristics about pointer variables have been covered. Specifically, each pointer variable:

1. Is a location in memory.
2. Contains a value, which is an address.
3. Can be used to obtain the indirect (**dereferenced**) value of the address that the pointer contains.

Given the following declaration,

int *iPointerVariable;

1. &iPointerVariable   Address of iPointerVariable
2. iPointerVariable   Contents of pointer variable (can be assigned an address).
3. *iPointerVariable   Indirect value which tells the contents at the address contained in iPointerVariable.

Therefore,

iPointerVariable = pointer	Assigns something to be the value of iPointerVariable, this will be interpreted as an address (pointer should be the address of an integer value.)
iNumber = *iPointerVariable;	Assigns the indirect value; finds the address in iPointerVariable, goes to that address and gets the value and then assigns that value to iNumber (iNumber should be an integer variable.)
int **iPtr = &iPointerVariable;	Assigns the address of iPointerVariable to a variable being declared as a pointer to a pointer to an integer value.

POINTERS TO POINTERS AND LEVELS OF INDIRECTION

You may have encountered the error message that reads "different levels of indirection." Exactly what does that mean and how can it be solved?

The level of indirection is the "distance" from the value.

```
int  iNumber = 5, *iPtr = & iNumber;
```

*iPtr has a 0 level of indirection because it refers directly to the value. On the other hand, the variable iPtr has a level of 1 because the address in iPtr has to be accessed to reach the value. Similarly, iNumber has a 0 level while &iNumber has a level of 1.

Errors are caused when values are assigned that are at different levels of indirection. All addresses are above the 0 level of indirection because they must be dereferenced to get to the indirect value.

```
int iNumber, iAmount;
```

Legal: iNumber = iAmount;

            iNumber is at indirection level 0;

            iAmount is at indirection level 0.

Illegal: iNumber = &iAmount;

            iNumber is at indirection level 0;

            &iAmount is at level 1 of indirection.

It would, of course, be illegal to assign the address of iAmount to iNumber or vice versa because they are not pointer variables. The * and & operators, as well as the declaration, determine what level a variable is. The * operator decreases the value of indirection as it dereferences to get toward the value. When the & operator is used, the level of indirection increases because the address of something is being referred to which is another level away from the actual value.

```
int    *iPtr, **iPtrPtr;
```

iPtr is at level 1 of indirection because the declaration is for a pointer that contains an address, not a value—must be dereferenced for the value; iPtrPtr is at level 2 by declaration because it contains an address that contains an address that contains a value.

*Decreases, &Increases

Notice that you can determine the level of indirection at the declaration by counting the iNumber of * preceding the variable. In the prior two examples, iNumber and iAmount had no * and were at level 0. In this example iPtr is at level 1 and iPrtPtr is at level 2.

After the declaration, the & and the * may be used when accessing a variable. Since the * dereferences, it brings the expression closer to the value, thereby decreasing the level of indirection. The & operator actually increases the level of indirection because it takes the address of a variable, moving it further from the actual value.

```
int iNumber, iAmount;
int *iPtr, **iPtrPtr;
```

Legal:
 iPtr = &iAmount;
 // assigns an address to a pointer
 iPtr is level 1
 &iAmount is level 1

Legal:
 *iPtr = iAmount;
 // assigns a value to a value
 *iPtr is level 0
 iAmount is level 0.

Illegal:
 iPtr = iAmount;
 iPtr is level 1
 iAmount is level 0.

Legal:
 iPtrPtr = &iPtr;
 &iPtr is up one level from iPtr (level 2)
 iPtrPtr is level 2.

Illegal:
 iPtrPtr = iPtr;
 iPtr is level 1
 iPtrPtr is level 2.

■ SELF-TEST

Give the levels of indirection for the following assignments. Which are legal?

float fAmount = 5, *fAmountPtr = &fAmount, **fPtrPtr = &fAmountPtr;

1. *fAmountPtr = fAmount;
2. fAmount = *fAmountPtr;
3. fAmountPtr = *fPtrPtr;
4. fAmountPtr = &fPtrPtr;
5. fAmount = *fPtrPtr;
6. fAmountPtr = fPtrPtr;
7. fAmount = &fAmountPtr;
8. *fAmountPtr = 10;
9. **fPtrPtr = 10;
10. fAmount = 10;

■ ANSWERS

At declaration,

fAmount is level 0
fAmountPtr is level 1
fPtrPtr is level 2

1. both level 0, legal   (* decreases level of fAmountPtr)
2. both level 0, legal   (* decreases level of fAmountPtr)
3. both level 1, legal   (* decreases level of fPtrPtr)
4. illegal:
   &fPtrPtr is level 3   (& increases level of fPtrPtr)
5. illegal:
   fPtrPtr is level 1   (decreases level but it still refers to an address, not a value)
6. illegal, different levels
7. illegal:
   &fAmountPtr is level 2   (& increases the distance from the value)
8. both level 0, legal   (* decreases level of fAmountPtr)
9. both level 0, legal   (** decreases level of fPtrPtr by 2)
10. both level 0, legal

POINTERS AS FUNCTION ARGUMENTS

The two primary reasons for passing a pointer to a function are to allow a local variable to be modified by another function or to pass an array. Recall that local variables are defined within a function and are visible to that function only. If an argument is passed to a function, we have passed the value of the original variable but the receiving function does not know where that original variable is really located. Therefore, the value of the original variable cannot be changed. The function may return a value, which is then assigned at the point where the function is called.

```
#include <iostream.h>
```

```
int Square(int iNumber);

void main()
{
    int iNum = 5, iSquare;

    iSquare = Square(iNum);
    cout << iNum << endl;
    cout << iSquare;
}


int Square(int iNumber)
{
    return(iNumber*iNumber);
}
```

A few problems with this approach include the following:
1. Only one value can be returned from a function.
    If a pointer is used to store the address, then the functions can change the contents at that memory address, even though the original variable name is unknown to the called function. No other function can alter the memory location; the variable is not visible except to the original function. Several pointers may be passed to a function and may thereby allow the function to change the value of multiple memory locations.
2. The original values cannot be changed by any other function. The variables could be changed to global and then the value could be changed. However, any and all functions would then have the ability to change the variable.

FUNCTION CALL BY REFERENCE TO A LOCAL VARIABLE ADDRESS

Take a look again at the Square program using a pointer as the argument. This eliminates the need for a return in the called function and an assignment in the calling function. In other words, the need for the variable square is eliminated. The print statement asks for each item to be printed to clarify what is happening. The address changes when you execute the program because the location is determined at run time.

```
#include <iostream.h>
int Square(int*);//Indicates an address of an integer variable as an argument

void main()
{
```

```
    int iNum = 5;

    cout << Square(&iNum);     //Pass the address of num
}

int Square(int *iNumber)
//Declare iNumber as a pointer variable to receive an address
{
    return *iNumber * *iNumber;  //Multiply the indirect values
}
```

By using a pointer, the memory location has been passed rather than passing a value. The value of the variable iNum in the main function was altered by the action of Square() upon the contents of the memory location *iNumber.

The declaration of iNumber in the Square() function required the asterisk notation since we had actually passed a pointer. This function must also know that it is dealing with a pointer.

REFERENCE OPERATOR

C++ introduced a new operator for working with data indirectly called a reference to a type.

> datatype &variable = value;

The variable is a reference to the datatype. One of the most convenient ways to use the new operator is in defining the receiving type of data in an argument list.

```
Square(int &iNum)
```

indicates that iNum will be a reference to an integer, in other words an address. However, within the function itself, the variable iNum does not need a dereference operator in order to access the value. This means that the function contents looks exactly the same whether a value or a reference is being sent.

```
#include <iostream.h>
int Square(int8);//Indicates a reference to  an integer variable as an argument

void main()
{
    int iNum = 5;

    cout << Square(iNum);    // passes the address of iNum
}

int Square(int &iNumber)
```

```
//Declare iNumber as a reference which to receive an address
{
        return iNumber * iNumber;    //Multiply the values
}
```

The primary advantage of the reference operator is that a function may be written the same and then the & inserted or not in the function header and prototype to indicate that a value or reference will be used. It also makes the function itself easier to read.

PASSING ADDRESSES OF FUNCTIONS

Using pointers it is also possible to send the address of a function. It may be necessary to use parentheses to make sure that the pointer references the function name and not the return type.

```
void (*Function)();
```

indicates that the pointer contains the address of a function that has a void return type. This is different than void *function(); which states that the function returns a pointer to a void data type.

The following structure for a menu item contains two data members; the first is the name of the menu item and the second is the address of the corresponding function.

```
struct MenuItem
{
        char stMenuCaption[20];
        void (*MenuFunction)();
};
```

A class for creating menus can then use the structure. The pointer that is used for the variable cOption allows us to treat the menu items as an array. Also note the second (overloaded) constructor that allows two items to be received. These will be the number of menu items that will be on the menu along with a pointer to the address of the first element in an array of menu items.

```
class Menu
{
        MenuItem *Option;
        int iNumOptions;
        char cChoice;
        void DrawMenu();
        void SelectOption();
public:
        Menu(){ iNumOptions = 0;}
        Menu(int, iMenuItem *);
        void RunMenu();
};
```

The header file also contains all of the functions to run the menu including the statement selecting the appropriate function.

```
if (iChoice > = 0 && iChoice < iNumOptions)
(*Option[iChoice].MenuFunction)();
```

MENU REVISITED

It is now time to reexamine the menu program using the structure that contains the menu item and the address of the function. Some of the parts of this program are placed in a header file that can be called from other programs as well.

The Header File

The header file for the menu program contains the class definition as well as the Pause() function. Notice the MenuItem structure as well as the definition of the constructors.

STRUCTURE

PROPERTIES	DATA TYPE	NAME
Caption for screen	character array	stMenuCaption
Function for menu selection	pointer to a function	*MenuFunction()

PROPERTIES	DATA TYPE	NAME
Menu option selection	character	cChoice
Number menu options	integer	iNumOptions
Menu item	array of MenuItem structure	*Options

METHOD	PURPOSE
Menu()	default constructor, no menu options
Menu(int, pointer to array)	constructor with size of array and address of menu array
PrintMenu	Draw the menu screen
SelectChoice	Select appropriate function using a switch
Run	Loop until quit is selected

```
//Menu.h
struct MenuItem
{
    char stMenuCaption[20];
    void (*MenuFunction)();
};
```

```cpp
class Menu
{
    MenuItem *Option;
    int iNumOptions;
    char cChoice;
    void DrawMenu();
    void SelectOption();
    public:
    Menu()                      //Number items not passed
    {
        iNumOptions = 0;
    }
    Menu(int, MenuItem[]);      //Overloaded constructor
    void Run();
};
void Menu::DrawMenu()
{
    cout << "Menu Selections\n";
    for(int i = 0; i < iNumOptions; i++)
    {
        cout << (i + 1) << ". "
             << Option[i].stMenuCaption
             << endl;
    }
    cout << "0. Quit\n";
    cout << "Your selection ======> ";
    cin > > cChoice;
}


void Menu::SelectOption()
{
    int iChoice = cChoice - 49; //convert from ASCII code to integer
    if (iChoice > = 0 && iChoice < iNumOptions)
        (*Option[iChoice].MenuFunction)();
    else
```

```cpp
            if (cChoice != '0')
                cout << "Error, Select by Number \n";
}


void Menu::Run()
{
    do
    {
        DrawMenu();
        SelectOption();
    }while(cChoice != '0');
}


Menu::Menu(int iSizeofArray, MenuItem MenuData[])
{
    //Assign value passed in constructor
    iNumOptions = iSizeofArray/sizeof(MenuItem);
    //Assign address of array of menu items to class member
    Option = MenuData;
}
```

The MENU Program

The program includes the header file and then will pass the menu names and the function names to the menu class when a menu object is created.

```cpp
// Ch08Pr01
#include <iostream.h>
#include <conio.h>
#include <string.h>
#include "Menu.h"

void Add(), List(), Edit();

void main()
{
    MenuItem MenuInfo[] = {
                {"Add a Client", Add},
                {"List all Clients", List},
```

```
                {"Edit Client Record",Edit}};

    Menu(sizeof(MenuInfo),MenuInfo).Run();
}


void Add()
{
        cout << "The Add function \n";
}


void List()
{
        cout << "The List function \n";
}


void Edit()
{
        cout << "The Edit function \n";
}
```

MULTIPLE LEVEL MENUS

The same menu class may be used multiple times within the same program by creating multiple menu objects. Such would be the case in a program in which a menu item calls up another menu. The following program demonstrates this application of the menu class.

```
// Ch08Pr02
#include <iostream.h>
#include <conio.h>
#include <string.h>
#include "menu.h"

void Add(), List(), Edit(), Dummy();

void main()
{
   MenuItem MenuInfo[] = { "Add", Add,
                "List", List,
```

```
                "Edit", Edit};

        Menu UpdateMenu(sizeof(MenuInfo),MenuInfo);
        UpdateMenu.Run();
}

void Add()
{
        cout << "The add function ";
        MenuItem MenuInfo[] = { "Item 1", Dummy,"Item 2",Dummy};
        Menu AddMenu(sizeof(MenuInfo),MenuInfo);
        AddMenu.Run();
}


void List()
{
        cout << "The list function is ";
        Dummy();
}


void Edit()
{
        cout << "The edit function is ";
        Dummy();
}


void Dummy()
{
        cout << "Not yet available" << endl;
}
```

INHERITANCE

Another major feature of programming in object oriented design is the ability to inherit characteristics from another class structure. Both data members and member functions may be inherited without modifying the original class.

An object can be derived from another object providing an object-oriented feature called **inheritance.** The original object is called the **base class.** The **derived class** contains all of the public data members and member functions of the base class. Additional items may be added to the derived class. The levels of derived classes are up to the needs of the application.

One advantage of inheritance is that changes may be made to an existing class by creating a derived class with all of the features of the original without actually making changes to the base class.

To indicate that a class is derived from another class, the : operator is used. The operator appears between the derived and base class names.

```
class derivedclass : baseclass
{

}
```

Inheritance provides the ability to create a new class that contains the characteristics of another class. The base class is not modified in any way by the inherited class and is not even "aware" of the inheritance. This feature allows us to add functionality or data items to existing code without altering the original code. A derived class may then become the base of another derived class. The relationship of base and derived classes is called the hierarchy of classes. The reusability of code without altering the base class reduces the chance of introducing errors into code that already works but allows the programmer to extend the versatility of a class. The inheritance operator is a : (semicolon).

```
class derivedclass : accessmode baseclass
```

```
struct derivedclass : accessmode baseclass
```

The access mode is optional but defaults to public for struct and to private for class. As with the keyword public and private within the definition of a class or struct the access mode provides the level to which functions and data elements may be used within the class and within the inherited classes.

BASE CLASS	INHERITANCE ACCESS MODE	DERIVED'S ACCESS TO BASE
public	public	public
private	public	cannot access
protected	public	protected
public	private	private
private	private	cannot access
protected	private	private

In other words if any member is to be inherited it should be protected rather than private. The private items from the base class cannot be inherited.

Example

Returning to the menu program you once again use the menu class in the header file for Chapter 7. However, the program inherits from the menu class and creates a new class called Menuwithtitle. The private members of the base class have been changed to protected to allow for the data to be inherited.

First, it will be necessary to modify the header file to change the mode of the private members to protected.

STRUCTURE

PROPERTIES	DATA TYPE	NAME
Caption for screen	character array	stMenuCaption

PROPERTIES	DATA TYPE	NAME
Menu option selection	character	cChoice
Number menu options	integer	iNumOptions
Menu item	array of MenuItem structure	MenuOptions[]
Title for the menu	character array	stTitle

METHOD	PURPOSE
PrintMenu	Draw the menu screen
SelectChoice	Select appropriate function using a switch
Run	Loop until quit is selected

Header File

```
//Menu.h

struct MenuItem
{
     char stMenuCaption[20];
     void (*MenuFunction)();
};

class Menu
{
     protected:
     MenuItem *Option;
     int iNumOptions;
     char cChoice;
     void DrawMenu();
     void SelectOption();
     public:
     Menu()                       //Number items not passed
```

```cpp
        {
                iNumOptions = 0;
        }
        Menu(int, MenuItem[]);   //Overloaded constructor
        void Run();
};
void Menu::DrawMenu()
{
        cout << "Menu Selections\n";
        for(int i = 0; i < iNumOptions; i++)
        {
                cout << (i + 1) << ". "
                        << Option[i].stMenuCaption
                        << endl;
        }
        cout << "0. Quit\n";
        cout << "Your selection ======> ";
        cin > > cChoice;
}

void Menu::SelectOption()
{
        int iChoice = cChoice - 49; //convert from ASCII code to integer
        if (iChoice > = 0 && iChoice < iNumOptions)
                (*Option[iChoice].MenuFunction)();
        else
                if (cChoice != '0')
                        cout << "Error, Select by Number \n";
}

void Menu::Run()
{
        do
        {
                DrawMenu();
                SelectOption();
        }while(cChoice != '0');
```

```cpp
                        }

                        Menu::Menu(int iSizeofArray, MenuItem MenuData[])
                        {
                            //Assign value passed in constructor
                            iNumOptions = iSizeofArray/sizeof(MenuItem);
                            //Assign address of array of menu items to class member
                            Option = MenuData;
                        }
```

Program File

```cpp
// ch08Pr03
#include <iostream.h>
#include <string.h>
#include "Menu.h"

void Add(), List(), Edit();

class Menuwithtitle:public Menu
{
    char stTitle[20];
    void DrawMenu(); //override old drawMenu
    public:
    Menuwithtitle(int iSizeOfArray, MenuItem MenuData[], char *stTitleInfo)
    {
    iNumOptions = iSizeOfArray/sizeof(MenuItem);
    Option = MenuData;
    strcpy(stTitle, stTitleInfo);
    }
    void Run(); //to force derived drawMenu()
};

void Menuwithtitle::DrawMenu()
{
    cout << stTitle << endl << endl;
    for(int i = 0; i < iNumOptions; i++)
    {
        cout << (i + 1) << ". " << Option[i].stMenuCaption << endl;
```

```cpp
        }
        cout << "0. Quit" << endl;
        cout << "Your selection ======> " << endl;
        cin >> cChoice;
}

void Menuwithtitle::Run()
{
        do
        {
                DrawMenu();
                SelectOption();
        }while(cChoice != '0');
}

void main()
{
  MenuItem Menuinfo[] = {{ "Add", Add,},
                         {"List", List,},
                         {"Edit", Edit}};
        char* stTitle = "Menu 1";
        Menuwithtitle UpdateMenu(sizeof(Menuinfo),Menuinfo, stTitle);
        UpdateMenu.Run();
}

void Add()
{
        cout << "The add function " << endl;
}

void List()
{
        cout << "The list function " << endl;
}

void Edit()
{
        cout << "The edit function " << endl;
}
```

Key Terms

address
address operator
buffer
default

dereference
indirection operator
indirect value
pointer

Chapter Summary

A pointer variable stores the address of a variable or a function. All addresses are integer, so the actual contents of a pointer variable will be an integer. Pointer variables may be used in limited types of calculations—incrementing or decrementing.

The declaration for a pointer variable indicates the type of data to which the pointer will be pointing. When a pointer variable is incremented by 1, the new address will increase by the size of the type of pointer. Thus, a float pointer when incremented will have the address increased by four bytes since each float data item occupies four bytes.

Pointers are especially useful for returning multiple values from a function or for allowing a function access to "private" data. A pointer to an array will allow an array to be returned from a function by returning the beginning address of the array.

When working with pointers, it is important to understand the levels of indirection to keep track of multiple layers of pointers. This eliminates many common errors. Another common error to be watchful for is a null pointer assignment, where a pointer does not really point to anything.

Data entry should check the validity of each character as it is entered. When the character is acceptable it is concatenated to a "good data" buffer. Using a data validation routine, it is also possible to set up a default value for a field. The purpose of data validation is to help ensure that the information being entered is as accurate as possible and to save time for the data entry person.

Review Questions

1. What is a pointer?
2. What type of data (integer, char, etc.) is the contents of a pointer variable?
3. When a pointer variable is incremented, how many bytes is it increased by?
4. Why use pointers? Give an example of a situation where a certain action could not be accomplished without pointers.
5. When we pass an array as a function argument, what are we really passing to the function?
6. How can a pointer be used to change the value of a variable that is local to a different function?
7. Why must a pointer variable be defined as the same data type as the variable to which it will point?
8. Why is the * operator not necessary when assigning an address to a pointer that has already been declared?
9. What is meant by the phrase "levels of indirection"?

Exercises

1. Using pointers to pass local variable values, write a program to calculate sales commissions.

Input:	Enter salesperson's name, commission level (1 or 2), and amount of sales.
Processing:	For commission level 1 the commission rate is 6%, for level 2 the commission rate is 8%.
Output:	
Titles:	Print appropriate titles and headings. The title must include a page number.
Detail:	Each detail line should include the salesperson's name, sales, and commission amount.
Total:	Print a report total for the sales and commissions totals.
Variables:	Page count-static local variable in titles module

Salesperson's name, level, and sales local to detail, passed as needed.

2. Use the header file from this chapter and modify your menu program from Chapter 7 so that it works with the header file. Your output will appear the same to the user.

3. Write a Menu program to retrieve information about project due dates.

Array:	Initialize parallel arrays containing project titles and completion dates.
Option 1:	Allow the user to enter a project title and have the completion date displayed on the screen.
Option 2:	Allow the user to enter a date and list all projects that are scheduled for completion as of that date. In testing, be certain to have duplicate dates.

4. Write a menu program that will find telephone numbers or give a listing (screen or printer) of all names and phone numbers.

Array:	Initialize parallel arrays with names and phone numbers
Option 1:	Enter a name and use a serial search to locate the appropriate phone number.
	Print the number on the screen and pause execution.
Option 2:	Prompt for screen or printer output.
	Produce a list as desired on the screen or on the printer, allowing for multipage or multiscreen output.

Hayley Office Supplies

Use the inventory structure array from Chapter 7. Find the cost value of the inventory on hand, by multiplying the cost by the quantity for each product in the array. Print a summary report that gives the inventory value on hand at cost and at retail.

CHAPTER 9

POINTERS AND ARRAYS

CHAPTER OBJECTIVES

By the end of this chapter you should be able to:
- Perform calculations with pointers.
- Access arrays with pointers instead of subscripts.
- Use pointers to access multidimensional arrays.
- Treat multidimensional arrays as single-dimensional arrays.
- Understand the concept of parallel arrays.
- Use multidimensional arrays.
- Visualize a multidimensional array as an array of arrays.
- Traverse a multidimensional array as though it were single dimensional.
- Sort data using an exchange sort or the qsort() function.
- Differentiate between a serial search and a binary search.
- Retrieve data using the bsearch() function.
- Apply pointers to structures of data.
- Use pointers to allow a function to access a memory location by reference rather than by value.
- Allocate memory with the new operator.

CHAPTER OVERVIEW

The relationship between pointers and array notation in C++ can improve your understanding of data storage. Through pointers, a reference to an array—including a string—may be passed to or returned from a function. Pointers may be used in some calculations. These incrementing and decrementing operations are discussed as well as the effect upon precedence.

Array names are actually a reference to the beginning address of an array. This creates a special relationship between arrays and pointers. Access of arrays through the use of pointers is covered. Multidimensional arrays are introduced along with their relationship to pointer access.

Performing searches is covered by creating functions as well as accessing existing functions. The difference between a serial search and a binary search will be discussed along with the advantages or limitations of each. Since the binary search requires sorted data, the *qsort()* function will be demonstrated.

POINTER CALCULATIONS

The address contained in a pointer variable may be incremented or decremented to point to the next or previous value in memory.

```
*iPtr + 2;
```

The previous expression means add 2 to the dereferenced or indirect value of *iPtr*. The * operator has a higher precedence than the + operator.

```
*(iPtr + 2);
```

While this expression means add to the address stored in *ptr* and then get the value at that location in memory. When working with pointers, it is important to consider the precedence compared to the other operators you have already been using.

```cpp
#include <iostream.h>

void main()
{
    int   iNumber = 5, *iPtr = &iNumber;
    cout << "*iPtr + 2 = " << *iPtr + 2 << endl;
    cout << "*(iPtr + 2) = " << *(iPtr + 2) << endl;
}
```

Output

```
*iPtr + 2 = 7
*(iPtr + 2) = 661680
```

Notice on the output that the first one added the 2 to the value of 5. The second line of output is a memory address. This number will likely be different if you try to run the program because the data may be stored in a different location each time it is loaded.

The pointer * and the incrementer ++ have the same precedence from right to left. Therefore, *iPtr++ gets the indirect value and increments the pointer to the next address. If you use parentheses to read (*iPtr)++, you have an operation that says get the value and then increment the value.

Let's determine what each of the following mean:

```
++*iPtr
*iPtr++
*++iPtr
```

The increment and the pointer * are at the same level and are associated from right to left. This can be used to interpret the previous examples with the following program, which deals with consecutive memory locations in an array.

1. ++*iPtr — references the value that is being pointed to and then increments that value.
2. *iPtr++ — the ++ binds to the iPtr first so that you take the address and do a postfix increment.
3. *++iPtr — increases the address and then finds the value in that new address.

POINTERS AND ARRAYS

The name of an array references an address. The array stName contains the address of the first element of the array. Strings, as you already know, are arrays. What the variable stName really refers to is &stName[0]. So you could say:

 stName is equivalent to &stName[0]

Since an array name is a pointer containing an address, it is possible to increment the pointer to access the elements in the array. The contents of the array can be obtained with the pointer rather than using subscripts. If:

```
int iNumber[] = {5,10,15}
```

then

```
iNumber[0] = 5
*iNumber = 5
iNumber[1] = 10
*(iNumber + 1) = 10
iNumber[2] = 15
*(iNumber + 2) = 15
```

Remember, the parentheses are required when incrementing the position in the array to add to the address itself and not to the contents of the address.

SELF-TEST

Given the following declarations and assignments, what operation will be performed according to the precedence of operators?

```
int iNum = 5, *iPtr = &iNum;
int iArray[] = {5,7,2,3,9,1};
```

1. iPtr += 5
2. iArray + 5
3. *(iArray + 5)
4. *iArray + 5
5. iNum + 5
6. iPtr++
7. *iPtr++
8. iArray++
9. (*iPtr)++
10. *++iPtr

ANSWERS

1. Since iPtr is a variable and not an array name, it can point to various items, such as a pointer variable. This statement changes the address stored in the pointer so that it contains an address 5 integer size fields beyond iNum.

2. Adds 5 to the address of the array and therefore points to iArray[5]. Remember that the name of an array is a pointer to the address of the array.

3. Adds 5 to the address and then gets the value of iArray[5].
4. Gets the value of iArray[0] and adds 5 to the value.
5. Adds 5 to the value of the variable iNum: no pointers here.
6. Increases the pointer to point to the address following iNum, actually changing the pointer to point to a different location.
7. Gets the value at the address and then increases the address stored in iPtr.
8. Can't do this. You are trying to say change the pointer address for the array to point to one address higher. An array name cannot be changed. You could say iArray + 1 which would not change iArray but would point to one position beyond the beginning of the array. The increment operator would attempt to actually change iArray, which cannot be done.
9. Dereferences and then increments.
10. Increments the address and then gets the value.

Accessing a Single-Dimensional Array with Pointers

Since the name of the array is the address of the first element, it is possible to increment the array name, thereby incrementing the address so it is pointing to the next element within the array. The address will automatically increment by the correct number of bytes because of the pointer declaration.

With a single dimension array, the data could also be read from the array as follows:

```
#include <fstream.h>

void main()
{
    int iNumber[] = {5,10,15};
    for(int i=0; i<3; i++)
        cout <<  iNumber[i] <<"\t" << *(iNumber + i) << endl;
}
```

OUTPUT

5	5
10	10
15	15

Caution: Because the name of an array contains an address it may be used similar to a pointer variable. However, it is not a variable and therefore cannot have an address assigned to the variable name or be incremented, decremented, etc.

Accessing a String Using Pointers

With a character array, the data can be accessed without a for loop. The end of the array is marked by a null character. Therefore, you can access a character array using a pointer and testing for a null character.

```
char stWord[] = "pointer";
char *stWordPtr = stWord;
```

```
while(*stWordPtr)
{
    cout << *stWordPtr++;
    // Loop will exit when it points to a null
}
```

OUTPUT

pointer

Note: The *static* storage class is required on some compilers if a local array is initialized at the time that it is declared.

SELF-TEST

Will the following calculations increment the contents or the address given Dates[3]?
1. Dates + 2
2. *(Dates + 2)
3. *Dates + 2
4. Write the loop using pointers that will find the average of the array grades.
   int iGrades[10];

ANSWERS

1. Address, dates + 2 is equivalent to &dates[2].
2. Address, adds to the address and then accesses the value—this means the contents of dates[2].
3. Contents, this will increase the contents of dates[0] by 2.
4.
```
for(i = 0; i < 10; i++)
{
    iSum += *(iGrades + i);
}
fAverage = iSum/10;
```

MULTIDIMENSIONAL ARRAYS

Arrays may have multiple levels of subscripts. A multidimensional array may be pictured as being an array of arrays. In memory, one array is followed by the next array. The first subscript refers to which array and the second subscript references the element within the array.

```
int iNum[3][5];
```

refers to an array that has three arrays with five elements in each array. With a multidimensional array of characters, there is a "list" or array each containing a "string."

```
char stWord[12][5];
```

sets up the storage for 12 words with 5 letters in each.

Initializing Multidimensional Arrays

Multidimensional arrays may also be initialized as they are declared. The initialization has sets of braces within braces.

```
int iNum[3][5] =  {
            {1,2,3,4,5},
            {6,7,8,9,10},
            {11,12,13,14,15}
            };
```

The subarrays do not need to be filled:

```
int iNum[3][5] =  {
            {1,2,3},
            {6,7,8,9,10},
            {11,12,13,14,15}
            };
```

When declaring character arrays, it is easier to eliminate the inner braces because the quotes delimit the string. A string is an array of characters.

```
char stWord[12][6]= {
            {"one"},
            {"two"},
            {"three"}
            };
```

Accessing a Two-Level Array with Nested Loops

Since the two-level array requires two subscripts, the array can be accessed with nested loops. The loops will be used when all elements of all arrays are to be processed.

```
#include <iostream.h>
int iNum[3][5] = {
            {1,2,3,4,5},
            {6,7,8,9,10},
            {11,12,13,14,15}
            };

void main()
{
for(int x=0; x<3; x++)
{
      for(int y=0; y<5; y++)
```

```
            cout << iNum[x][y]<< " ";
    }
}
```

OUTPUT

| 1 2 3 4 5 6 7 8 9 10 11 12 13 14 15 |

The order of the loops affects the sequence in which the array is accessed. Consider the following:

```
#include <iostream.h>

void main()
{
int iNum[3][5] = {
                {1,2,3,4,5},
                {6,7,8,9,10},
                {11,12,13,14,15}
                };
//Print out first element in each array, then second in each array etc.
for(int y=0; y<5; y++)
{
    for(int x=0; x<3; x++)
        cout << iNum[x][y]<< " ";
}
}
```

OUTPUT

| 1 6 11 2 7 12 3 8 13 4 9 14 5 10 15 |

■ SELF-TEST

1. Write the statements to find the sum of the elements in the following array:
   ```
   float  sales[5][7];
   ```

2. What prints?
   ```
   #include <iostream.h>
   int iNum[3][5] = {
                   {10,21},
                   {67,89,10}; change; to,
                   {11,12,13}
   ```

```
                    };

void main()
{
for(int x=0; x<3; x++)
{
    for(int y=0; y<5; y++)
    {
        cout << iNum[x][y]<< " ";
    }
    cout << endl;
}
}
```

■ **ANSWERS**

1.

```
float fTotal;
for(int x=0, fTotal = 0; x<5; x++)
{
for(int y=0; y<7; y++)
{
    fTotal+= fSales[x][y]<< " ";
}
}
```

2.
```
10  21  0   0   0
67  89  10  0   0
11  12  13  0   0
```

MULTIDIMENSIONAL ARRAYS AND POINTERS

Pointers can also be used with multidimensional arrays. This may require a pointer to a pointer.

Pointers to Pointers and Multidimensional Arrays

Consider the declaration of a two-dimensional array. The following array declares five arrays, each of which is a subarray containing 10 elements.

`int iNumber[5][10];`

The "iNumber" contains the address of the first element of the entire array. It is also the address of the first subarray of 10 elements.

`iNumber == &iNumber[0]`

and

`&iNumber[0] == &iNumber[0][0];`

Even though the address of the entire array, the subarray, and the address of the first element are all the same, there is a difference when doing pointer calculations.

Incrementing the address of the subarray should take us to the next subarray while incrementing the entire array, or the first element takes you to the address of the next element.

The difference between the levels is as follows:

iNumber	The address of the entire array
*iNumber	The address of the first subarray
**iNumber	The value in the first element

Incrementing the Pointers

Although *iNumber and iNumber holds the same address, there is a difference when they are incremented.

INUMBER	Is a pointer to an array of 5 elements, each one containing 10 integers. iNumber + 1 points to the address of the next subarray, incrementing the address by the size of 10 integers.
*INUMBER	Is a pointer to an integer. *iNumber + 1 points to the address of the next integer element 2 will be added to the address, to account for 1 integer.

As a result of precedence, the array can be incremented to either the first subscript or to the second subscript depending on the use of parentheses.

*(iNumber + 1)	Yields iNumber[0][1].
*(iNumber + 2)	Yields iNumber[0][2].
*iNumber + 1	Yields iNumber[1][0].
*iNumber + 2	Yields iNumber[2][0].

Summary of Relationships

```
iNumber[0][0] == *iNumber[0] == **iNumber
iNumber[1][0] == *iNumber[1] == *(*(iNumber + 1))
iNumber[2][3] == *(iNumber[2] + 3) == *(*(iNumber + 2) + 3)
iNumber[x][y] == *(iNumber[x] + y) == *(*(iNumber + x) + y)
&iNumber[0][0] == iNumber[0] == *iNumber
&iNumber[1][0] == iNumber[1] == *(iNumber + 1)
```

Accessing a Multidimensional Array with Pointers

Using the pointer notation, *(*(iNumber + x) + y), all of the elements in a two-dimensional array can be accessed using two loops. One loop controls the value of x and the second controls y. The x relates to the column and the y to the row of each element within the array.

```
int iQuantity[5][4] = {{12,4,6,8},
           {1,3,5,7},
           {3,6,9,12},
           {0,1,2,3},
           {3,2,1,0}};
int iRow, iCol, iTotal = 0;


//Add up all elements in the table
for(iRow = 0; iRow < 5; iRow++)
{
    for(iCol = 0; iCol < 4; iCol++)
    {
    iTotal += *(*(iQuantity + iRow) + iCol);
    }
}
cout << "The total is " << iTotal << endl;
```

OUTPUT

> The total is 88

Accessing a Multidimensional Array as a Single Array

Since an array can be accessed with pointers, a multidimensional array can be accessed as though it were one long single-dimensional array. The following example really has two lists with three elements in each list. However, it may be treated as one list of six elements.

```
int iNumber[2][3] =  {{2,4,6},{8,1,2}};
// access a 2 level array as a single level array
for(int i=0; i<6; i++)
{
    cout <<   *(iNumber[0] + i);
}
```

Another way that this two-dimensional array could be perceived is as a single array of pointers. The first pointer points to the first list of three elements and the second pointer holds the address of the second list.

Thus:

```
iNumber[2][3] == *iNumber[6]
int *iNumber[] = {2,4,6,8,1,2};
for(int i=0; i<6; i++)
{
    cout <<   *(iNumber+i);
}
```

■ SELF-TEST

1. Use pointer notation to add up the elements in the array:

   float fSales[7][10];

■ ANSWERS

1. ```
   for(i=0; i < 70; i++)
   {
       fTotal +=*(fSales[0] + i);
   }
   ```

Accessing Data in an Array

Data in an array can be accessed through **direct access** or **indirect access**. In direct access the subscript is known and the element may be found through the use of the subscript iNumber. With indirect access the subscript iNumber must be determined.

An example of direct access would be an account iNumber assigned starting with 0 to correspond to the position within the array.

```
char stClient[9][7] =   {"Adams","Baker","Doe","Evans","Jones",
             "Mills", "Nguyen", "Olsen", "Smith"};
```

SUBSCRIPT	stCLIENT	SUBSCRIPT	stCLIENT
0	Adams	5	Mills
1	Baker	6	Nguyen
2	Doe	7	Olsen
3	Evans	8	Smith
4	Jones		

If the client's "account number" is known, their name could easily be accessed. For example, account number 7 relates to Olsen. If the account numbers were not sequential or if the account number is not known, a search is needed to look up the appropriate data.
```

SEARCHING AN ARRAY

A search is used to match an item with another item from a list (array) or from a file. There are two types of search logic: a serial search and a binary search. These methods of look up are examples of indirect access to the array.

A serial search compares each item in the list sequentially with the key field. Key field refers to the item to be found. In a serial search the key field will be compared to the first item in the array. If it does not match, the subscript will be incremented and the key field will then be compared to the next element in the array. If the item to be found was located in the last element in the array, it would have been necessary to compare the key field with every element in the array. With a 100-element array, it may take 100 comparisons to find a match.

A binary search is faster but requires that the data be sorted in order prior to the search. With a binary search on a list of 100 elements, the maximum number of comparisons is 7.

A binary search of a sorted list compares the item in the middle of the list with the item to be found, the key field, and then determines whether the middle item is too large or too small or a match. The next comparison will then be with the middle item in the appropriate half of the list, the top half if the middle element was too small, or the lower half if the middle element was too small. The search will continue to divide the remaining elements in half and then compare with the next middle item until a match is found.

Serial Search

Consider two arrays: the first array contains account numbers and the second array contains client names. Create a search routine that will locate a name given the account number.

```
int iAccount[9] = {10,20,30,45,55,65,75,85,99};
char stClient[9][7] =   {"Adams","Baker","Doe","Evans","Jones",
            "Mills", "Nguyen", "Olsen", "Smith"};
```

SUBSCRIPT	iACCOUNT[]	stCLIENT[]
0	10	Adams
1	20	Baker
2	30	Doe
3	45	Evans
4	55	Jones
5	65	Mills
6	75	Nguyen
7	85	Olsen
8	99	Smith

Notice that each of the arrays have the same number of elements. The account numbers belong to the corresponding name. iAccount 30 is the third account number and Doe is the third name. Two is the subscript for both elements, therefore we can see that the elements and subscripts correspond between the two arrays. These could be called parallel arrays because of the correspondence between them.

To search for a name to match an account number, first look for the position of the account number within the first array. Next, print the corresponding position within the second array.

PSEUDOCODE

- Set a found switch to No.
- Ask for the account number key.
- In a loop, compare the key with each element in the account number array until end of array or item is found.

IF A MATCH IS FOUND

- Set the found switch to Yes
- Print the corresponding name (same subscript) from the client array
- Exit the loop
- At the end of the loop check if the found switch is still set to No. If it is, then no match was found.
- Pause the screen to display the name or the not found message.

The search function to find the name associated with an account number is as follows:

```
void Search()
{
    char cFound = 'n';              //Set found switch to no
    int iAccountIn;                 //Account number to search for
    cout << "Account Number   ";    //Prompt for key field
    cin >> iAccountIn;              //Input key field
    /*Loop sequentially through the loop comparing
        the key with each element in account array */
    for(int i=0; i<9 && cFound == 'n'; i++)
    {
        if(iAccountIn == iAccount[i])
        {
            cFound = 'y';
            cout << "Client:      " << stClient[i];
        }
    }
    if (cFound == 'n')
    {
        cout << "Client not found - check number ";
    }
}
```

■ SELF-TEST

1. Write the search routine to find the room number when a course name is entered. Assume that the following arrays have been declared and initialized.

   ```
   int iRoomNum[5] = {112, 4, 310, 308, 17};
   char stCourse[5][6] = { "COBOL",
                           "BASIC",
                           "CICS",
                           "RPG",
                           "C++"};
   ```

2. How would the function change if we knew the room number and were looking for the course that meets in that room?

3. Using a structure for the array, rewrite the search

   ```
   struct
   {
       int iRoomNum.;
       char stCourse[6];
   }Class[5];
   ```

■ ANSWERS

1.
```cpp
void Search()
{
    char cFound = 'n';
    char stCourseIn[5];

    cout << "Course Name   ";
    cin << stCourseIn;
    for(int i=0; i<5 && cFound == 'n'; i++)
    {
        if(strcmp(stCourseIn, stCourse[i])== 0)
        {
            cFfound = 'y';
            cout << "Room Number:    " << iRoomNum[i];
        }
    }
    if (cfound == 'n')
    {
        cout << "Course not found - check spelling ";
    }
}
```

2. Change the key to ask for the room number. Change the comparison to compare the key with the room number array. Print the corresponding course name.
3.
```
void Search()
{
    char cFound = 'n';
    char stCourseIn[5];

    cout << "Course Name   ";
    cin << stCourseIn;
    for(int i=0; i<5 && cFound == 'n'; i++)
    {
        if(strcmp(stCourseIn, Class[i].stCourse)== 0)
        {
            cFfound = 'y';
            cout << "Room Number:      " <<      Class[i].iRoomNum;
        }
    }
    if (cfound == 'n')
    {
        cout << "Course not found - check spelling ";
    }
}
```

Binary Search

A binary search in C++ can be accomplished via the *bsearch()* function. This function performs a binary search on a sorted array with a specific number of elements each with a specific width. You must specify the base of the array to be searched and a key field to be searched for. In order to access the *bsearch()* function you must include the *stdlib.h* header file.

The format of the bsearch() is:

bsearch(key,base,num,width,compare);

- **key** is the item to be searched for;
- **base** is the name of the array;
- **num** gives the number of elements in the array;
- **width** is the width in bytes of each item in the array; and
- **compare** is a function that performs the comparison.

The program may determine the number of elements in the array by dividing the size of the entire array by the size of a single element.

In the header file definition of the binary search function, the prototype for the comparison function incorporates void pointers. Therefore, it is necessary to typecast the function to correspond to the header file. The easiest way to do this is to include the following typedef in your program and then use it as the typecast.

> typedef int (*fptr)(const void*, const void*);

The (fptr) is then placed in front of the compare function name in the call to bsearch().

The bsearch() returns the address of the item if a match is found, otherwise the function returns a NULL. The actual search and looping takes place in the function from the header file.

The compare function will be used by the binary search but is defined by the programmer. This is necessary in order to specify the type of data that is going to be compared. The compare function must return an integer:

Negative	if element1 < element2
Zero	if element1 = element2
Positive	if element1 > element2

Example

Suppose we have a list of department names and a list of department numbers. We can use the bsearch() to find the position of the department name if we enter a department name to be found.

SUBSCRIPT	DEPARTMENT	DEPARTMENT NAME
0	331	Accounting
1	633	Information Services
2	425	Marketing
3	124	Production
4	515	Sales

The department names are in alphabetic order, making it possible to do a binary search by department name. The return value of the binary search will be assigned to a field to hold an address of the department where the match was found.

```
Dept *Result;
```

The assignment is

```
Result=(Dept*)bsearch(stKey,Department,sizeof(Department)/sizeof(Dept),sizeof(Key),
(fptr)compareit);
```

The key is the same size as a single department name in the array because it holds the name of the department to be found. The compare function is compareit() as defined within the program. Since the department names are of type char[], compareit() uses the string compare function.

When a match is found, the address of the appropriate department name is known within the department structure. The difference between the beginning of the array and the location of the match gives the subscript that can be used for the department number.

```
int iSubscript = (Result - Department);
```

PLANNING

PROPERTIES	DATA TYPE	NAME
Department Name	char array	stName
Department Number	integer	iNumber

```cpp
//Ch09Pr01
#include <iostream.h>
#include <stdlib.h>
#include <string.h>

typedef int (*fptr)(const void*, const void*);
int Compareit(char  Item1[], char Item2[]);

struct Dept
{
    char stName[21];
    int iNumber;
}Department[] = {{"Accounting",331},
        {"Information Services",  633},
        {"Marketing", 425},
        {"Production", 124},
        {"Sales", 515}};

void main()
{
    char stKey[21];
    cout << "Enter Department Name:    ";
    cin >> stKey;

    Dept *Result =(Dept *)bsearch(stKey,Department,
    sizeof(Department)/sizeof(Dept),sizeof(Dept),(fptr) Compareit);

    if(Result == NULL)
        cout <<"Department not found\n";
    else
    {
```

```
        int iSubscript = Result-Department;
        cout << "\nDepartment number is "
             << Department[iSubscript].iNumber;
    }
}

int Compareit(char  Item1[], char Item2[])
{
        return(stricmp(Item1, Item2));
}
```

Example 2

Reverse the situation, and look up the department number to determine the department name. The data needs to be arranged in order by department number, because the search will be performed on that field.

SUBSCRIPT	DEPARTMENT #	DEPARTMENT NAME
0	124	Production
1	331	Accounting
2	425	Marketing
3	515	Sales
4	633	Information Services

The key field will now be of type integer because the search is for a department number. The compare function must also be modified to work with integer numbers.

PLANNING

PROPERTIES	DATA TYPE	NAME
Department Name	char array	stName
Department Number	integer	iNumber

```
// Ch09Pr02
#include <iostream.h>
#include <stdlib.h>
#include <string.h>

typedef int (*fptr)(const void*, const void*);
int CompareIt(int *Item1,int *Item2);

struct Dept
```

```
{
char stName[21];
int iNumber;
}Department[] = { {"Production", 124},
            {"Accounting",331},
            {"Marketing", 425},
            {"Sales", 515},
            {"Information Services",633}};

void main()
{
  int iKey;
  cout << "Enter Department Number:    ";
  cin > > iKey;

  Dept *Result =(Dept *)bsearch(&iKey,&Department[0].iNumber,
  sizeof(Department)/sizeof(Dept),sizeof(Dept),
                   (fptr)CompareIt);

  if(Result == NULL)
      cout <<"Department not found\n";
  else
  {
      int iSubscript = Result-Department;
      cout << "\nDepartment name is "
           << Department[iSubscript].stName;
  }
}


int CompareIt(int *Item1,int *Item2)
{
      return *Item1 - *Item2;
}
```

Notice that the key requires an & to explicitly specify "address of". In the first example the address operator was assumed because the key field is an array.

■ SELF-TEST

1. Write the bsearch() to find the client name from the example in the linear search logic section.

2. Why is the sizeof operator preferable to just keying in the size of an element in the array?

■ ANSWERS

1. `bsearch(account_in, account, 10, sizeof(account_in),(fptr)compare);`
2. The size of data types may differ from one type of machine to another, the sizeof operator provides greater portability.

SORTING DATA IN AN ARRAY

In order to put data into sequential order, either ascending or descending, a sort may be made. The sort works on either numeric or string data depending on whether relational operators or the string functions are used.

The sort may be coded in the program or the quicksort function called qsort() may be used. Let's look at the logic for doing a sort first, then consider the qsort() function. Either sort may be used on the array prior to performing a bsearch().

An Exchange Sort

An exchange sort routine is about the easiest sort logic to follow. It is efficient if the array has fewer than 10 elements, which, of course, is not very often. We will do an example with a 10-element array called num.

```
#include <iostream.h>

void Sort(), PrintArray();

int iNum[5] = {456,123,781,213,377};

void main()
{
    PrintArray();          // print array before sort
    Sort();                // Sort the array
    PrintArray();          // print the sorted array
}


/*--------------------------
    Perform an exchange Sort on an array
--------------------------*/
void Sort()
{
```

```
int a,b, iTemp;

for(a =0;a<4;a++)
{
    for(b = a+1;b<5;b++)
    {
        if(iNum[a] >  iNum[b])
        {
            iTemp = iNum[a];    //Store in temporary
            iNum[a]=iNum[b];    //Exchange the values
            iNum[b] = iTemp;
        }
    }
}
}

/*--------------------------
Print contents of array
--------------------------*/
void PrintArray()
{
    for(int a=0; a<5; a++)
    cout << iNum[a] << endl;}
}
```

OUTPUT

```
456
123
781
213
377
123
213
377
456
781
```

Using the qsort() Function

The *qsort()* function, which is declared in *stdlib.h*, is used for performing a quick sort. The sort arguments are similar to those used in the *bsearch()* function.

> qsort(base,num,width,(compare)());

The base gives the name of the array to be sorted. The num is the number of elements in the array, and the width is the width of each element in the array. The compare() function is one from your program and can use whatever name you wish.

```cpp
// use the qsort() function to sort
#include <stdlib.h>
#include <iostream.h>

void PrintArray();
int Compare(char Arg1[],char Arg2[]);

char stName[5][6] = {"Mary","Bob", "Laura","Susan","David"};

void main()
{
    PrintArray();
    qsort(stName,5,6, Compare); //Call to stdlib.h sort
    PrintArray();
}

/*------------------------
Compare for the qsort()
------------------------*/
int Compare(char Arg1[],char Arg2[])
{
return(stricmp(Arg1,Arg2));
}

/*------------------------
print contents of the array
------------------------*/
void PrintArray()
{
    for(int i=0;i<5;i++)
    cout << stName[i] << " ";}
    cout << endl;
}
```

OUTPUT:

> Mary Bob Laura Susan David
> Bob David Laura Mary Susan

The *qsort()* function could also take advantage of the operators or functions within C++ to determine the width and the number of elements.

```
qsort(stName,sizeof(stName),sizeof(stName[0]),Compare());
```

THE COMPARE FUNCTION IN QSORT() AND BSEARCH()

The function used for comparison should return a 1 if the value of the first element is greater than the value of the second. If the two values are equal then a 0 will be returned and a -1 if the value of the first is less than the second.

For string comparisons, *strcmp()* takes care of this very nicely. When doing numeric comparisons, we may use the following compare functions.

```
int Compare( unsigned *Elem1, unsigned *Elem2 )
{
if( *Elem1 >  *Elem2 )
      return 1;
else if( *Elem1 < *Elem2 )
      return -1;
else
      return 0;
}
```

or

```
int Compare(int *iNum1, int *iNum2)
{
return(*iNum1-*iNum2);
}
```

Take a look at another example that performs a quick sort on an array of integers. The compare function is different than the one that used on the names in the earlier example.

```
#include <stdlib.h>
#include <iostream.h>


int iNum[5] = {3,4,1,2,5};
int Compare(int *iNum1, int *iNum2);


void main()
```

```
{
    qsort(iNum,5,sizeof(int),Compare);
    for(int i = 0; i< 5; i++)
        cout << iNum[i];
}


/*--------------------
   Compare function for integers,
   returns 0 if equal
--------------------*/
int Compare(int *iNum1, int *iNum2)
{
    return(*iNum1 - *iNum2);
}
```

SELF-TEST

1. Write the bubble sort loop to sort the 100 elements in an array called iNumint[].
2. Write the qsort call for sorting the 100 elements in an array called iNumint[].

ANSWERS

1.
```
for(a =0; a<100; a++)
{
    for(b = a+1; b<99; b++)
    {
        if(iNumint[a] >  iNumint[b])
        {
            temp = iNumint[a];
            iNum[a]=iNumint[b];
            iNumint[b] = temp;
        }
    }
}
```

2. `qsort(iNumint, 100, sizeof(int), compare);`

POINTERS AND STRUCTURES

A structure can also use a pointer to access the members of the structure. A pointer to a structure is declared the same as other pointer variables. There is, though, a new operator for accessing the elements of a structure. The operator is ->, which is typed by following a hyphen with a greater than symbol.

```
struct FullName
{
    char stFirst[15];
    char stLast[10];
}

struct Person
{
    Fullname Name;
    char stPhone[15];
}


Person *Their;
```

The *Their points to a structure of type person. This variable does not yet contain the address of a particular item.

```
Person Friends[20] = {{"Tricia", "Mills","(714) 555-1111"}
         {"Mitzi", "Johnston","(818) 555,2222"}}};
Their = Friends;   //Assign the array to the pointer
```

Now:

Their	contains &Friends[0]
Their + 1	&Friends[1]

To access individual elements of the structure:

`Their->stPhone`

would access the phone number of the first structure within the array.

`(Their + 1)->stPhone`

accesses the phone number for the second structure in the array. The parentheses are necessary to avoid having the 1 bind with the pointer, which would be meaningless, not to mention an error.

```
#include <iostream.h>
const  iNUM  = 2;

struct FullName
```

```cpp
{
  char stFirst[10];
  char stLast[15];
};

struct Person
{
    FullName Name;
    char stPhone[15];
};
Person Friends[iNUM] ={
            {"Tricia", "Mills","(714)555-1111"},
            "Mitzi","Johnston","(818)555-2222"}};

Person *Their = Friends;

void main()
{
    int i;
    for( i=0; i< iNUM; i++)
    {
        cout << "Name:  " << (Their+i)->Name.stLast << endl;
        cout << "Phone: " << (Their+i)->stPhone << endl;
    }
    cout << Their->stPhone; //Points to first structure
}
```

SELF-TEST

1. Write a loop to print out the title and author of each of the books.

   ```cpp
   struct Bibliography
   {
     char stTitle[30];
     char stAuthor[30];
     char stPublisher[30];
     char stISBN[15];
   }Book[1000];

   Bibliography *Bib;
   ```

ANSWER

```
1. for(i = 0; i < 1000; i++)
   {
        cout << (Bib+i)->stTitle <<(Bib+i)->stAuthor;
   }
```

THE NEW AND DELETE OPERATORS

To effectively use memory it makes more sense to assign it as needed rather than automatically reserve it. To this point all character arrays have specified a size if they were not initialized immediately. Often the size of the array is set to a sufficient size to handle most situations causing some bytes to be left unused after the null is assigned to the end of the string variable.

Memory can be dynamically allocated when it is needed through the use of the new operator. This operator assigns the appropriate amount of memory when needed if enough memory is available. When the programmer takes responsibility for allocating memory the rules for the scope of a data item are no longer of concern. It becomes the programmer's responsibility to release the memory when it is no longer needed. This is accomplished with the delete operator.

A common usage of the new and delete operators is to create structures with pointers to items where the number of items is not known. This might be to replace a character array or to replace an array of structures. The following example uses a pointer for the string desc, which indicates that the address of the beginning of a character array is stored. The variable name for the structure is actually a pointer to the structure so it likewise contains the address of an item structure—this may also replace an array. Storage will then be allocated when the structure is actually used—when an object is created.

```
struct Item   //This structure name will be used with the "new" operator
{
    char *stDesc;
    int iQuantity;
    float fPrice;
}*Product;
```

Remember that when an object is created a constructor will be called. At that point the storage can be allocated to store the new object. The same memory can be released when the object ceases to exist, which can take place in the destructor.

```
//Ch09Pr04
// This program contains a class with overloaded constructors
//   uses new to allocate memory when an object is created
//   the destructor releases memory when the object goes out of scope
#include <iostream.h>
#include <string.h>
#include <iomanip.h>

class Inventory
```

```cpp
{
   struct Item   // this structure name will be used with the "new" operator
   {
      char *stDescription;
      int iQuantity;
      float fPrice;
   }*Product;
public:
   Inventory()
   {
      Product = new Item;
      Product->stDescription = new char(NULL);
      Product->fPrice = 0.0;
      Product->iQuantity = 0;
   }
   Inventory(char *NewstDescription, float NewfPrice, int NewiQuantity)
   {
      Product = new Item;
      Product->stDescription = new char[strlen(NewstDescription)+1];
      strcpy(Product->stDescription, NewstDescription);
      Product->fPrice = NewfPrice;
      Product->iQuantity = NewiQuantity;
   }
   ~Inventory()
   { delete Product;}
   void print()
   {
      cout << setw(20) << Product->stDescription
         << setw(10) << setiosflags(ios::right) << Product->iQuantity
         << setw(10) << setiosflags(ios::fixed|ios::showpoint) << Product->fPrice
         << endl;
   }
};

void main()
{
   Inventory Item1;   //Default constructor is called
```

```
    Item1.print(); //Nothing will print

    Inventory Item2("Widget",5.00,4);  //Call constructor with arguments
    Item2.print();
} //End of scope, the destructor is called for both Item1 and Item2
```

PROGRAMMING/DEBUGGING TIP

Another unique thing about an array in C++ is that the subscript and array name can be reversed. What?? Consider the following code segment:

```
#include <iostream.h>

int a[3] = {550,661,772};

void main()
{
    int i= 2;

    cout << "a[i]  = " << a[i] << endl;
    cout << "i[a]  = " << i[a] << endl;
}
```

OUTPUT

a[i] = 772
i[a] = 772

Key Terms

binary search
key field
multidimensional array
parallel arrays

search
serial search
sort

Chapter Summary

An array is a type of data structure that can contain multiple values at the same time. Another way to think of an array is as a variable that contains a list of values.

Each value is called an element within the array. In order to specify which element we are referring to, every access to the array must include a subscript. A subscript is an index to a position within the array. The subscript must evaluate as an integer value but it may be a constant, a variable, or an expression.

A for loop can be used to access an array using the subscript as a variable. Multi-dimensional arrays require multiple subscripts to reference each of the dimensions. A two-dimensional array may be considered to have rows and columns and would require a subscript to specify the row and a subscript to specify the column. To accomplish access to the entire array, you may use nested for loops.

Data can be accessed from an array either directly or indirectly. With direct access, the subscript is known from some other factor or variable. For example, the month portion of the date contains an integer that could directly refer to the appropriate position in an array of month names.

Indirect access requires a search operation. This search may be either binary or serial. A binary search requires that the arrays be sorted in order prior to the search. With a serial search, the elements of the array are accessed sequentially. The search will frequently be performed on one array and then the subscript used to reference the same position in a "parallel" array.

To put the elements in the array in order, they must be sorted. This can be accomplished by writing a routine or by calling the C++ quicksort function.

Review Questions

1. What is the relationship between arrays and pointers?
2. Give the array size for the following multidimensional values.

    ```
    {
        {1,3,5,7},
        {2,4,6,8},
        {9,9,9,9},
    }
    ```

3. What are the subscripts of the value 4 in the array values in question 8?
4. Give the subscript for the value 4 in the previous array, if the array is accessed as a single-dimensional array.
5. Why is it possible in C++ to handle a multidimensional array as though it were a single dimension?
6. How is a multidimensional array stored in memory?
7. If an array has been declared as

    `int number[5][6];`

    how can the first element of the second array be accessed?
8. What occurs during a sort process to the elements in an array?
9. How can the values of two elements be swapped during the sort process?
10. What type of sort is the sort function contained in the C++ library?

Exercises

1. Write a program for a grocery checkout. The program produces a receipt containing the description, qty @ unit price, and the extended price. At the end of the receipt include the subtotal, the amount of tax, and the total amount.

    Tables: Create tables to contain the product code, the description, and the unit price. The first character of the product code determines the department. The variety and liquor departments are taxable.

#	DEPARTMENTS
1	Bakery
2	Deli
3	Produce
4	Dairy
5	Variety
6	Liquor
7	General Foods

Input: The input screen will be designed to include the store name. The program will prompt for the product code and the quantity. (The product code must be verified as valid by confirming that it is in the table before asking for the quantity.)

Output: Each detail line will include the description, the extended price, and a tx if the item is taxable. If a quantity of more than one has been requested, print a line with: qty @ unit price.

PRODUCT CODE	DESCRIPTION	UNIT PRICE
101	Whole wheat rolls—doz.	1.79
102	Croissants—pack of 4	1.29
103	Carrot cake	5.27
201	Potato salad	1.19
202	Ham	3.49
301	Lettuce	.79
302	Onions	.49
303	Potatoes	1.29
401	Whole milk	.98
402	Cottage cheese	.79
501	Cold tablets	2.50
502	Pencils	.59
601	Beer	2.99
701	Tomato soup	.49

Calculations: Use a sales tax rate of 6% for taxable items.

Sample Output:

```
Your Neighborhood Grocers


Lettuce            .79
```

```
              Potatoes      2 @ 1.29       2.58
              Cold tablets                 2.50   tx


              Subtotal                     5.87
              Tax                           .15
              Total                        6.02
```

2. Write a program that finds the yearly total for each year, the quarterly average for the same quarter over the three years, and the yearly averages for sales for 1996 through 1998.

   Sample Data:
   ```
   int iSales[3][4] = {
                       {5000,5025,6800,3750},
                       {5555,5050,7000,4590},
                       {6000,6000,6700,7000}
                      };
   ```

   Sample Output:
   ```
            Year            Sales
            1996            20575
            1997            22195
            1998            25700
                            Yearly average:        $22823


                        Quarterly Averages
       1st Qtr        2nd Qtr        3rd Qtr        4th Qtr
       5518           5358           6833           5113
   ```

3. Write a program that will produce a list of the sales for each salesperson and print out the percent of total sales that each salesperson has maintained.

   Input: Place the names of the salespeople and the amount of sales into 2 arrays.

   Output: Produce a report of the salespeople and percents.
   Use appropriate titles and column headings.
   Each detail line should include the salesperson's name, the amount of sales and the percent of total sales.

   Processing: Accumulate the total sales for all salespeople and use the total as the base by dividing the individual's sales by the total sales and multiplying by 100.

4. Write a program that tallies total calendar sales for each girl in a Girl Scout Troop.

   Array: Create an array that contains the girls' names and an array to accumulate the total sales.

Input: Enter the girl's name and the quantity sold.

Output: Produce a report that lists the total sales by girl.

The report should contain appropriate titles and column headings.

Each detail line will print a girl's name and the total number sold by that girl.

Print a summary line containing the total sold for all girls.

Processing: Add the quantity sold to the proper element in the total sales array for the girl making the sale

Test Data:

Girl Scouts:	Sales:
Laurie	5
Julie	5
Heather	4
Lisa	10
Christine	7

5. Write a program to track the responses to an interactive survey about potential success in a programming course. A summary report will be produced on the printer at the conclusion of the program to indicate the number of responses that were received for each response for each question.

Initialization:

Load an array to hold the following questions:

Do you attend class consistently?

Do you read the text thoroughly?

Do you test short programs to understand concepts?

Do you do assignments promptly?

Do you chart before coding?

Gathering Responses:

Welcome Screen:

Create a screen that will welcome the survey respondent and prompt for a name. Loop until no name is entered.

1. Print a screen containing a question from the array and possible answers.

   Sample:

   Programming Success Survey

   Do you do test short programs to understand concepts?

   1. Never

   2. Occasionally

   3. Usually

   4. Frequently

   Enter NUMBER for your response _

2. Add 1 to an appropriate two-dimension table according to the question number and the response.

Print the Report:

At summary time, print the table and the accumulated responses for each question.

Hayley Office Supplies

Create parallel arrays to store the product items and to store the aisle numbers where the products can be found.

1. Write a program that will "lookup" the aisle number when the product description is entered. Use the strncmp() to compare the number of characters entered with the table entry—for example, if pen is entered, a match should be found for pens and pencils.
2. Modify the program to use a binary search. Sort the array, if necessary.

Sample Data:

PRODUCT	AISLE
Staples	11
Notebooks	8
Pens and pencils	1
Desk chairs	17
Computers	16
Typewriters	16
Printers	16
Drafting tables	17
Forms	8
Calendars	9
Diskettes	15

FILE INPUT/OUTPUT USING STRUCTURES

CHAPTER OBJECTIVES

By the end of this chapter you should be able to:
- Understand the difference between sequential and random file access.
- Demonstrate the use of structures in data files.
- Learn how to create and access a random file.
- Use file functions to update a random file including add a record, delete a record, and edit.
- Develop hashing algorithms for use in C++.

CHAPTER OVERVIEW

In order to access a data file it must be opened as a stream. The mode in which it will be accessed must be specified. Files in C++ may be produced using familiar input/output operations.

Files can also be created using data structures. The structure data type provides a convenient way to deal with data as a unit or record. With the file commands that deal with structures, it is possible to read or write an entire array of structures with a single function call.

This chapter will also discuss a file update, including adding records, deleting records, and editing records. The update program will be menu driven and will contain options for listing the data.

SEQUENTIAL VS. RANDOM FILE ACCESS

Data files may be accessed for update either randomly or sequentially. A **sequential** requires that every record be read in order to access data later in the file. With a **random file** a record towards the end of the file may be accessed directly.

To illustrate the difference between sequential and random access considers media for audio. Access on a cassette tape for music is normally sequential while a compact disc can be accessed randomly by specifying the track and the song number.

Because the size of each record may vary with a sequential file, it is impossible to go directly to a specific record.

In order to randomly select a record, the size of each record must be known. Fixed length records can be created with a structure.

Using Structures in Data Files

Although data may be written to the disk one variable at a time, the use of structures can greatly ease file access. With a structure defined to contain all of the information for one record, an entire record or file can be accessed with a single read or write. With the structure, you needn't worry about what constitutes a record at the time you are reading or writing to the file because the declaration of the fields is specified at the time the structure is declared.

RANDOM FILE ACCESS

It is possible to access the records randomly if structures are used because the length of each record becomes a set size. The *sizeof* operator gives the size of a data type. With a random file it is not necessary to access each record in sequence. If you know the record number we can go directly to the appropriate record. The beginning byte of the record within the file will be the record number times the size of one record (structure).

Data Files

A **stream** is the term used in C++ input/output to refer to a sequence of data. Sometimes the term stream is used synonymously with file. By opening the file a name will be assigned to the file that is used as the stream name. The familiar *cout* is a stream object declared in the *iostream.h* file.

In working with data files, the *fstream* class is used. This class is derived from the *ifstream* for input files and the *ofstream* class for output files.

Each disk file that is to be accessed must have its own name. This is not the name of the file on the disk (the **physical file name**), but rather a name that will be referred to in the program when we want to access that specific file (**logical file name**). The logical file name is internal to the program code and will follow the guidelines for naming identifiers in C++. For DOS-based systems, the physical file name must follow DOS naming constraints, including an extension if desired.

A file that will be referenced as *clientfile* would be declared as an object of type *fstream*:

```
fstream ClientFile;
```

The physical file name that is on the disk will be associated with the logical name at the time that the object is created or with the open() member function.

File Modes

As the file is opened, you may specify the mode in which the file will be accessed. The modes available include:

FILE MODE	PURPOSE	FILE POINTER POSITION
in	reading	beginning
out	writing	beginning
ate	reading	ending
	writing	
app	reading	ending
	writing*	

* will only write at the end of the file

The modes will be referenced with ios to specify where they are defined:

> ios::in
> ios::out

They may also be combined using the | operator.

> ios::in | ios::out

Attaching a File to a stream

The physical file may be attached to the logical file at the time the stream object is declared. The stream may be an object of type *fstream* (file stream), *ofstream* (output file stream), or *ifstream* (input file stream). A file that is created as on *ofstream* will automatically be opened for writing while an *ifstream* object is used for reading.

```
ofstream MyFile("datafile");
// the physical file datafile may be used for output


ifstream FileIn("accounts");
//the physical file accounts may be used for input.
```

The declaration of these objects is passing a value to one of the constructors. (If no value is passed a different constructor is executed.) The constructor opens the file and sets the default mode of access.)

The stream *myfile* may now be referenced as the stream name in write functions and *filein* is accessible for reading.

Another constructor allows for the mode and the file name to be specified at the time that an object is declared.

```
ofstream MyFile("datafile",ios::ate);
```

THE OPEN() FUNCTION

An object can be created that does not call a constructor and is therefore not associated with a specific file. The file may then be connected with the object with an *open()* function, which is a data member of the *fstream* class. The *open()* function has two parameters, the file path and the mode. The *open()* member function of *fstream* is assigned to a stream as follows:

> stream.open("physical file name", "file mode");

The function that opens the file will specify the file mode in which the file will be accessed and associate the file with a stream.

```
fstream MyFile;
MyFile.open("A:data",ios::in);
```

Examples

```
ClientReportFile.open("datafile",ios::out);
ClientFile.open("c:\\acct\\data",ios::in);  //File with a specific path
UpdateFile.open("myfile",ios::in|ios::out);
```

226 CHAPTER 10 **File Input/Output Using Structures**

Two declarations specify that streams called *clientfile* and *clientreportfile* are of class *fstream*. The first statement opens a physical file on the disk called "datafile" for output mode and assigns the file to the name *clientreportfile*.

The second statement opens a file for a mode of read only. Notice that the entire path is used. The file name may contain any required path notation.

The final open allows the file to be accessed for input or for output.

Closing a File

After the access to the data file is complete it may be closed by using the *close()* member function. The format for this statement:

```
objectname.close();
```

The close function releases the file from the object, allowing the object to access a different file or to use a different mode. The close also transfers any data remaining in a file buffer to the disk.

■ SELF-TEST

1. Write the fstream declaration and the open() to assign the streamname of inv_file to the disk file INVEN.DAT in an append mode that can be used for read and write.

2. What is wrong with the following:

    ```
    //Write the record next
    fstream Pay;
    Pay.open("Payroll.Dat",ios::in);
    ....
    ```

3. What is wrong with the following:

    ```
    fstream Count;
    Number.open("Count",ios:app)
    ...
    ```

4. Given the following open statement:

    Inventory.open("invtry.dat",ios::app);

    a. Can the file be used for input or output?
    b. What is the physical name of the file on the disk?
    c. Write the appropriate close statement for this file.

■ ANSWERS

1. ```
   fstream InventoryFile;
   InventoryFile.open("Inven.Dat",ios::app);
   ```

2. The file mode of ios::in can only be used for reading from a file, not for writing to it.

3. The object name on the fstream declaration was count but in the remaining statements it is number.
   ```

4. a. This particular file is opened for append, which means that the record pointer will be set to point to the end of the file. Any new records are added to the end but to read you must set the pointer back further in the file.
   b. The physical name on the disk is invtry.dat on the default drive.
   c. Inventory.close();

Testing if the File Exists

Even though some file modes will create a file if one does not exist, there are some occasions where we need to see if the file is on the disk. If the file is not there to open it may indicate that the user has the wrong disk or that the wrong file name was given. When a file is not successfully opened, the open() function returns a NULL. The NULL can be tested for when an attempt is made to open the file with an option for some alternative to be taken if the open() was not successful.

```
ifstream InventoryFile("inventry");   //open file Input

if(InventoryFile)                      //test if file exists
{
    FindRecordCount();
}
else
    iNumberRecords = 0;
```

If the file exists, a function will be called to determine the number of records in the file, otherwise the number of records variable will be set to 0.

Writing to the File

Records may be written to a file that has a mode for writing. The member function used to place data on the disk is *write()*. The parameters are the specified data and the number of bytes. The data will frequently be a structure that contains all of the fields associated with a specific record of information.

> MyFile.write((char *)&recordname, sizeof(record));

The (char *) is a type cast which causes the recordname to be treated as a character string; it is used to force the structure to meet the data type in the argument list of the definition of the *write()* function. Notice the & prior to the structure name. This is required for accurate results.

Assuming that we have a structure defined called employee, the format is

```
MyFile.write((char *)&Employee, sizeof(Employee));
```

■ SELF-TEST

1. Code a statement to write one record to disk, using the object name of InventoryFile, that contains the following fields:

   ```
   struct
   {
       char stDescription[15];
       int iQuantity;
       float fCost;
   }Product;
   ```

2. Assume that two files, ClientfFile and ClientReportFile, are currently open. Write the statement to close only the ClientFile object.

3. What is wrong with the following:

   ```
   fstream Sales;
   Sales.open("Sales.dat",ios::out);
   ...
   Sales.dat.write((char *)&SalesInfo, sizeof(Sales));
   ```

■ **ANSWERS**

1. InventoryFile.write((char *)&Product, sizeof(Product));
2. ClientFile.close();
3. The write() must contain the logical name, not the physical name. In this case the object is Sales, not sales.dat.

Reading Data from a Disk File

To read a record from a file using the ifstream class, a call is made to the *read()* member function. The *read()* function has the same parameters as the *write()* function.

```
myfile.read((char *)&recordname, sizeof(record));
```

■ **SELF-TEST**

1. Write the statement to read a record of the following structure type to a file opened with the stream name of DataFile.

   ```
   struct Inventory
   {
       char stDescription[20];
       float fUnitPrice;
       int iQtyOnHand;
       Date LastOrderDate;
       int iMinOrderQty;
   } InventoryRecord;
   ```

2. Why does the use of structures in a data file allow us to do random updates to the file?

3. How many records are read when a read() is executed?

■ **ANSWER**

1. DataFile.read((char *)&InventoryRecord, sizeof(InventoryRecord));
2. When using a structure, there is a fixed length record, making it possible to determine the beginning byte of each record.
3. Depends on the sizeof operator in the read function. It is possible to access multiple records but typically we will access one record at a time.

The seekp() function

The *seekp()* member function of the *ifstream* can be used to control the location of the next record to be accessed. Using the *seekp()*, the file pointer may be set to the beginning of the data, to the end, or to any point in between.

> object.seekp(offset, location constant);

The available constants are:

CONSTANT	LOCATION OF POINTER
ios::beg	beginning of the file
ios::cur	current location in the file
ios::end	end of the file

The offset is a long integer that indicates the number of bytes; the pointer should be set from the location constant. Normally we will offset by 0 bytes. To indicate this as a data type of long, use 0L.

```
DataFile.seekp(0L, ios::beg);
```

This function call will set the file pointer to the beginning of a file that has been opened with as an object *DataFile*. This may be necessary to do if we are working on a file and then decide we want to list the records or search the file from the beginning of the file. If the file were to be closed and reopened the file pointer is reset. The *seekp()* can change the pointer position without closing the file.

Perhaps a file is being edited, and a record needs to be added to the end of the file. Once again, it will be possible to reposition the pointer without closing the file.

```
DataFile.seekp(0L, ios::end);
```

The previous function call will set the pointer immediately behind the last record in the file.

The seekg() function

The corresponding member function of the *ifstream* objects is the *seekg()*. This function controls the position of the file pointer for input access to the file. Think of the p for "put" and the g for "get" from the file. The two pointers work in a similar manner but both exist while the program is executing.

This means that every time you need to read or write to a file consideration should be made of where the appropriate pointer is located. Although you may have positioned the pointer for reading the file, a different pointer needs to be adjusted for rewriting the same record back to the file as would occur with an edit.

Assume that we would like to read the tenth record from a file. Each record will be held in a structure called *employee*. The *seekg()* function could be:

```
EmployeeFile.seekg(10*sizeof(Employee));
```

The tellg() Function

Another handy member function of *ifstream* is the *tellg()* function. This function returns the position of the get file pointer. If you set the file pointer to the end of the file and then ask for the *tellg()* result, you can determine the number of bytes in the file. This number may be used to determine the number of records in a fixed length file if the result of the *tellg()* is divided by the size of a single record. This can be done with the *sizeof* operator.

```
InventoryFile.seekg(0,ios::end);         //Set input pointer to end of file
long lFileLength = InventoryFile.tellg(); //Find out where pointer is
iNumberRecords = lFileLength/sizeof(Item);
```

■ SELF-TEST

1. Given a file opened for input as PatientFile, find the number of records in the file. Assume that each structure is called Patient.
2. Code the statement(s) to print the fifth record in the file.
3. Differentiate between a seekg() and a seekp().
4. If a file is opened for both input and output does it have two file pointers?

■ ANSWERS

1. `PatientFile.seekg(0,ios::end);`

   `long lFileLength = PatientFile.tellg();`
   `iNumberRecords = lFileLength/sizeof(Patient);`

2. `PatientFile.seekg(4*sizeof(Patient), ios::beg);`

   `PatientFile.Read((char*)&Patient ,sizeof(Patient));`
   `cout << ...;`

3. The seekg() is the pointer for records being read from the file, the seekp() pointer indicates where a record will be written.
4. Yes, one for reading and one for writing.

UPDATING A RANDOM FILE

A file update needs to provide the user with the ability to add records to the file, to delete records, and to edit existing records. In addition, it is handy to have an option to list the records to the screen or to the printer. The easiest way to present this program in a useful manner, is to use a menu program. The last item on the menu will be an option to exit the update.

At the beginning of the program the file will be opened to a mode of append. The file will remain open until just before the program is terminated. While the file is open we will position the cursor to the desired location using the *seekp()*. Because of the append mode being used, it would be desirable to display a message if there are no records in the file. We can do this in each of the modules.

UPDATE MENU

1. Add a record
2. Delete a record
3. Edit/Change a record
4. List Records
5. Exit

The Class for the File

The class will contain screens for data entry and for reading and writing the records. The reading/writing will be considered in the following sections. The class constructor will check if the file exists. If there is no file the number of records (a data member is needed for this) will be set to 0 and the file is created, otherwise, the constructor will open the file and determine the number of records in the file and assign the count to the number of records data member.

```
struct Item
{
    char stDescription[20];
    int iQuantity;
    float fPrice;
};

class InventoryFile
{
    protected:
    Item Data;
    int iNumberRecords;
    int iCurrentRecord;
    void DataScreen(), EnterData(),Read();
    void Write(), List(char *,int);
    int GetRecordNum(), Search(char *);
    void EditMenu(),PrintData(int);
    public:
    InventoryFile();
    virtual void AddRecord(), ListRecord(), DeleteRecord(), EditRecord();
};

InventoryFile::InventoryFile()    //Constructor
{
    // Initialize number of Records field
    ifstream InventoryFile("inventry"); //Open File Input
    if(InventoryFile)
    {
        InventoryFile.seekg(0,ios::end);
    long lFileLength = InventoryFile.tellg();
        iNumberRecords = lFileLength/sizeof(Item);
    }
```

```
            else
                    iNumberRecords = 0;
    }
```

DATA MEMBERS	PURPOSE
Item Data;	a data record
iNumberRecords;	number of records in the file
iCurrentRecord;	record number for the file pointers

MEMBER FUNCTIONS	PURPOSE
AddRecord()	Control the add from the menu
Datascreen()	Data input screen
DeleteRecord()	Control the delete function from the menu
EditMenu()	Add numbers to data display for editing
EditRecord()	Control the delete function from the menu
Enterdata()	Data entry for add
Getrecordnum()	Prompt for record number, determine if search needed
InventoryFile()	Constructor, opens file and sets numberrecords field if file exists
List()	Prints the information to screen or printer
ListRecord()	Control the list function from the menu
PrintData()	Display the data of requested record for edit or delete
Read()	Positions the pointer and inputs a record from disk
Search()	Find the requested record by the key field
Write()	Positions the pointer and outputs a record to disk

The Write Routine

The function that writes to the disk needs to position the pointer to the desired location and then perform the write. It is desirable to have a single write function that is then called by the add routine, the edit routine, and the delete routine.

The file pointer is controlled by a data member from the class called *currentrecord*. This value will be set by the routine that is requesting that a write be performed.

```
void InventoryFile::Write()
{
    ofstream InventoryFile("inventry",ios::ate);
    InventoryFile.seekp(sizeof(Item)*iCurrentRecord,ios::beg);
    InventoryFile.write((char*)&Data, sizeof(Item));
}
```

The Read Routine

Similarly there will be a single read function. This will be used by the edit and delete routines to find the proper record when the record number is not known. It will also be used by the list routine for reading the records from the file. Each call to the read function will position the file pointer.

```
void InventoryFile::Read()
{
    ifstream InventoryFile("inventry");
    InventoryFile.seekg(sizeof(Item)*iCurrentRecord,ios::beg);
    InventoryFile.read((char*)&Data, sizeof(Item));
}
```

Using the Same Screen

Your user will be more comfortable with your program design if you keep the screen design consistent. For that reason the following code sections will reuse the same screen design for adding a record, deleting a record, and for editing a record. The DataScreen() and the EnterData() functions work from the same screen without clearing. This is accomplished by positioning the cursor using DOS commands. As with the other DOS commands you must have Ansi.sys setup in your system configuration.

The following function positions the cursor at the horizontal position of x and the vertical position of y:

```
void inline gotoxy(int x, int y)
{
    cout << "\033[" << y << ";" << x << "H";
}
```

The screen may be cleared using the DOS system function or with the following code:

```
void inline ClearScreen()
{
    cout << "\033[2J";
{
```

You will call these functions when you display information to the screen.

```
void InventoryFile::DataScreen()
{
    ClearScreen();
    gotoxy(35,5);
    cout << "ABC Incorporated";
    gotoxy(15,8);
    cout << "Product Description";
    gotoxy(15,10);
    cout << "Quantity on hand";
```

```
            gotoxy(15,12);
            cout << "Selling Price";
    }


    void InventoryFile::EnterData()
    {
            gotoxy(35,8);
            cin >> Data.stDescription;
            gotoxy(35,10);
            cin >> Data.iQuantity;
            gotoxy(35,12);
            cin >> Data.fPrice;
    }
```

Adding Records to the File

To add a record to the file, place the file pointer to the end of the file. Adding records is the same as originally creating the file. It is not necessary to have two separate programs or routines to create and to add record. If the file is opened in ate mode, records may be added to the end of the file. If the file is being created for the first time, the end of the file is the beginning of the file and that is where the records will be placed.

```
    //          Add Routine
    void InventoryFile::AddRecord()
    {
            DataScreen();
            EnterData();
            iCurrentRecord = ++iNumberRecords;
            Write();
    }
```

THE STEPS TO ADD A RECORD ARE:
1. Get data from the keyboard. 2. Position the pointer to the end of the file. 3. Write to the file.

Deleting or Editing a Record

To delete or edit an existing record, we must begin by finding out which record is to be deleted/processed. If the user knows the record number of the record to be deleted, we could go directly to that position in the file. If not, we will have to ask for a field in the record. We will then search for this record in the file. Recall from Chapter 7 that the field being searched for is called the key. If the data was sorted in the array by the key field, we could use the *bsearch()*.

After the record is located, we should display the information from the record and verify that this is the proper record. If the answer is yes, the record will then be processed.

How is the record deleted? One way would be to rewrite the file and just not write this record back in. This method is slow and it also changes the record number for all of the records following it. Another alternative would be to use a **flag** to mark the record as deleted or inactive.

FLAGGING A RECORD FOR DELETE

There are two common ways to flag a record for delete. If you've worked with DOS you are probably aware that files are not really deleted from the disk immediately but instead the first letter of the file name is deleted in the directory table. Next time a file is saved, this space will appear as available. With this method, some form of delete code is used in the key field.

```
Data.stDescription[0] = '*';
cout << "Record  Deleted";
Write();
```

A second method is to set up an extra field which will contain a code to determine if the record is active or inactive. This method is especially desirable when there is a good chance that records will need to be "undeleted."

USING A DELETE CODE

Sometimes it is desirable to maintain the information in a deleted record. An example may be a file in which records are active or inactive, as indicated earlier. In order to do this an extra field will be added to each record that contains the status of the record.

```
struct Patient
{
      char stName[25];
      char cRoom[1];
      int iDays;
      char cDeleteCode;
}PatientRecord[iMAX];
```

In order to delete the record, the delete code would be changed to inactive, rather than using the *. To give the menu option to undelete records, all records that contain a delete code of inactive would be listed.

STEPS IN DELETING A RECORD
1. Get the record number or a key field of the record to be deleted.
2. Find the record.
3. Verify that the record that is found is the one the user wishes to delete.
4. Flag the record as deleted.

> **LOCATING THE REQUESTED RECORD**
>
> Several routines are shared for both delete and edit.
>
> *Shared routines for Delete and Edit:*
>   GetRecordnum()
>   Search()
>   Verify()
>   Print_data()

1. Get the record number or a key field of the record to be deleted.

```
int InventoryFile::GetRecordNum()
{
      int iRecordNum;
      char stKey[15], cAnswer;

      gotoxy(5,10);
      cout << "Enter Record Number(if known) or type a 0    ";
      gotoxy(50,10);
      cin >> iRecordNum;
      if(iRecordNum == 0)
      {
            gotoxy(5,10);
            cout << "Enter Description of product to be found   ";
            cin >> stKey;       // Get the key of Record to be deleted
            iRecordNum = Search(stKey);
      }
      if(iRecordNum != 0)    //Record was found
      {
            DataScreen();
            PrintData(iRecordNum);
            gotoxy(15,20);
            cout << "Is this the Record to be edited/deleted (Y/N)";
            gotoxy(60,20);
            cin >> cAnswer;
            if(cAnswer!='Y' && cAnswer!='y')      //Is it the correct Record
                  iRecordNum = 0;
      }
      return iRecordNum;
}
```

2. Find the record.

```
int InventoryFile::Search(char stKey[])      //Find the Record
{
    for(int i = 0; i < iNumberRecords; i++)
    {
        iCurrentRecord = i;
        Read();
        if(strncmp(Data.stDescription, stKey, strlen(stKey)) == 0)
            return(i);
    }
    return -1;
}
```

3. Verify that the record that is found is the one the user wishes to delete.

```
if(iRecordNum != 0)      //Record was found
{
    DataScreen();
    PrintData(iRecordNum);
    gotoxy(15,20);
    cout << "Is this the Record to be edited/deleted (Y/N)";
    gotoxy(60,20);
    cin >> cAnswer;
    if(cAnswer!='Y' && cAnswer!='y')     //Is it the correct Record
        iRecordNum = 0;
}
```

Editing Records

To edit a record, we must first locate it just as we did with the delete option. After the record is found, we then need to know which changes the user wishes to make. Once again, there are different approaches to this problem. Some programs simply treat an edit like an add and all field must be re-entered. However, this does not seem very "user-friendly."

Another approach would be to give the user a menu and then permit them to select the field to be changed. This would be placed in a loop that would terminate when the user chose an option for "No More Changes."

The menu screen will use the search and display functions from the delete to print the field names and the data. Once the fields and the data from the record are displayed on the screen, we can then place menu numbers in front of the field names.

```
//                              Edit Routine
void InventoryFile::EditRecord()
{
```

```cpp
            iCurrentRecord = -1;
            ClearScreen();
            gotoxy(30,7);
            cout << "Edit Option";
            iCurrentRecord = GetRecordNum();
            if(iCurrentRecord >= 1)
            {
                EditMenu();
                Write();
            }
            else
            {
                gotoxy(30,21);
                cout << "Record not found";
                Pause();
            }
}

void InventoryFile::EditMenu()
{
    char cOption;

    do
    {
        gotoxy(7,8);
        cout << "1.";
        gotoxy(7,10);
        cout << "2.";
        gotoxy(7,12);
        cout << "3. ";
        gotoxy(7,14);
        cout << "0. No more changes";
        gotoxy(15,20);
        cout << "Select option =============>";
        gotoxy(50,20);
```

```
        cin >> cOption;

    switch(cOption)
    {
        case '1':
                gotoxy(35,8);
                cout << SPACES;
                gotoxy(35,8);
                cin >> Data.stDescription;
                break;
        case '2':
                gotoxy(35,10);
                cout << SPACES;
                gotoxy(35,10);
                cin >> Data.iQuantity;
                break;
        case '3':
                gotoxy(35,12);
                cout << SPACES;
                gotoxy(35,12);
                cin >> Data.fPrice;
        case '0':
                break;
        default:
                gotoxy(15,20);
                cout << "Please enter an appropriate letter or number ";
                gotoxy(40,17);
                cin >> cOption;
}
    }while(cOption != '0');
    }
```

Listing Records from the File

When we are listing records, we will only want to display or print the active records, which will necessitate checking for the delete code. This requires a decision statement.

```
if(Data.stDescription[0] != '*')     //Check if deleted
{
```

```
            cprn << "\t" << setiosflags(ios::left)
                 << setw(35) <<Data.stDescription
                 << setw(10) << Data.iQuantity << endl;
            iLineCount++;
}
```

PRINTING TO THE SCREEN

When printing to the screen the program must count lines to determine when the screen is full. When the screen is filled, the screen should pause until the user is ready to continue. At that point, the screen will be cleared and the titles reprinted. This will continue until all records have been printed.

PRINTING TO THE PRINTER

A printed listing of records should contain the logic for multipage output. This routine will differ from the screen in the number of lines per page and also in using a form feed rather than a clear screen.

THE LIST ROUTINE

The following code uses a menu for the user to select screen or printer for the destination of the output. The response from the user then determines the device name and the number of lines to be sent to the print function.

```
//              List Routine
void InventoryFile::ListRecord()
{
    char cOption;

    ClearScreen();
    gotoxy(30,7);
    cout << "Listing Option";
    gotoxy(20,10);
    cout << "1. Send to the Printer";
    gotoxy(20,12);
    cout << "2. Display on the Screen";
    gotoxy(18,15);
    cout << "Enter your Choice (1 or 2)";
    gotoxy(48, 15);
    cin >> cOption;

    ClearScreen();
    switch (cOption)
```

```cpp
        {
            case '1': case 'P': case 'p':
                List("PRN",24); break;
            case '2': case 'S': case 's':
                List("CON", 8); break;
            default:
                cout << "Please enter an appropriate letter or number ";
                cin >> cOption;
        }
    }
}
void InventoryFile::List(char *stDevice,int iNumLines)
{
    ofstream cprn(stDevice);
    int  iPageCount = 0,
    iLineCount = iNumLines + 1;   //Force title on first page/screen

    for(int i = 1; i < iNumberRecords; i++) //Loop for number of Records
    {
        if(iLineCount > iNumLines)       //Check for new page/screen
        {
            if(strcmp(stDevice,"CON")==0)   // Check if output to screen
            {ClearScreen();}
            iLineCount = 0;                 //Reset linecount
            iPageCount++;
            cprn << "\t\tInventory Listing\tPage " << iPageCount << endl;
            cprn << "\n\tDescription                     Quantity\n\n";
        }
        iCurrentRecord = i;              //Tell which Record to read
        Read();
        if(Data.stDescription[0] != '*')   //Check if deleted
        {
            cprn << "\t" << setiosflags(ios::left)
                 << setw(35) <<Data.stDescription
                 << setw(10) << Data.iQuantity << endl;
            iLineCount++;
        }
```

```
        }
        if(strcmp(stDevice,"CON")==0)          // Check if output to screen
        {
                Pause();
                ClearScreen();
        }
}
```

Replacing Deleted Record Positions during Add

If the possibility of undeleting records is not going to be used, a record that is being added could be placed in a record position that contains a deleted record marked by an *.

To replace deleted records when adding a record a loop will be used to find the first record location that contains an * in the appropriate field. If no records have been deleted, the new record will be placed at the end of the file.

```
for(int i = 1; i < iNumberRecords; i++)
{
        iCurrentRecord = i;
        Read();
        if(Data.stDescription[0] == '*')
                break;
}
```

If a break is encountered prior to the end of the file, that is where the new record will be placed, otherwise there are no deletes and the new record will be placed at the end of the file.

COMPLETE UPDATE CLASS

PLANNING

ITEM PROPERTIES	DATA TYPE	NAME
Description	char array	stDescription
Price	float	fPrice
Quantity	integer	iQuantity

DATA MEMBERS	PURPOSE
Item Data;	a data record
iNumberRecords;	number of records in the file
iCurrentRecord;	record number for the file pointers

MEMBER FUNCTIONS	PURPOSE
AddRecord()	Control the add from the menu
Datascreen()	Data input screen
DeleteRecord()	Control the delete function from the menu
EditMenu()	Add numbers to data display for editing
EditRecord()	Control the delete function from the menu
Enterdata()	Data entry for add
Getrecordnum()	Prompt for record number, determine if search needed
InventoryFile()	Constructor, opens file and sets numberrecords field if file exists
List()	Prints the information to screen or printer
ListRecord()	Control the list function from the menu
PrintData()	Display the data of requested record for edit or delete
Read()	Positions the pointer and inputs a record from disk
Search()	Find the requested record by the key field
Write()	Positions the pointer and outputs a record to disk

```
//Ch10Pr01.h
#include <fstream.h>
#include <conio.h>
#include <string.h>
#include <iomanip.h>

void inline ClearScreen()
{
      cout << "\033[2J";
}

void inline gotoxy(int x, int y)
{
      cout << "\033[" << y << ";" << x << "H";
}

const char SPACES[] = "                                        ";

void inline Pause()
{
```

```cpp
        gotoxy(35,20);
        cout << "Press Any Key to Continue";
        getche();
}

struct Item
{
        char stDescription[20];
        int iQuantity;
        float fPrice;
};

class InventoryFile
{
        protected:
        Item Data;
        int iNumberRecords;
        int iCurrentRecord;
        void DataScreen(), EnterData(),Read();
        void Write(), List(char *,int);
        int GetRecordNum(), Search(char *);
        void EditMenu(),PrintData(int);
        public:
        InventoryFile();
        virtual void AddRecord(), ListRecord(), DeleteRecord(), EditRecord();
};

InventoryFile::InventoryFile()     //Constructor
{
        // Initialize number of Records field
        ifstream InventoryFile("inventry"); //Open File Input
        if(InventoryFile)
        {
                InventoryFile.seekg(0,ios::end);
                long lFileLength = InventoryFile.tellg();
                iNumberRecords = lFileLength/sizeof(Item);
        }
```

```cpp
        else
                iNumberRecords = 0;
}


void InventoryFile::DataScreen()
{
        ClearScreen();
        gotoxy(35,5);
        cout << "ABC Incorporated";
        gotoxy(15,8);
        cout << "Product Description";
        gotoxy(15,10);
        cout << "Quantity on hand";
        gotoxy(15,12);
        cout << "Selling Price";
}


void InventoryFile::EnterData()
{
        gotoxy(35,8);
        cin >> Data.stDescription;
        gotoxy(35,10);
        cin >> Data.iQuantity;
        gotoxy(35,12);
        cin >> Data.fPrice;
}


//       Add Routine
void InventoryFile::AddRecord()
{
        DataScreen();
        EnterData();
        iCurrentRecord = ++iNumberRecords;
        Write();
}


void InventoryFile::Write()
```

```cpp
{
    ofstream InventoryFile("inventry",ios::ate);
    InventoryFile.seekp(sizeof(Item)*iCurrentRecord,ios::beg);
    InventoryFile.write((char*)&Data, sizeof(Item));
}



void InventoryFile::List(char *stDevice,int iNumLines)
{
    ofstream cprn(stDevice);
    cprn << "\033[2J";   //Clear screen
    int iPageCount = 0;
    int iLineCount = iNumLines + 1;   //Force title on first page/screen

    for(int i = 1; i < iNumberRecords; i++) //Loop for number of Records
    {
        if(iLineCount > iNumLines)              //Check for new page/screen
        {
            if(strcmp(stDevice,"CON")==0)   // Check if output to screen
            {ClearScreen();}
            iLineCount = 0;                   //Reset linecount
            iPageCount++;
            cprn << "\t\tInventory Listing\tPage " << iPageCount << endl;
            cprn << "\n\tDescription                   Quantity\n\n";
        }
        iCurrentRecord = i;                 //Tell which Record to read
        Read();
        if(Data.stDescription[0] != '*')    //Check if deleted
        {
            cprn << "\t" << setiosflags(ios::left)
                 << setw(35) <<Data.stDescription
                 << setw(10) << Data.iQuantity << endl;
            iLineCount++;
        }
    }
    if(strcmp(stDevice,"CON")==0)       // Check if output to screen
    {
```

```cpp
            Pause();
            ClearScreen();
        }
}


void InventoryFile::Read()
{
    ifstream InventoryFile("inventry");
    InventoryFile.seekg(sizeof(Item)*iCurrentRecord,ios::beg);
    InventoryFile.read((char*)&Data, sizeof(Item));
}


//              List Routine
void InventoryFile::ListRecord()
{
    char cOption;

    ClearScreen();
    gotoxy(30,7);
    cout << "Listing Option";
    gotoxy(20,10);
    cout << "1. Send to the Printer";
    gotoxy(20,12);
    cout << "2. Display on the Screen";
    gotoxy(18,15);
    cout << "Enter your Choice (1 or 2)";
    gotoxy(48, 15);
    cin >> cOption;

    switch (cOption)
    {
            case '1': case 'P': case 'p':
                List("PRN",24); break;
            case '2': case 'S': case 's':
                List("CON", 8); break;
            default:
                gotoxy(20,20);
```

```cpp
                cout << "Please enter an appropriate letter or number ";
                gotoxy(48,14);
                cin >> cOption;
        }
}



//           Delete Routine
void InventoryFile::DeleteRecord()
{
        ClearScreen();
        gotoxy(30,7);
        cout << "Delete Option";
        iCurrentRecord = GetRecordNum();
        if(iCurrentRecord >= 0)
        {
                Data.stDescription[0] = '*';
                gotoxy(30,21);
                cout << "Record  Deleted";
                Write();
        }
        else
        {
                gotoxy(30,21);
                cout << "Record not found";
                Pause();
        }
}


//           Shared routines for Delete and Edit
/*               GetRecordNum()
             Search()
             Verify()
             PrintData()*/
int InventoryFile::GetRecordNum()
{
        int iRecordNum;
```

```cpp
        char stKey[15], cAnswer;

        gotoxy(5,10);
        cout << "Enter Record Number(if known) or type a 0    ";
        gotoxy(50,10);
        cin >> iRecordNum;
        if(iRecordNum == 0)
        {
            gotoxy(5,10);
            cout << "Enter Description of product to be found    ";
            cin >> stKey;      // Get the key of Record to be deleted
            iRecordNum = Search(stKey);
        }
        if(iRecordNum != 0)    //Record was found
        {
            DataScreen();
            PrintData(iRecordNum);
            gotoxy(15,20);
            cout << "Is this the Record to be edited/deleted (Y/N)";
            gotoxy(60,20);
            cin >> cAnswer;
            if(cAnswer!='Y' && cAnswer!='y')    //Is it the correct Record
                iRecordNum = 0;
        }
        return iRecordNum;
}

int InventoryFile::Search(char stKey[])    //Find the Record
{
        for(int i = 1; i < iNumberRecords; i++)
        {
            iCurrentRecord = i;
            Read();
            if(strncmp(Data.stDescription, stKey, strlen(stKey)) == 0)
                return(i);
        }
        return -1;
```

```cpp
}


void InventoryFile::PrintData(int iRecordNum)
{
    // Fill in data from Record to data screen
    iCurrentRecord = iRecordNum;
    Read();
    gotoxy(35,8);
    cout << Data.stDescription;
    gotoxy(35,10);
    cout << Data.iQuantity;
    gotoxy(35,12);
    cout << Data.fPrice;
}


//                          Edit Routine
void InventoryFile::EditRecord()
{
    ClearScreen();
    gotoxy(30,7);
    cout << "Edit Option";
    iCurrentRecord = GetRecordNum();
    if(iCurrentRecord >= 1)
    {
        EditMenu();
        Write();
    }
    else
    {
        gotoxy(30,21);
        cout << "Record not found";
        Pause();
    }
}


void InventoryFile::EditMenu()
{
```

```cpp
    char cOption;

do
{
        gotoxy(7,8);
        cout << "1.";
        gotoxy(7,10);
        cout << "2.";
        gotoxy(7,12);
        cout << "3. ";
        gotoxy(7,14);
        cout << "0. No more changes";
        gotoxy(15,20);
        cout << "Select option =============>";
        gotoxy(50,20);
        cin >> cOption;

        switch(cOption)
        {
                case '1':
                        gotoxy(35,8);
                        cout << SPACES;
                        gotoxy(35,8);
                        cin >> Data.stDescription;
                        break;
                case '2':
                        gotoxy(35,10);
                        cout << SPACES;
                        gotoxy(35,10);
                        cin >> Data.iQuantity;
                        break;
                case '3':
                        gotoxy(35,12);
                        cout << SPACES;
                        gotoxy(35,12);
                        cin >> Data.fPrice;
```

```cpp
                        case '0':
                                break;
                        default:
                                gotoxy(15,20);
                                cout <<"Please enter an appropriate letter or number ";
                                gotoxy(40,17);
                                cin >> cOption;
                }
        }while(cOption != '0');
}


//Ch10Pr01
////////////////////////////////////////////////////////////
//      Programmer:
//      Date:
//      Description: Uses a highlighted menu bar for file update
////////////////////////////////////////////////////////////
#include<conio.h>
#include <iostream.h>
#include <stdlib.h>
#include "Ch10Pr01.h"

InventoryFile MyFile;

void ColorOn()
{
        cout << "\033[7m";
}

void ColorOff()
{
        cout << "\033[0m";
}


const bool FALSE = 0;
const bool TRUE = 1;

char MenuItem[5][20] = {"Add an item",
```

```
                        "Delete an item",
                        "Edit/Change",
                        "List all items",
                        "Quit"};
class Menu
{
   void Choice(), Validate(), DisplayMenu();
   int iSelection, iValidExit, iValidChoice;
   int iNumberOptions;
   public:
   Menu(int iNumber);
   void Run();
};

void main()
{
   Menu(5).Run();
}

Menu::Menu(int iNumber)
{
   iNumberOptions = iNumber;
   iSelection = 0; iValidExit = FALSE; iValidChoice = FALSE;
}

void Menu::Run()
{
   while(!iValidExit)
   {
      DisplayMenu();
      Choice();
      Validate();
   };
}

void Menu::DisplayMenu()
{
```

```cpp
            ClearScreen();
            gotoxy(25,7);
            cout << "File Update Menu\n\n";
            for(int x = 0; x < iNumberOptions; x++)
            {
                    if(iSelection == x)
                            ColorOn();
                    else
                            ColorOff();
                    gotoxy(25, 7 + x+2);
                    cout << MenuItem[x];
                    ColorOff();
                    cout << endl;
            }
    }

    void Menu::Choice()
    {
       char cKey;
       cKey = getche();
       switch(cKey)
       {
         case 72: //up arrow
           iSelection--;
           break;
         case 80: //down arrow
           iSelection++;
           break;
         case 13:
           iValidChoice = TRUE;
       }
    }

    void Menu::Validate()
    {
            if(iSelection < 0) iSelection = iNumberOptions - 1;
            if(iSelection > iNumberOptions - 1) iSelection = 0;
```

```
        while(iValidChoice)
        {
                switch(iSelection)
                {
                        case 0:
                                MyFile.AddRecord(); break;
                        case 1:
                                MyFile.DeleteRecord(); break;
                        case 2:
                                MyFile.EditRecord(); break;
                        case 3:
                                MyFile.ListRecord(); break;
                        case 4:
                                iValidExit = TRUE;
                }
                iValidChoice = FALSE;
        }
}
```

PROGRAMMING/DEBUGGING TIP

Hash Addressing

Hash Addressing is the programming technique in which the key field is used to generate a record number for a random file. The field such as name has an algorithm applied to it to determine a record number within the file size. This record number, sometimes called a **hash key,** can then be used for direct access to a random file using the *seekg()*.

An overflow area for records with duplicate keys is required because it cannot be guaranteed that all key fields will produce a unique record number. When a key generates a record number that has already been assigned, a **collision** occurs. The same hashing function may yield a different rate of collisions depending on the type of data used for the key field (string or numeric). In general, the steps in hash addressing are:

1. Change the key to a record number.
2. Get the record.
3. If the record is blank, write the data; if not blank, chain to next available record number in the overflow area.

Hashing Algorithm

The algorithm used should not be too complicated and must minimize collisions. The following method starts by entering the key field, converting each of the characters to ASCII code, and finding the sum of the ASCII codes. A prime number close to the file size is used in finding the record number.

Example

Use a sum of the ASCII codes and a modulus assuming a file size of 100 to determine a hash key for the following fields:

Jones
Johnson
Johnston
Jensen
Johns

```
//Ch10Pr02
/////////////////////////////////////////////////////////
//      Programmer:
//      Date:
//      Description: Implement hashing algorithms
//                   to find a record number
/////////////////////////////////////////////////////////
#include <fstream.h>
#include <iomanip.h>
#include <conio.h>



char stName[5][9] = {"Jones",
                     "Johnson",
                     "Johnston",
                     "Jensen",
                     "Johns"};
int iAsciiSum(char stName[]);

void main()
{
    int iKey, iSum;

    ofstream Screen("CON");
    Screen << setiosflags(ios::left)
           << setw(15) << "Name"
           << setw(15) << "ASCII Sum"
           << setw(10) << "Key" << endl << endl;
    for(int i =0; i < 5; i++)
    {
```

```
        iSum = (int)iAsciiSum(stName[i]);
        iKey = iSum % 101;      // Use modulus and a prime number */
        Screen << setw(15) << stName[i]
               << setw(15) << iSum
               << setw(10) << iKey << endl;
   }
   getche();
}


/*------------------------
    Find the sum of the ASCII code for
    each letter in a name
-------------------------*/
int iAsciiSum(char stName[])
{
     int iSum=0;

     for(int i=0; stName[i] != NULL; i++)
     {
          iSum += (int)(stName[i]);    //Type cast each letter to integer
          }
          return iSum;
}
```

OUTPUT

NAME	ASCII SUM	KEY
Jones	511	6
Johnson	735	28
Johnston	851	43
Jensen	611	5
Johns	514	9

Key Terms

- append
- collision
- delete code
- edit
- file mode
- file update
- flag
- hash address
- hashing algorithm
- logical file name
- physical file name
- random access
- sequential access
- stream

Chapter Summary

Disk files may be accessed sequentially or randomly. In order to access data as a random file, the record length will be fixed. Data can be written to a disk file using stream classes. Summary of file commands:

fstream stream	Declares object name for disk storage.
stream.Open("diskfile name",mode)	Opens the file in the desired mode and assigns the physical disk name to the streamname that will be used in the program.
stream.Write()	Write to a file.
stream.Read()	Read from a file.
stream.Close()	Close the file buffer.

A file update includes routines for adding records, deleting records, editing records, and for listing the data from the file.

A hashing algorithm provides a method for generating a random record number from a key field. A random file that is accessed using a hashing algorithm must have an overflow area to provide for collisions. A collision occurs when multiple key fields generate the same record number.

Review Questions

1. What statement is used to read a record?
2. List the arguments necessary to do a write().
3. When accessing a file of structures, how can you find out how many records to read?
4. If the array size is set at 100, and the file contains 4253 records, how can all of the records be processed?
5. What are the advantages of using a delete code rather than just changing an existing field?
6. In the example program, why does the list file check for an * before printing?
7. What are the steps necessary to do an edit to an existing record?
8. What is meant by an index?
9. What is the purpose of hashing?
10. What is meant by the phrase "hashing algorithm"?
11. Give an example of a hashing algorithm.
12. What is a "collision"?

Exercises

1. Write a program that will input data from the keyboard and create a file of inventory records using the following structure.

```
struct Inventory
{
```

```
     char stDescription[20];
     float fUnitPrice;
     int iQuantityOnHand;
     struct date LastOrderDate;
     int iMinOrderQuantity;
   }   InventoryRecord;
```

2. Write a program that will produce a report to the screen or to the printer listing the records from the inventory file created in exercise 2.

3. Write a program that will create a sequential data file for a used car dealership. Each inventory record will consist of the manufacturer, model name, year, vehicle number, and market value. The vehicle number is a 15 character string field and the market value will be float.

   Output:

   Read the records from the data file and produce a list of the data with appropriate titles and column headings.

   Data:

   Chevrolet, Blazer, 87, AND042049, 12000
   Chevrolet, Camaro, 69, TOM022765, 5000
   Dodge, Ramcharger, 79, CAB070480, 6000
   Ford, Mustang, 69, ERI032075, 5000
   Ford, 150-Pickup, 90, ART062137, 19000
   Ford, Thunderbird, 89, WEN984567, 12500
   Honda, LXI, 88, GEN092330, 4500
   Honda, Civic, 91, LES11234, 5500
   Honda, Civic, 92, MES21334, 6500
   Jeep, Scout, 75, ALP122720, 1000
   Jeep, Scout, 85, ABB432189, 3000
   Mazda, 323, 90, GOG123456, 6000
   Mazda, 626, 84, TRI082573, 4000
   Peugeot, 505S, 84, ANI081650, 4000

4. Create a random file using the data from the used car dealership in exercise 3. Each structure will consist of the manufacturer, model name, year, vehicle number, and market value. The vehicle number is a 15 character string field and the market value will be float.

   Output:

   Read the records from the data file and produce a list of the data with appropriate titles and column headings.

5. Create a data file for a bowling league. Each record will contain the team name, the bowler name, the number of games played this season, the total pins, and the high series. Records for females will contain an asterisk.

Data:

Team Supreme	Al Argus	18	3135	572
Team Supreme	Mary Menace	15	2024	420 *
Team Supreme	Bob Menace	18	3004	550
Team Supreme	Karin Dee	18	3030	525 *
Alley Gators	Chris Carson	18	2788	479 *
Alley Gators	Audy Carson	18	3011	590
Alley Gators	Eddie Tomas	15	2275	455
Alley Gators	Cindy Tomas	15	1788	395 *
Lucky Strikes	Andy Marvin	18	3055	602
Lucky Strikes	Ann Marvin	18	2020	398 *
Lucky Strikes	Linda Noon	18	2550	456 *
Lucky Strikes	Scott Noon	18	2888	522
Sub	Lou Garcia	6	2088	488 *

6. Write a program that will create and update an employee file. For each employee, you must use a structure to store the information.

   Each record will include:
   - Last Name
   - First Name
   - Middle Initial
   - Social Security Number
   - Date Hired
   - Vanpool (Yes or No)
   - Salary Code—S for salaried H for hourly
   - Salary level, may be an hourly rate or an annual salary
   - Year to date income
   - Year to date federal income taxes
   - Year to date state income taxes

   The update program must be menu driven and must include options for adding a record, deleting a record, editing a record, and for listing the records to the screen or to the printer. The list option should print the employees in order by last name.

7. Write a program to create a payroll report from the employee file created in program 6.

   Input: Design an input screen that will print the employee name and Social Security name on the screen from the file. Prompt the user to enter the number of hours worked if hourly. If the individual is salaried, ask for number, if any, of sick or personal leave days.

Output:

Title: The title will include a page number and the report date. Create column headings for name.

Detail Line:

The detail line will include

1. Employee Name
2. Regular Pay
3. Overtime Hours
4. Overtime Pay
5. Deductions
6. Gross Pay

Summary: The summary line should contain totals for overtime hours, overtime pay, and gross pay.

Processing:

Overtime:

For hourly employees, calculate overtime at a rate of time and one half for all hours over 40.

Deductions:

VanPool, if Yes, deduct 14.50

Federal Taxes, use 15%

State Taxes, use 8%

FICA

8. Create a program that will input a last name and then will print the address calculated by using four different hashing algorithms.
    Test the program for 20 different last names and print a summary of the number of collisions created by each method.

9. Modify the grocery store program from Chapter 8, Exercise 1 so that the product information is stored in a data file and then loaded into an array from the constructor function.

Hayley Office Supplies

Use the structure created in Chapter 6 for the inventory items to create a file. Each structure will contain the product number, product description, the aisle number, current cost, quantity on hand, minimum order quantity, vendor.

Use the file to create a program for sales transactions. The sale transaction screen will allow the user to enter the product number, or if not known (press Enter), the product description. The price will be calculated as a 35% markup. Assume all items are taxable.

The results will be an invoice calculating the amount due, and an update to the structure quantity field.

For this example, make up sample data and enter it into the array of structures at the beginning of the program to simulate a data file.

GLOSSARY

Address operator: Indicated by an ampersand (&), the address operator is read as "the address of" and as the "pass by reference" operator.

Address: A location in memory that may contain a variable, a function, or another pointer.

Append: A method of adding records to a file, deleting records, or editing existing records.

Argument: Any items that are enclosed inside of parentheses; also known as values.

Arithmetic conversion: The result when the binary arithmetic operators cause a conversion of the data type depending on the operator and on the type of the operands.

Assignment operator: Value on left of operator is assigned to right. May be combined with arithmetic operation. Unary increment and decrement operators are frequently considered to be assignment operators.

Base class: The broadest type of class in a system that uses inheritance and object-oriented models. A derived class will have similar features and actions but require greater specificity than the base class with which it is associated. The automobile would be a derived class from vehicle base class.

Binary operator: Used to perform calculations, a binary operator has two factors or operands.

Binary search: A search that requires data to be sorted in order prior to the search.

Bind: The way in which operators combine according to precedence.

Block: A series of declarations and statements that are enclosed inside of braces.

Braces ({}): Used to enclose the statements or instructions within a function.

Break: A statement that terminates a loop, case, or if. Used to indicate the end of the statement(s) for each case, or the execution of the program will continue to flow through the remaining cases without testing the case conditions.

Case: One of several possible values in a switch.

Class: Encapsulates things. The word "class" refers to the object-oriented data and functions. Defaults to private access mode.

Collision: The result when a key generates a record number that has already been assigned.

Comment: Information contained in the source code that is not translated by the compiler, symbolized by two slashes (//).

Compiler: The portion of C++ that translates source code into object code (machine instructions). As the compiler attempts to perform this translation, it will be able to locate any syntax errors punctuation or spelling that cannot be translated by the compiler).

Compound condition: Conditions combined with || or && that may be used together in the same expression if more than two conditions are to be tested.

Concatenation: Combining two string fields.

Conditional operator: An operator that will express an entire conditional in a single statement. A conditional operator is a ternary operator, meaning that it requires three operands: the condition, the action if true, and the action if false.

Const: A reserved word used to assign a name to a constant value.

Constant: Data that remains unchanged during execution of a program.

Constructor: A specialized function that automatically executes when an object is created. The constructor name is the same as the structure or class to which it belongs.

Data member: Variables or properties of class or structure.

Data type: The types of data in C++ are integer, floating point, double precision, and character. These may be modified as long integer, short integer, signed integer, or unsigned integer.

Declaration: To declare a variable, the type of data is followed by the variable name.

Decrement: An operator that will decrease the value of an integer variable by one.

Default: A built-in error-checking factor that may be used when none of the cases have been met.

Delete code: A method of maintaining information in a deleted record; for example, by adding a field that will generate a file in which records are active or inactive.

Dereference: A dereference operator (*) can be used to get the indirect value of a pointer variable.

Derived class: The more specific type of class in a hierarchy system. A derived class will have similar features and actions but require greater specificity than the base class with which it is associated. The automobile would be a derived class from vehicle base class.

Destructor: A destructor function is automatically executed when an object goes "out of scope." This usually occurs at the end of the function in which the object was declared.

Detail: The main body of a report, which would contain an output line for each transaction.

double: One of the basic types of data in C++; the others are integer, long integer, float, and character.

Encapsulation: The process of combining data members with the actions that are used to manipulate the type of data. In C++ encapsulation is denoted with a structure or class that contains both data and functions.

Entry condition: A condition placed at the beginning of a loop.

Escape sequences: Typically used to represent white space, such as a tab or new line, or to represent unprintable characters, such as the bell; escape sequences are preceded by a backslash (\).

Exit condition: A condition placed at the end of the loop.

Expression: Comparing numeric data that will become a part of a statement. A semicolon does not follow the expression because it is not a complete statement.

File mode: As the file is opened, a programmer may specify the mode in which the file will be accessed to determine whether the programmer will use the file for reading or writing.

File update: Includes routines for adding records, deleting records, editing records, and listing the data from the file.

Flag: A tag the programmer can use to mark a record as deleted or inactive.

Float: One of the basic types of data in C++.

Function: A calculation or task to be performed in C++. A main() function controls execution of the entire program; the program will always begin and end execution in the main() function.

Global variable: Variables declared outside of a function, usually before the main() function; also called external variables.

Hash address: The programming technique in which the key field is used to generate a record number for a random file.

Hashing algorithm: Something that provides a method for generating a random record number from a key field. A random file that is accessed using a hashing algorithm must have an overflow area to provide for collisions.

Header file: Files from the library with an .h extension are called header files and contain definitions that will be used in the program.

Hierarchy: The relationship of classes. Hierarchy promotes reusability of code and allows features to be added to a C++ program without altering code that is already in use.

Identifier: A name made up by the programmer for a variable.

Increment: The increment operator performs an addition operation and an assignment, increasing the value of the variable by one.

Indirect value: The contents (value) stored at the location being pointed to by a pointer variable.

Indirection operator: Indicated by an asterisk (*), the indirection operator is used when referring to the contents (value) stored at the location being pointed to (the indirect value of the pointer).

Inheritance: A feature of object-oriented models that allows one class to be derived from another class.

Instance: Another term for "object," an instance is the actual variable that is associated with a struct or class and its encapsulated properties and methods.

integer: One of the basic types of data in C++; the others are float, long integer, double, and character.

Key field: The item to be found in a search.

Linker: The C++ feature that is accessed after a program is compiled to combine all necessary object files and data files.

Local variable: Variables that are declared inside a block that are visible only to that block and can be changed only by statements in the block.

Logical file name: A name that will be referred to in the program when a programmer wants to access that specific file, distinguished from a physical file name. The logical file name is internal to the program code and must follow the guidelines for naming identifiers in C++

Loop: A logic construct that allows for a statement or block of statements to be repeated.

main() function: A main() function controls execution of the entire program; the program will always begin and end execution in the main() function.

Manipulators: Features that control the output of the data, such as column width, justification, precision of decimal numbers, and the number of decimal places.

Member functions: Methods of an object that are declared inside the structure. Methods may be defined within the structure or have a prototype declared within the structure and the function definition outside of the structure.

Menu: A program that displays several different options that may be selected.

Methods: Another term for "member functions," these are declared inside of the structure. They may be defined within the structure or have a prototype declared within the structure and the function definition outside the structure.

Modulus: An operator used to find a remainder. It performs a division and then returns the remainder as the result of the operation.

Multidimensional array: Arrays may have multiple levels of subscripts, and a multidimensional array may be pictured as being an array of arrays.

Nested if: An "if" inside of an "if" that is used when more than one condition is to be tested. The second condition will be tested only if the first condition is true.

Object code: Machine instructions.

Object-oriented programming (OOP): The analysis of data and related functions into abstract classifications or classes.

Object: The actual variable that is associated with a struct or class and its encapsulated properties and methods; also referred to as an instance.

Operand: Another word for factor.

Operator: Used to perform operations including calculations and comparisons.

Overloading: Another term for "polymorphism." The ability to have many versions of the same function and to select the appropriate version at run time.

Parallel arrays: Related arrays having elements at the same subscript position corresponding to the element in the other array at the same subscript position.

Physical file name: The name of a file on a disk, as opposed to the logical file name.

Pointer: A variable that contains an address or a location in memory.

Polymorphism: The ability to have many versions of the same function and to select the appropriate version at run time. Polymorphism allows functions to be written for various data types; the compiler selects the proper function to be used in a particular execution of the program. In C++ polymorphism is referred to as overloading. Both functions and operators can be overloaded.

Postfix: Increment and decrement operators may be placed either before or after a variable. A postfix operator evaluates the expression and then increments the variable, while with a prefix operator, the calculation is done prior to the evaluation of the remainder of the expression or statement.

Precedence: The sequence in which the operators will combine with the operands.

Prefix: Increment and decrement operators may be placed either before or after the variable. A postfix operator evaluates the expression and then increments the variable, while with a prefix operator, the calculation is done prior to the evaluation of the remainder of the expression or statement.

Preprocessor directive: An order in C++ that specifies some action to be taken prior to the compilation of the program, it is preceded by #.

Priming input: By using a priming input and putting the input as the last statement in the loop, the programmer can terminate execution of a loop as soon as the user enters the value for which the programmer is testing.

Private: One of two default access types of the variables and the functions. In a structure, the contents are considered public by default and can be accessed by an object within a program as well as by the methods. In a class, all members (data and functions) are private by default, limiting their access only to methods (member functions) of the class. In both a class and a structure the programmer can explicitly specify any property or method as public or private by using the keyword public or private.

Prompt: A cout statement or question that will ask the user for specific data input.

Properties: The data members, or variables, of an object.

Prototype: The function declaration. The programmer may divide programs into functions that serve a specific purpose. Each function must be declared in a prototype and be defined.

Prototype: Declaration of a function including return type and datatype of arguments.

Public: One of two default access types of the variables and the functions. In a structure, the contents are considered public by default and can be accessed by an object within a program as well as by the methods. In a class, all members (data and functions) are private by default, limiting their access only to methods (member functions) of the class. In both a class and a structure the programmer can explicitly specify any property or method as public or private by using the keyword public or private.

Random access: A method of accessing data files that allows the user to obtain a record within the file directly (as compared with a sequential access).

Relational operator: Operators that provide the ability to create conditions.

Scope resolution operator: Used when defining a method outside of the structure or class to associate the function with the appropriate structure or class.

Scope: Determines the visibility and lifetime of a variable or object.

Search: A search is used to match an item with another item from a list (array) or from a file. Two types of search logic: a serial search and a binary search.

Sequential access: A way of accessing data files that requires that every record be read in order to access data later in the file.

Serial search: A search that compares each item in a list sequentially with the key field.

Sort: A function used to put data in sequential order, either ascending or descending. A sort works on either numeric or string data depending on whether relational operators or the string functions are used.

Source code: Another term for programming code.

Stream: The term used in C++ input/output to refer to a sequence of data; sometimes used synonymously with "file."

String length: The number of characters up to, but not including, the null character.

String literal: A constant containing multiple characters that is enclosed in double quotes.

switch: A statement that allows a variable to be tested for several possible values (called "cases").

system: A function that allows the C++ program to "shell" out to the operating system. The program can be requested to run another program (an .EXE, .BAT, or .COM file) or to perform a DOS command.

Text editor: Used to enter the program into the machine to provide the ability to easily edit your programming code (source code). These edit features usually include cut and paste and searching operations.

Unary operator: Used to perform calculations, a unary operator has only one factor or operand on which the operation is performed.

Variable: Data that may be changed during the execution of the program.

INDEX

: (colon), 47, 97
: (colon operator), 181
. (period), dot operator, 37, 48
; (semicolon), 5, 23, 110, 115
:: (scope resolution operator), 46
& (ampersand)
    address of operator (&), 166, 171
    logical AND operator (&&), 86–87, 94–96
    reference operator (&), 174–175
    dereference operator (*), 168
    indirection operator (*), 166, 171, 190
\ (backslash), 6, 20
{ } (braces)
    positioning of, 14, 90, 110
    structural function of, 5, 12–13
= (equal sign)
    assignment operator (=), 68
    equals operator (==), 84
>> (extraction operator), 32
/ (forward slash)
    // (comment), 5, 11–12
    /*-*/ (slash-asterisk), 11
<< (insertion operator), 6–7, 28
- (minus sign)
    decrement operator (--), 66–68
    points-to operator (->), 213
% (modulus operator), 65
! (NOT operator), 84–85
() (parentheses), function of, 5, 191
| (piping symbol)
    || logical OR operator, 87, 94–96
    and flag combinations, 29–30, 225
+ (plus sign)
    addition operator (+), 190
    increment (++), 66–68, 101–102, 190
(pound sign), 5, 6
" (quotation marks)
    double (""), 6, 20
    single ('), 138
[] (square brackets), 122, 123
~ (tilde), 58

A

Accessing methods
    for array data, 198, 199, 200–212
    and inheritance, 181
    pointers as, 165, 191–193, 196–199
    public vs. private, 47, 48, 181
    random vs. sequential file, 223–230
    for updating files, 231–232
Add() function, 233, 236, 240–241
Addition operators
    addition (+), 190
    increment (++), 66–68, 101–102, 190
Address of operator (&), 166, 171
Addresses, 165, 175–176, 191–192

Advancing to new line (\n), 7–8
Allocation, memory, 47, 165, 215–217
American National Standards Institute (ANSI), 2
Ampersand (&)
    address of operator (&), 166, 171
    logical AND operator (&&), 86–87, 94–96
    reference operator (&), 174–175
Arguments
    and constructors, 54
    definition, 5
    and overloaded functions, 56
Arithmetic conversion, 70
Arithmetic operators. See Mathematical operators.
Array names, 189, 191
Arrays, 121
    accessing methods for, 198, 199, 200–212
    character, 23, 25, 51 72, 84, 124–125
    dynamic memory allocation, 215–217
    and for loops, 124–128
    multidimensional, 193–199
    and pointers, 165, 191–193, 196–199
    single-dimensional, 121–123, 192, 198–199
    subscripts, 123, 191, 193, 197, 217
ASCII code table, 85
Assignment, 26–28, 166–167
Assignment operators, 68, 68–70, 100–102
Asterisk (*)
    dereference operator (*), 168
    indirection operator (*), 166, 171, 190

B

Backslash (\), 6, 20
Bars, menu, 158–161
Base class, 2, 180–181
Binary operators, 63, 63–64, 67, 70
Binary search, 203–208
Binding and precedence, 100
Blank lines, skipping of, 10
Block, 24
Braces ({ })
    positioning of, 14, 90, 110
    structural function of, 5, 12–13
Brackets ([]), 122, 123
Break statements, 138
bsearch() function, 203–212, 233
Buffers
    ClearBuffer() function, 33
    file, 226
    keyboard, 32–33
Bugs, programming. See Debugging hints.

C

C programming language, history of, 2
C++ programming language
    advantages and disadvantages, 3–4
    history of, 1–2
    overview of program structure, 4–11
    reusable code as goal of, 153
Calculation operators. See Mathematical operators.
Calling of functions, 13–14, 49
Capabilities classes, 2, 180–181
Carriage return (\r), 10
Case of letters, and string comparisons, 89
Case statements, 137–138
Character reference parameters (get() function), 146
Character variables
    in arrays, 23, 25, 51 72, 84
    constants, 20
    vs. numerical, 124–125, 138, 150–151, 166
    and relational operators, 84–85
cin object, and data entry, 32–35
cin.get() function, 32
cin.getline() function, 32
Classes
    accessing for file update, 231–232
    and declaration of data types, 47–48
    definition, 1, 2
    menu, 153–156, 178–179
    overloaded functions and, 56
    and reusable code, 153
    static storage, 122, 193
    stream, 9, 224, 225, 229–230, 256
    vs. structure, 45, 47
    versatility of, 180–181
ClearBuffer() function, 33
Clearing of screen between menu options, 157
Close() member function, 226
Closing a file, 226
Code, programming
    reusability of, 153
    types of, 4
    See also Readability of code.
Collision, record number, 255
Colon (:)
    in conditional operators, 97, 181
    and public/private access, 47
Column width, 29
Comments (// or /*), 5, 11–12
Compare() function, 210–212
Compareit() function, 204–207
Compiler, 4
Compound conditions, 87, 93–95, 116
Concatenation, 73, 73–74
Condition, for loop, 114–116

Conditional operators (?:), 96
    if statement, 90–100
    logical operators, 84–88
    and string functions, 88–90
const (reserve word), 22–23
Constants, 19
    characteristics of, 20
    and const, 22–23
    naming conventions, 22
    string, 27
Constructor() functions, 48–49
    with arguments, 54
    and attaching files to streams, 225
    in menu programs, 158–159, 176–177
    overloading of, 54
    and updating of files, 231–232
Conversion operators, 70
Copying of strings, 27–28
cout statement, 5, 6

D
Data
    entry of, 32–35
    reading from disk file, 228, 233
    sorting of, 208–211
    storage of, 122, 189, 193
    See also Variables.
Data files, and streams, 224
Data items
    vs. data types, 19–20
    as variables, 23
Data members, 46
See also Variables.
Data types, 19–20
    declaration of, 47–48
    for functions, 50–54
    mixing of, 70–71
    naming conventions, 22
    and pointer variables, 168–169
    structure as, 38–40
Debugging hints
    hash addressing, 254
    menu programs, 161–162
    subscript and array reversals, 217
    See also Error-checking.
Decimal numbers, setting precision of, 30
Declarations, 12
    array, 122
    data type, 47–48
    pointer, 166, 167, 171
    stream object, 225
    structure, 35–36, 46
    variable, 23–24, 25
Decrement operator (--), 66, 66–68
Default statement, 137
Defining process, 12–13
Delete operator, 215–217
Deleting records from a file, 233–236, 240–241
Dereference operator (*), 168
Dereferenced value, 166, 168, **170,** 170–172
Derivation (inheritance), 2, 180–181
Derived classes, 2, 180–181
Destructors, 58, 217
Device assignment statement, 9
Direct access for array data, 199
Do loops, 109–110, 113–114
Documentation, and readability, 11–12
DOS commands, running from menu programs, 156–158
Dot operator (.), 37, 48
Double slashes (//), comment, 5, 11–12
Dynamic memory allocation, 215–217

E
Editing of records, 236–238
Element of an array, 121–122
Else statement, 90
Encapsulation, 2
Ending a line (endl), 8
Endless loops, 110–112
Entry condition, 110
Entry of data, 32–35, 224–230, 233, 236, 240–241
Equal sign (=)
    assignment operator (=), 68
    equals operator (==), 84
Error-checking
    default features for switch statements, 137
    and pointers, 4, 170–172
    See also Debugging hints.
Escape sequence, 8, **20**
Eternal loops, 110–112
Exchange sort, 208–209
Exclamation (!) (NOT operator), 84–85
Executable files, running from menu programs, 156–158
Exit condition, 110
Exponentiation, 72
Expression, 84
Extraction operator (>>), 32

F
\f (formfeed), 10
Fields
    entering data for, 32
    key, 200
    in structures, 37
File buffer, 226
Files
    accessing classes for data types, 47–48
    adding records to, 224–230, 233, 236, 240–241
    closing of, 226
    and constructor functions, 225
    deleting records from, 233–236, 240–241
    executable, 156–158
    updating, 230–253
    See also Header files.
Finding data. *See* Search functions.
Fixed format flag, 29
Flags, setting of, 29–31, **235**
float data type, 20
for loops, 114–117, 124–128, 194–195, 218, 240–241
Formfeed (\f), 10
fstream (file stream) classes, 224
Functions, 12
    add(), 233, 236, 240–241
    bsearch(), 203–212, 233
    cin(), 32–35
    ClearBuffer(), 33
    close() member, 226
    compare(), 210–212
    compareit(), 204–207
    creation of, 12–14
    data types for, 50–54
    double(), 20
    get(), 146
    inline, 49–50
    main(), 5, 13
    open() member, 224, 225–226, 227
    overloading of, 56
    Pause(), 176–177
    and pointer variables, 172–176
    pow(), 72
    PrintMenu(), 146
    qsort(), 209–210
    read(), 228, 233
    resetiosflags(), 31
    Run(), 47, 146
    search, 200–212
    seekg(), 229, 254
    seekp(), 229
    setiosflags(), 29
    setprecision(), 30
    setw(), 29
    Square(), 174
    string, 27–28, 73–74, 88–90
    and structures, 46
    system(), 156–158
    tellg(), 229–230
    write(), 227, 232
    See also Constructor() functions.

G
Global variables, 24

H
Hash addressing, 255
Hash key, 255
Header files, 5
    in binary searches, 203–204
    creation of, 59–60
    function of, 6, 176
    and menu programs, 176–178
Hierarchy of classes, 2, 181
Highest/lowest logic, 120–121

I

Identifiers, 21–22, 22, 24, 35–36
  See also Names.
if statements, 83, 90–100, 143
Ifstream (input stream) class, 224, 225, 229–230
Implied conditions, 86
Implied objects, 60
Include directive, 6
Increment operator (++), **66,** 66–68, 101–102, 190
Incrementation, 114–116, 197
Indirect access for array data, 199, 200–212
Indirect value, 166, 168, 170–172
Indirection levels, and pointer variables, 170–172
Indirection operator (*), **166,** 171, 190
Infinite loops, 110–112
Inheritance, 2, 180–181
Initialization
  arrays, 122, 194
  for loop, 114–116
  variables, 25–26
Inline functions, 49–50
Input/output flag, 29
Input/Output methods
  cin, 32–35
  cout, 5, 6
  creation of, 6–11
  flags, 29
  inputting to a file, 224–230
  and manipulators, 29–31
  priming of input, 112–113
  random vs. sequential file access, 223–224
  updating a file, 230–253
  See also Printing.
Insertion operator (<<), 6–7, 28
Instance, 48
  See also Objects.
Integers, 20, 168–169
I/O (input/output) methods. See Input/Output methods.
Ios flags, 29, 31, 225
Iteration. See Loops.

J

Justification, 29

K

Key fields, use of, 200
Keyboard buffer, 32–33

L

Line
  advancing to new (\n), 7–8
  ending of (endl), 8
Linkers, 4
Linking to calling location, 49

Listing records from a file, 238–240
Literals, string, 21, 23, 25
Local variables, 24, 172–174
Logic, highest/lowest, 120–121
Logical operators, 84–88, 94–96, 100–101, 102
Logical vs. physical file names, 224, 225
Loops, 109
  for, 114–117, 124–128, 218, 240–241
  and array access, 124–128, 198
  do, 109–110, 113–114
  endless, 110–112
  if statements in, 120–121
  in menu programs, 146
  nested, 118–119, 194–195
  while, 109–112

M

Machine language, 4
main() function, 5, 13
Manipulators, 29–31
Mathematical operators, 63–77
  addition, 190
  equals, 84
  increment/decrement, 66–68, 101–102, 190
  sizeof, 37, 72, 224, 230
Math.h file, 72
Member functions, 46
  See also Functions.
Memory allocation, 47, 165, 215–217
Menu object, 178, 179
Menu programs, 145
  debugging hint, 161–162
  definition and structure, 145–149
  designing options for, 149–151
  and do loops, 113
  generic menu classes, 153–156
  menu bars, 158–161
  and pointers, 175–185
  programming hints, 151–153
  running of executable files/DOS commands from, 156–158
  and updating of files, 230
Methods, 46
  and if statements, 93
  vs. non-methods, 47
  using calculations in, 73
  See also Functions.
Modulus operator (%), **65**
Multidimensional arrays, 193–199
Multiple values, 143
Multiple variables, 25, 26–27
Multiple-level menus, 179–180

N

\n (newline character), 7–8
Names
  of arrays, 189, 191
  logical vs. physical file, 224, 225
  See also Identifiers.

Nested if statements, 93–95
Nested loops, 118–119, 194–195
New operator, 215–217
Newline character (\n), 7–8
NOT operator (!), 84–85
Null character, 23–24, 28
Numerical variables
  vs. characters, 124–125, 138, 150–151, 166
  and relational operators, 84–85
Numerical variables
  constants, 19, 20, 22–23, 27

O

Object code, 4
Object-oriented programming (OOP), 2
  characteristics of, 2–3
  and inheritance advantages, 180
  origins of C++ as, 1–2
  and reusable code, 153
Objects, 46–48
  cin, 32–35
  cout, 5, 6
  implied, 60
  and inheritance, 180–181
  menu, 178, 179
  printer, 9–10
  stream, 224, 225, 256
  See also Classes; Variables.
ofstream (output stream) class, 9, 224, 225
OOP (object-oriented programming). See Object-oriented programming (OOP).
open() member function, 224, 225–226, 227
Operand, 63
Operators, 57–58
  address of (&), 166, 171
  assignment, 68–70, 100–102
  calculation, 63–77, 190
  conditional (?:), 84–100
  delete, 215–217
  dereference (*), 168
  dot (.), 37, 48
  extraction (>>), 32
  increment/decrement, 66–68, 101–102, 190
  indirection (*), 166, 171, 190
  insertion (<<), 6–7, 28
  logical, 84–88, 94–96, 100–101, 102
  new, 215–217
  pointer, 166
  points-to (->), 213
  pros and cons of C++, 3
  and readability of code, 104–105
  reference (&), 174–175
  relational, 83–88
  scope resolution (::), 46
  sizeof, 37, 72, 224, 230
  and strings, 27, 88–90

INDEX

Output
    cout, 5, 6
    creation of, 6–11
    and listing records from a file, 238–240
    and manipulators, 29–31
    See also Printing.
Overloading, 55
    of constructors, 54–57
    definition, 3
    of operators, 57–58
    and reusable code, 153

P

Parallel arrays, 200
Parentheses (), 5, 191
Partially filled array, 123, 125–127
Passing of addresses of functions, 175–176
Pause() function, 176–177
Period (.), dot operator, 37, 48
Physical vs. logical file names, 224, 225
Piping symbol (|)
    and flag combinations, 29–30, 225
    logical OR operator (||), 87, 94–96
Plus sign (+)
    addition (+), 190
    increment (++), 66–68, 101–102, 190
Pointers, 165
    and arrays, 191–193, 196–199
    characteristics of, 165–170
    and dynamic memory allocation, 215–217
    and error detection problems, 4
    as function arguments, 172–176
    and indirection levels, 170–172
    and menu programs, 175–185
    and structures, 212–214
Points-to operator (->), 213
Polymorphism, 2–3, 55
    See also Overloading.
Postfix operator, 67
Pound sign (#), 5, 6
pow() function, 72
Precedence of operators, 64–65, 67–68, 70, 100–101, 190
Prefix operator, 66–67
Preprocessor directives, 5, 6
Priming of input, 112–113
Printing
    flexibility of, 15
    and listing records from a file, 238–240
    and manipulators, 31
    and menu program output, 162
    objects for, 9–10
    to screen, 6–7, 15, 238
    troubleshooting, 14
    of variables, 28
PrintMenu() function, 146
Private access method, 47, 48, 181
Programming code, 4
Prompts, 33–35
Properties of objects, 46, 47
    See also Variables.
Prototypes, 12, 50
Public access method, 47, 48, 181

Q

qsort() function, 209–210
Quotation marks
    double (""), 6, 20
    single ('), 138

R

\r (carriage return), 10
Random file access, 223, 224–230
Range of values, and switch statements, 143–144
read() function, 228, 233
Readability of code
    importance of, 3, 11–12
    and identifiers, 22
    and operator usage, 104–105
    and programming style, 14, 40
Records, manipulation of, 233–238, 240–241
Reference operator (&), 174–175
Relational operators, 83, 83–88
Resetiosflags() function, 31
Return statement, 50–51
Reusable code, as goal of C++, 153
Reverse video/image, 161
Richie, Dennis, 2
Run() function, 47, 146

S

Scope of variable, 24
Scope resolution operator (::), 46
Screen
    clearing of, 157
    printing to, 6–7, 15, 238
Search functions
    and compare functions, 211–212
    serial and binary, 200–208
    and sorting, 208–211
seekg() function, 229, 254
seekp() function, 229
Semicolon (;), 5, 23, 110, 115
Sequential vs. random file access, **223,** 223–224
Serial search, 200–203
setiosflags() function, 29
setprecision() manipulator function, 30
setw() manipulator function, 29
Single-dimensional array, 121–123, 192, 198–199
sizeof operator, 37, 72, 224, 230
Skipping of blank lines, 10
Slash-asterisk (/*-*/), comment, 11
Slashes
    backslash (\), 6, 20
    forward (/), **5,** 11–12

Sorting data in arrays, 208–211
Source code, 4
Square brackets ([]), 122, 123
Static storage type, 122, 193
Stdlib.h file, 203
Storage of data, 122, 189, 193
strcat() function, 73–74
strcmp() function, 88
strcpy() function, 27–28
Stream objects, 9, **224,** 225, 229–230, 256
stricmp() function, 89
String field, entering data for, 32
String length, 89
String literals, 21, 23, 25
Strings
    accessing using pointers, 192–193
    and character vs. numeric arrays, 125
    definition, 23–24, 25
    and DOS commands from menus, 156
    functions using, 27–28, 73–74, 88–90
    initialization of, 25
    and loops, 111, 115–116
    manipulation of, 73–77, 122
    pointers for accessing, 165
    See also Arrays.
Strlen() function, 89
Strncat() function, 74
Strncmp() function, 88
Strncpy() function, 28
Stroustrup, Bjarne, 1
Structures
    vs. classes, 45, 47
    functions declared outside of, 46
    and pointers, 212–214
    properties of, 35–40
    and random file access, 223–224
Style guidelines. *See* Readability of code.
Subscripts, 123, 191, 193, 197, 217
Switch statements, 137–145, 149–150
Symbol table, 49
Symbolic constants, 123
    See also Constants.
Syntax errors, 4
    See also Error checking.
system() function, 156–158

T

Tags, 35–36
Tellg() function, 229–230
Ternary operator, conditional operator as, 96
Text editor, 4
Tilde (~), 58
Troubleshooting. *See* Debugging hints.
True/false determination, 86

U

Unary operators, 63, 66–68
Updating of random files, 230–253

V

Values
- assignment to variables, 26–28
- dereferenced, 166, 168, 170–172
- indirect, 166, 168, 170–172
- multiple, 143
- and switch statements, 143–144
- void, 5

Variable names. *See* Identifiers.
Variables, 19
- vs. arrays, 121
- assigning of values to, 26–28
- declaration of, 23–24, 25
- global, 24
- initializing of, 25–26
- local, 24, 172–174
- and relational operators, 84
- structure, 36
- *See also* Character variables; Pointers.

Void value, 5

W

while loop, 109–112
write() function, 227, 232